LESSONS FROM AMERICA

THE CONTRIBUTORS

Reyner Banham
  History of Architecture, University of London

Marcus Cunliffe
  American Studies, University of Sussex

Nicholas Deakin
  Department of Planning and Transportation, Greater
  London Council

Hugh Heclo
  Research Associate, The Brookings Institution

Tom Hooson
  European Director, Benton and Bowles International

A. N. Little
  Head of Reference Division, Community Relations
  Commission of Great Britain

H. G. Nicholas
  Rhodes Professor of American Institutions, Oxford

Jim Potter
  Economic History, London School of Economics

Richard Rose
  Politics, University of Strathclyde, Glasgow

John Whale
  Journalist, *Sunday Times*, London

Esmond Wright
  United States Institute, University of London

LESSONS FROM AMERICA:

An Exploration

Edited by

Richard Rose
University of Strathclyde

America, thou half-brother of the world;
With something good and bad of every land.

Philip James Bailey,
Festus: The Surface

A HALSTED PRESS BOOK

JOHN WILEY & SONS
New York – Toronto

First published in the United Kingdom 1974 by
THE MACMILLAN PRESS LTD

Published in the U.S.A. and
Canada by Halsted Press, a
Division of John Wiley & Sons, Inc.,
New York

ISBN 0 470 73350 0
Library of Congress Catalog Card No. 74–925

Printed in Great Britain

Dedicated to
THOSE WHO CAME OUT

Contents

Acknowledgements

Like Phineas Fogg's trip around the world in eighty days, this book owes its origin to a casual remark at the Reform Club, London. The editor is therefore indebted to the late Sir Charles Barry, architect of the Club, for providing such an attractive place to meet for conversation. He is also indebted to Robin Winks, Professor of History at Yale University, for making him wonder aloud what would result from a careful examination of the casual assertion that what happens in America today must happen elsewhere tomorrow.

Dr Wayne Wilcox, Cultural Affairs Officer of the American Embassy, London, provided assistance in bringing the contributors together for three days beside Loch Long in the Western Highlands of Scotland. The weather kept us inside Knockderry Castle long enough to get through a considerable amount of valuable discussion. Scottish Television provided material assistance. Mrs R. West and Mrs K. M. E. Liston substantially aided the quick production of the final typescript. S. M. Miller, Martin Rein and Rupert Wilkinson made very useful contributions to our discussion of manuscripts.

RICHARD ROSE

4 July 1973

America: Inevitable or Inimitable?

RICHARD ROSE

Professor of Politics, University of Strathclyde

Two themes have always dominated the dialogue between Americans and Europeans. The first is America's uniqueness; no place else on earth can compare with the great colossus of the New World. The second is that America is a forerunner of what European societies will become tomorrow. While the former idea presupposes that America is inimitable, the latter assumes that it inevitably foretokens the fate of all Western societies. The two assumptions are mutually exclusive: both cannot be true. Yet the very familiarity and plausibility of each is a reminder of how greatly our thinking about America is based upon contradictions, rather than upon logical analysis or the sceptical commonsense of a Philadelphia *philosophe*.

The object of this book is deceptively simple: to consider to what extent American experience is unique to the United States, and to what extent it provides a model for the rest of the world. In so far as the American experience is not unique, then Europeans may, by looking at America, foresee what their own country will be like tomorrow. In this uncertain age, few are likely to be so confident that anything is inevitable. If Europeans see things in American society that they do not wish to follow, then America can provide lessons in how to avoid problems of post-industrial society. Alternatively, Europeans can use American examples to prod their fellow-citizens to abandon obsolescent ways, thus hastening the day when the fruits as well as the thorns of post-industrial life spread across the Atlantic.

Americans have a particular stake in ascertaining whether their society is unique or a prototype for the rest of the world. If American civilization is not for export, then a significant part of its foreign policy is built on false premises; the effort to make the world safe for democracy by reshaping distant and often exotic societies in the image of the United States is doomed to failure. The history of the Philippine Islands, the land where the United States has had longest to exert its influence, suggests that American ideas and institutions are not easily transferred. Latter-day experience elsewhere in Asia underscores this point. Even if the United States is not able to remake the world in its image, it can still exert great influence on the lives of many societies, in spheres as different as work, leisure, politics and architecture. There is both pleasure and reward for Americans in acting as missionaries for secular change. A European might also note that if the rest of the world can draw practical lessons from America, perhaps the citizens of the New World might also find something beside antiques worth importing from the Old.

Within the confines of a single volume, not all the questions that arise in America's relations with Europe can be answered. But many can be raised. This volume is not intended to provide slick but misleading answers, but rather to ensure that the right questions are asked. It cannot be assumed that each reader would wish to draw the same lesson from an agreed body of knowledge. Evidence and argument in the pages that follow cover a wide variety of subjects, from the history of architecture (an engineering subject in America, as it is an aesthetic subject in Europe) to politics and economics. Each chapter should make each reader self-conscious about the problems of projecting experience across the Atlantic to demonstrate what can or can't happen here.

American society and the literature about it is vast and complex. Any effort to generalize must involve people with specialist knowledge in a variety of very different fields. The contributors to this volume exemplify the breadth of subjects touched by the American experience. Collectively, their biographies show how varied are the motives that first lead people to explore American society. In several cases there was an explicit desire to learn from American experience in race relations, education and advertising. For others, there was no motive more definite than the desire to see a new part of the world, and the existence of generous scholarships for transatlantic study. The two American-born authors were spurred by the same motives, but travel led them in the opposite direction. In every case the result has been the same. Each has become involved in the business of translating American experience into European terms, and vice versa. Friendships, work and sometimes marriage make the contributors more than students of Americanizing influences; they are also subject to them.

I. THE CROSSING

Ties between Europe and America are a fact established by history, as well as by present-day influences. The movement across the Atlantic has always been two-way traffic. European explorers brought to the New World such things unknown to the Indians as gunpowder and the Bible; they brought back as first instalments of a continuing exchange such exotic and unfamiliar products as tobacco and the potato.

For the first two centuries of settled existence, the colonists of the New World were inevitably conscious of their connection with the Old, for England, France, Spain and Russia held sovereign claim to parts of the territory that today constitutes the United States. Political ties meant economic links; the colonies, like their latter-day counterparts in other countries, were seen as trading outposts for European sovereigns. They quickly became places of settlement. When the impetus for settlement was rejection of the Old World, the settlers' values made them stress America's unique attractiveness as an Eden free of troubles. The new environment and the experience of exploring a scarcely settled continent made Americans different from their cousins left behind. As Mark Twain and Charles Dickens each noted, travellers across the Atlantic were surprised at how different their cousins were from themselves. Material artefacts take on different meaning in disparate contexts. In Daniel Boone's last home, stone-built with loopholes for rifles to use against Indians, eighteenth-century English furniture assumes a significance lacking in an English country rectory. Reciprocally, blue jeans in London or Paris were once as rare and noteworthy as a Stetson hat would still be today. The fact that America is a transplant of many different European experiences ensures some points of similarity with other countries. The fact that it is a

hybrid, a plant that has flowered in remote, strange and virgin soil, has made its total character unique and distinct from
its European inheritance. The nearest one could come to asserting an identity between the two worlds would be to quote
Marcus Cunliffe's notion that perhaps 'America is the same as
Europe only more so'.

In the soil of the New World a new society not only flourished but found itself growing beyond its original territory.
The American outward thrust first led away from Europe to
the unexplored trans-Mississippi West, which was never
under a British flag, nor properly settled by the French. Once
the Pacific coast was reached, Asia beckoned across the Pacific.
Just as Europeans approach Asia through the Middle East
and India, so Americans approach it from San Francisco,
Hawaii and barren islands with names such as Midway and
Guam. Americans turned north, sometimes fearful of attack
from the Tories who had emigrated to Canada, then latterly
in the assumption (not necessarily shared by their neighbours) that Canadians too partake of the American way of
life. Involvement of the United States with Latin America
has taken many turns through the centuries, from the time
when the first permanent settlement was established on
American soil at St Augustine, Florida, by explorers from
Spanish America.

When Americans started voyaging east across the Atlantic,
they were sailing as explorers to a continent that had many
things as strange to them, e.g. medieval cathedrals or hereditary aristocracy, as log-cabins or Indians were familiar. The
experience of white Americans in Europe was no more a
homecoming than that of latter-day American blacks returning to Africa. In both cases the shock of recognition was the
shock of strangeness. Even when Americans tried hardest to
assimilate, by settling into the language and civilization of
the older country, they could but help, in Ezra Pound's
phrase, to 'make it new'. T. S. Eliot, an articulate and committed exponent of writing with an awareness of tradition,
not only knew the metres of Shakespeare and Milton, but also
the ragtime rhythms of his native St Louis. 'The Love Song of
J. Alfred Prufrock' is no ordinary *chanson d'amour*. The
tourist who thought the Louvre would sure hold a lot of hay

had a sense of architecture different from the man who built
it. The Yanks have come, but they have not come home.

Modern communications technology has made transatlantic travel a part of everyone's existence – even for those who
stay at home. The common domestic recreation of Europeans
today is viewing television; here the influence of American
programmes is palpably great. If one travels to Brussels, the
city proclaimed the capital of the New Europe, the first
buildings that one is likely to see coming in from the airport
are the European outlets of such well-known American firms
as Goodyear, Esso, Holiday Inns and IBM. The readiness to
move across the established boundaries of European states is
understandable. After all, from London to Frankfurt or Paris
to Milan is a lesser distance than from New York to Chicago.
People who seem different from each other may have one
homogenizing characteristic to American exporters: they are
all Europeans. The proponents of a United States of Europe
may owe America something more than the analogue of a
name.

The most isolationist of Americans today must also be conscious of Europe's influence upon his life. This consciousness
may be negative, a reaction against two world wars and a cold
war. These events led his government to abandon isolationism with results that are sometimes cited by isolationists as
proof that no good can ever come of Americans mixing in
Europe's troubles. The devaluation of 1971 showed Americans that the dollar, while ubiquitous, was not necessarily almighty. Changes in the world economy provide Europeans
once again with the opportunity to export their material products to America; even the movie Western may be taken over
by the Italians. If the exchange of ideas and goods continues
long enough, the two continents may converge in their ways
of life. Yet even if this were to happen, Americans would expect to get to the point of convergence first!

Intellectual technology almost always lags behind communications technology. The dominant language of communication in the Western world today is no longer French
or the Queen's English. Instead it is a speech perhaps best
described as the President's American. The persons most in-
sensitive to nuances of communication when using this lan-

guage are not necessarily Europeans: sometimes they are Americans, even Presidents. An increase in transatlantic travel does not lead inevitably to an increase in understanding across the Atlantic. Professors with Pan-American chairs, flying from one conference to another, may find it difficult to study the lands they traverse with the care of a Tocqueville and Beaumont, travelling by stage-coach, horseback and riverboat to the interior of America. Nor will many travellers generalize as carefully and as challengingly as those early nineteenth-century French students of society.

II. OH SAY, CAN YOU SEE?

Comparisons made across national boundaries often tell one more about the observer than about what is observed. Some writers fall victim to the appeal of distant greenness: the further away the grass, the greener it is thought to be. On a dull December day in London, the grass may look greener in California than at home, just as in the heat of a summer race riot, someone from Los Angeles may prefer the peaceful image of a distant English garden. In both cases the land is the same: only the observers' values differ. Some writers are like the astronomer with muddy boots: they are better at contemplating distant stars than they are at regarding the ground before them. For example, a diplomat or a foreign correspondent may be an acute observer of a land to which he is sent as a stranger, yet make misleading comparisons between it and his native country because his picture of the latter is distorted by memory and the indiscipline of casual recollections. Writers who seek to draw lessons from a committed viewpoint often delude themselves into believing that what is foreign must be good, because what they know best they think bad. They import sticks – whether cricket bats, shillelaghs or alpenstocks – with which to beat their native institutions, oblivious of the fact that when doing so they have a fifty-fifty chance of picking up the wrong end of the stick.

When comparing changes across time within American society, even an experienced observer risks generalizing about a trend that may turn out to be a 'non-event'. One may argue that events of the present, such as violence, represent a new trend in American society only by ignoring what has happened in the past. Alternatively, experts in the past may assume that the things they know best continue to persist. For example, some American historians suggest that the political ideas of the Founding Fathers remain dominant today. Yet when historians purport to generalize about the present, their conclusions are likely to strike their readers as far more contentious than their judgements about the past. When studies involve comparisons between the past and present in both America and Europe, there is a greatly increased risk of seeing things that are, in fact, not there.

The first part of this volume is entitled 'Myth and History', because so much of what passes for common knowledge is the former rather than the latter. Marcus Cunliffe's chapter demonstrates that it is as easy to draw an antithesis between different visions of America as it is to draw an antithesis across the Atlantic. Esmond Wright's concluding chapter shows how confusion about the past and present affects Americans' perceptions of themselves, as well as images important in international comparison. In the world of design and architecture, Reyner Banham suggests that the myth has usually been at least as important to Europeans as the reality.

One difficulty in sorting myth from reality is that there are many different Americas. The word can conjure up immediately an image of California or New York; Charleston, South Carolina, or Santa Fé; Chicago or a small New England town. The statements made about America will differ greatly, according to which place is taken as the point of reference. It is often forgotten that Europe is heterogeneous too. An American visitor to Avignon or Arles cannot help but be impressed by its antiquity, just as an American visitor to Coventry will be struck by how the city is in most respects newer than Boston or Baltimore. A European visiting both Long Island and Mississippi will see great contrasts in wealth; he could find this in Milan and Calabria as well. Galway and Galicia are both peasant societies, but they differ as much as a rural community in Kansas differs from a rural community in Louisiana.

The point of reference selected for comparison must be adapted to subject-matter. Anyone concerned with the world of advertising will think of New York City as the capital of 'his' America, just as a student of politics will regard Washington as central, and a movie fan Hollywood, or perhaps Monument Valley, Arizona, made famous by John Ford in his Westerns. A European academic may think of Berkeley, California, or Cambridge, Massachusetts, as typically American. Even people who think of New York City as the centre of America may be thinking of different parts of Manhattan. A banker will know the area around Wall Street, a theatre critic the Manhattan of Broadway and Off-Broadway, and a student of race relations, Harlem. Many of these choices of 'typically' American cities would strike Americans as odd. It is worth noting that the centre of population gravity in America is remote from every place cited in this paragraph: it is in an industrial wasteland near East St Louis, Illinois.

The European element of any comparison must also change with the subject. (Cf. the remark of the cosmopolitan Habsburg monarch, Charles V: 'I speak Spanish to God, Italian to women, French to men and German to my horse.') If England represents the height of civilization, judged in political or literary terms, then France symbolizes the height of European cuisine, Italy of art and architecture, and German-speaking lands the centre-point of music. There is no necessity that one European country be the central point in any professional or intellectual field. Professional worlds can be polycentric in Europe, just as in America there is a West Coast and an East Coast entertainment industry, and a Chicago, a Berkeley and a Columbia school of sociology. Europeans will dispute among themselves which country today is the leading centre of literature or art. In high finance Brussels, Frankfurt, Paris, Zürich and London each have some significance.

It follows from these differences that there must be variations from chapter to chapter in the geographical focus of comparisons. For example, H. G. Nicholas could not write about Tocqueville without calling attention to his French background as well as his relationship to English society, both facts significant for understanding Tocqueville's ideas about

America. Tom Hooson's chapter on consumer behaviour calls attention to differences and similarities within a mass market of 200 million American consumers and within a potential mass market of greater size in Europe.

In this volume England is the basic point for European comparisons with America. It was to England that Americans first looked for their ideas of what Europe is about, even if the Scots, Welsh, Irish and Ulstermen (the Scotch-Irish) who came to America looked at England differently from those remaining in typically English parts of the United Kingdom. (Even today, a Yank at Oxford may well wonder whether his student compatriot, resident as a Yank at Salford, is actually living in the same country.) A citizen of one of the six founding members of the European Community may not regard any Englishman as typically European, but rather as insullar. An Englishman might reply by noting that Americans too are insular in outlook, albeit insular on a continental scale.

Notwithstanding such complications, common origins and frequent contact make the transfer of ideas and institutions most likely between England and America. Conversely, in so far as America appears unique by comparison with England, then uniqueness is even more likely to be demonstrated by comparison with France, Germany, Italy or other European societies.

III. THE ART OF DRAWING LESSONS

The statement that America is inimitable is true when it is most trivial. No other country in the world today is exactly like the United States. For that matter, the United States today is not identical with the America of yesterday. But this extreme assertion of uniqueness does not destroy the prospect of drawing lessons from America. The morals that Americans try to draw for the future from their distant past might be less relevant to present circumstances than the morals that Europeans might draw across a distance less great in space. The argument that America's present is inevitably the future of Europe is – for the moment at least – incapable of proof or disproof. It is a hypothesis that one can accept or reject; like any other wager on the future, there is a risk of mistaking a conjecture for a certainty.

If America is in part inimitable, by the same token it must in part be capable of imitation. For example, while trends in American society arising from the legacy of slavery have no counterpart in modern Europe, the American response to this unique experience has produced innovations in race relations, education and community development that British governments have consciously considered imitating, as is shown in the chapters by Alan Little and Nicholas Deakin. No country likes to admit that it is consciously imitating another. When the term 'Americanization' first became used in England in the 1830s, it is no accident that it was a term of abuse.

The variety of ways in which American influences appear in Europe defeats any simple assertion about the inevitability of Americanization. What is often called Americanization may be no more than a set of experiences common to all (or most) Western industrial societies. For example, every Western nation has at some time had to face the problem of providing political representation for masses of people excluded from the franchise. America was the first to resolve the problem by basing government upon popular election. When Europeans slowly came to the same general conclusion, no country copied American electoral law. It remains unique in the Western world today. The problem of how to maintain the elderly, the handicapped and the workless is another common problem of modern Western societies. Hugh Heclo's chapter about the absence of a welfare state in America illustrates that America is not always in the forefront of change.

Americanization most obviously occurs when American products or personnel are imported to Europe. Salesmen of everything from Singer sewing machines to IBM computers have found Europe a ready market for their exports. American social science textbooks sell well, not only in England, where similarity of language might account for their use, but also in Germany, the Netherlands and Scandinavia, where books are read in spite of rather than because of their language. The process of Americanization often involves imitation more than importation. As any travelling American will testify, European hamburger and hot-dog stands do not import their meat from America; instead they produce an imitation that resembles, but fails to equal, the 100 per cent American hot dog or hamburger. By imitation, Europeans pay the sincerest form of flattery to American goods.

Confronted with a variety of things American to experience, import, imitate or avoid, Europeans need not feel themselves trapped by historical determinism. Europeans are no more prisoners of an American future than they are prisoners of their own past. Everyone must co-exist with both. Those who are conscious that their position provides openings (including vulnerable points) to more than one tradition have the greatest opportunity to exert conscious influence on their own future. People can learn, by a process of trial and error, what lessons they wish to follow in the American experience, and what they wish to try to avoid.

Lesson-drawing is a difficult art. One must be clear about the subject for study. It is particularly important to stipulate the basis for making comparisons. Is the best in Europe, e.g. the oldest and most famous of its universities, to be compared with the average American college, or is an attempt to be made to compare like with like? Careful studies face problems not capable of easy resolution. For example, a comparison of the living standard of an average automobile worker in America and France may be complicated by the fact that the two men value different things, some of which cannot be priced in money terms. One must also be clear about what kind of evidence is appropriate to show what is happening on each side of the Atlantic: travellers' impressions, government statistics or opinion surveys? One must also consider what are the causes of the events described, and what are the chief pressures for change. The object is to formulate a reasonable descriptive model of contemporary affairs in America. With such a model, one can then begin to consider the implications for transferring its parts to another society. For example, if one finds in America that family differences influence children's educational achievement more than classroom differences between schools, one can ask whether family influences similarly affect the education of

European children. If so, then one starts the next cycle of
analysis, asking what steps Americans have taken to combat
the effects of cultural deprivation upon education, and to
what extent these ideas can (or should) be imported or imi-
tated in Europe.

In some subjects, transatlantic analysis stimulates reflection
rather than the simple drawing of lessons. It is often easier to
see what the similarities and differences are between two
societies than what can be done about these facts. This is most
obviously true in politics and economics. Even if a writer decided that the American Presidency is superior to the British
form of government, he would have great difficulty in teaching this lesson to the occupant of 10 Downing Street. In a
reciprocal manner, American scholars who have concluded
that a parliamentary form of government is superior to the
American model have yet to win acceptance for this conclusion in the American Congress. The chapter by Jim Potter
records the ways in which the American economy remains
elusively incomparable to the British – as well as similarities
in certain post-war economic achievements and problems.
The chapter on government suggests that while the institutions of politics may differ, some problems of government
occur in every modern society.

While the studies in 'Myth and History' are primarily concerned with contrasting real and imagined societies, chapters
in the second half of this book seek lessons from particular
facets of the American experience. Even when facts are
agreed, the lessons that can be drawn are sometimes in conflict. The contributions by John Whale, a professional journalist, and Tom Hooson, a professional advertising man,
evaluate the undoubted force of salesmanship in American
society today differently. They differ less in what they perceive than in what they prefer in what they see. Nicholas
Deakin and Alan Little describe admiringly the very considerable efforts made by American society to come to grips
with the problems of race and deprivation. The authors
chronicle the disillusion that has followed in America from
learning that large inputs of money, legislation and administrative effort cannot be mechanically translated into great
outpourings of benefits. The chapter on education suggests

that England can learn from American experience not to expect too much from education reform. By contrast, Deakin shows more admiration for the government that attempts much, even if it has more failures. Anyone who has ever calculated whether it would be better to be ill or indigent in America or England will not be surprised by Hugh Heclo's conclusion that in these fields the lessons that America has to teach are negative ones.

Many discussions of the relationship between America and Europe explicitly compare two societies at *different* points in time. America is said to resemble Europe, because it has adopted institutions and ways of thinking that were first developed in the Old World. In the middle of the nineteenth century, when England's industrialization had given it a living standard that was different from as well as materially better than that of any other country, Continental visitors to England made comments that today might be applied to America, the country that has replaced it as the world's leading economic power. In 1835 Tocqueville said of England: 'Money is the hallmark, not of wealth alone but of power, reputation and glory.' A quarter-century later, the French critic, Hippolyte Taine, wrote from London: 'Everything here is on a larger scale; the clubs are palaces, the hotels are monumental, the river is an arm of the sea, and the cabs move twice as fast.' Today the relationship is reversed. America is the land where money speaks loudest, everything is on a larger scale, and cars and cabs move twice as fast. Even though the reaction time is becoming less, Europe often lags behind where America leads.

Comparisons couched in terms of 'leading' and 'lagging' have evaluative as well as analytic significance. In a society such as America, where the words 'new' and 'big' are honoured as well as familiar, it is always assumed that the nation that is ahead by these criteria is also ahead in some moral sense. Even Nikita Khrushchev accepted this. His boast that the Soviet Union would one day bury America showed a very American respect for massive material achievements. When he and Richard Nixon debated the merits of the two countries, Nixon was fortunate in staging the dispute on his own terrain: an American-style kitchen erected in a Moscow exhibit to show the Russians, in terms they might understand, how much their society lagged behind America. In England, standards are different. An Englishman might say, in mock-polite language: 'How fortunate it is that the Americans value things that are new and big. This is just what the Americans are good at.' In England the old receives more respect than the new, and size of itself has little claim to merit.

In a competition where there is uncertainty about the standards of evaluation, every society can be ahead in something. Well-educated Indians may cite their country's poverty as evidence that India is morally superior to America, because it has transcended (or failed to attain) material well-being. Often a visitor may admire novel attributes of another society, precisely because these are the attributes that are scarcest in his own society. A professor at Oxford and a professor at Stanford University could exchange jobs and houses for a year very happily, marvelling at the contrast between their temporary home and their normal surroundings. At the end of the year, habit being what it is, each would return home with some regrets about leaving, but satisfied that his familiar surroundings provided the best nest for people like himself.

Often it is difficult to distinguish between prediction and evaluation. The statement that what happens in America today *will* happen in Europe tomorrow is confused with the statement that what happens in America today *should* happen in Europe tomorrow. Marxists and Calvinists are not the only propagandists who like to feel that history is on their side. One of the attractions of living in America is the belief that history is on your side, that you and those around you *are* the wave of the future. (One reason why American intellectuals ignore the American South, a not insignificant portion of the country, is the feeling that there 'history has already happened'.) Similarly, Europeans sometimes study American society in the belief that it helps anticipate the future of Europe.

It is all very well to be in the vanguard of history, when history is heading in the right direction. In the 1970s Americans and, *a fortiori*, Europeans are no longer confident that this is the case. Only time will tell whether the last part of the twentieth century will deserve the accolade of the American century. The prospect beyond is even less certain. Within America, critics of the society challenge its perceived trends. Some argue that change should be accelerated in a novel, even revolutionary direction. Others argue that the first priority is to arrest the march of progress, when progress means more and more of things that people want less and less.

Whatever the future holds, American society today faces challenges on a scale that dwarfs those of any single European society. If Americans retain a Biblical faith, the settlers of Eden must sometimes wonder whether they must now endure the trials of Job. Certainty and innocence are gone. In the words of one European-American writer: 'Until yesterday, America believed itself immune from the hereditary plagues of mankind. It could not credit the danger of being suffocated or infected by any sinister principle.' These words, from a study of *Character and Opinion in the United States,* are specially apt for the Nixon era. Their aptness is not dimmed by the fact that they were written by George Santayana more than half a century ago.

In earlier times the challenge of the wilderness forced Americans to become masters of the art of improvising what Reyner Banham here calls a 'neat engineering solution'. To-day, in the jungles of the cities, Americans are once again challenged, this time to produce solutions through social engineering. Whether there is such a thing as a 'neat' solution of social problems is a matter of debate. As long as urban problems are political issues there cannot be a tidy outcome, because politics is about the resolution of conflict, and conflict is inevitably a messy process. The settlement of the American West in less than half a century demonstrated that however great the plains, they could be tamed by the strength of man. The settlement of American cities has produced problems that appear at least equally challenging. But tools which contributed so much to the taming of the West, like the tractor, barbed wire or the Winchester rifle, are unlikely to be so useful in coping with problems of American urban life today.

Whatever conclusions are drawn from individual cases, a few generalizations are of persisting significance. The first is that the past must be accepted as a given. Whatever is done for the future, the past cannot be undone. The chapters in this volume that refer to the American past are also those that most emphasize America's uniqueness. The inheritance from the past is mixed. Just as America today faces world military commitments far greater than those of any European nation, for more than a century it enjoyed splendid isolation from Europe's troubles. Accepting the past – warts and all – is safer than trying to ignore it.

Another moral is that one can understand what cannot be changed. The facile engineer – whether civil or social – believes that understanding should lead to the statement of procedures by which one can solve a problem. Americans are beginning to learn in their efforts to remake the non-Western world in their own image that the more one understands cultural differences, the less one expects change. On both sides of the Atlantic today citizens must understand that many circumstances of their lives cannot be easily changed. Americans cannot gain (or regain) the putative advantages of a rural society. European workers cannot enjoy today (whatever may happen tomorrow) all the benefits of an American consumer society, because the national wealth of European societies is not yet sufficient to pay for them.

Many judgements depend upon circumstances. The experienced traveller learns to avoid dogmatic statements without qualification of time or place. For example, the American who says that he only drinks coffee for breakfast may find himself switching to tea after a few mornings in a London hotel, just as an Englishman may interrupt a lifetime of tea-drinking by favouring coffee in an American setting. The art of drawing lessons is to know when generalizations are truly general – or at least broad enough to stretch across the Atlantic – and when they are so narrow in scope that they may not even reach from America's East Coast to the Middle West.

Part One
Myth and History

1 New World, Old World: The Historical Antithesis*

Marcus Cunliffe

Professor of American Studies, University of Sussex

I. PROBLEMS

1. *What is American history?*

It would be silly to pretend that the history of the United States can be or has been discussed from exactly the same position as that of the history of Western Europe. America has undergone various experiences both actually and figuratively remote from the preoccupations of Europe. If the American time-dimension has been smaller, the space-dimension has been larger. American attitudes to their national past sometimes appear 'un-European' in a paradoxical way. The New World, that is, is apt to fall back upon historical precedent in a search for solutions to controversies of the moment – mingling past and present with a readiness that can puzzle observers from the Old World. 'History' is never an easy word to define, since it embraces not only the record of what has happened but also successive layers of interpretation or myth as to what is thought to have happened. Long before the United States became an independent nation, 'America' was a fable. Something of this large, abstract quality was incorporated into the thought-patterns of the new nation. 'Our fate,' according to the American historian Richard Hofstadter, 'is not to have an ideology but to be one.'

Novelties of circumstance, reinforced by a long-continuing self-conscious effort to put this American essence into words, have led American scholars as well as imaginative writers to make 'Americanness' or 'Americanity' a central theme. The

* I am indebted to Herbert Nicholas for suggestions on some of these matters, and to some of the work of J. R. Pole. I have also benefited from comments by Richard Rose and Rupert Wilkinson.

process perhaps reached its height in the 1940s and 1950s. By then the greatest power in the world, the United States was also a leader among the nations in science, literature and the arts. There was an understandable desire to present and to analyse this achievement, in such books as F. O. Matthiessen's *The American Renaissance* (1941) and Henry Nash Smith's *Virgin Land: The American West as Symbol and Myth* (1950). Several brilliant and illuminating studies emerged. Nor were the Matthiessens and Smiths chauvinist in outlook. They were not concerned to prove that the United States had the finest culture in the world, but simply that it possessed a distinctive culture, whose products might or might not be 'distinguished' in another sense.

In the universities this development was associated with the new 'American Studies' approach. The idea behind 'area studies' was that every society or nation has its own special character, a unique configuration of traditions, values and styles of behaviour. Anthropologists like Ruth Benedict and Clyde Kluckhohn, who had already applied these notions to 'primitive' communities, now enlarged the inquiry to cover modern nations. Scholars in a number of fields were stimulated to hunt for an American tradition (sometimes called 'the American Dream') in the novel, in poetry, in humour, in folklore, in politics, in music, in the evolution of American nationalism. One historian, Merle Curti, explored *The Roots of American Loyalty* (1946). In *The Uprooted* (1951), Oscar Handlin saw immigration as a principal key to the understanding of national character. *People of Plenty* (1954) by a third historian, David M. Potter, was subtitled 'Economic Abundance and the American Character'.

None of these was a naïve investigation, flag-waving in type. Curti treated patriotism dispassionately, and was critical of the American version of what Germans call *Hurrapatriotismus*. Handlin implied that immigration was a disturbing and even traumatic business for the 35 million Europeans who crossed the North Atlantic: the settlers were *un*settled first of all. Potter began his book with a survey of the inadequacies of the usual treatment of national character at the hands of his fellow-academics.

Nevertheless, the assumption that the Americans were set

apart from other peoples was taken as almost axiomatic. And despite Potter's attempt to clarify, the controlling generalizations about American character, or that of other nations, remained vague. One of the ablest contributions was that of the 'psycho-historian' Erik H. Erikson. But take this passage from his *Childhood and Society* (1950):

> It is a commonplace to state that whatever one may come to consider a truly American trait can be shown to have its equally characteristic opposite. This, one suspects, is true of all 'national characters', or (as I would prefer to call them) national identities – so true, in fact, that one may begin rather than end with the proposition that a nation's identity is derived from the ways in which history has, as it were, counterpointed certain opposite potentialities; the ways in which it lifts this counterpoint to a unique style of civilization, or lets it disintegrate into mere contradiction.

Here surely we begin to run into difficulties. If every nation defines itself by means of a set of polar opposites (law-abiding – lawless, sociable – individualistic, etc.), can any nation be said to embody a clear, congruent identity? Or does each contain large exceptions, contradictions, dissents – such as those of the South in relation to the rest of the United States? If so, perhaps national character/identity is a dangerously loose conception, apt to turn into self-congratulation or anecdote. Even in Erikson, there is the supposition that national identity is a state of equilibrium – leading to a 'unique style of civilization' which is clearly deemed preferable to 'mere contradiction'.

One may regret the lack of precision in analyses of national character, yet still believe there are undoubted if unquantifiable differences between nation A and nation B. An Englishman and a Japanese, for instance, can sense deep differences of 'character' in each other. But their two societies, and the admired or deplored forms of conduct they have generated, reflect conspicuous differences of heritage and environment. It is much harder to be sure about Euro-American or Anglo-American differences. For after all, the American colonies were once English. Neither the indigenous Indian

nor the Negro slave population had much voice in colonial
life; their influence was indirect and negative. When the
colonies became independent, the United States continued to
be closely linked with the Old World. How then can we pro-
nounce with confidence on presumed aspects of American
national uniqueness? Thus, enumerations of American characteristics almost always include 'pragmatism' – the habit of
thinking practically rather than theoretically. But this has
also often been said about the English. An Englishwoman
tells me that one of her schoolteachers used to begin each
lesson with the catechistic query 'What are we English?', to
which the class was trained to chorus in reply: 'Empiricists!'
How should we set about assessing and accounting for the
pragmatic or empirical element in American life? Did it
come from Britain in the first place, then evolve in special
American ways? If so, how and when?

Historians are interested in movement and change through
time. The concept of national character, as employed in a
good deal of writing about the American past, tends to be
static. It assumes that, once formed, the national character acquired permanent lineaments. A prevalent idea is that
Americanness was a sort of igneous formation: a coalescence
produced by the intense heat of the crisis of the American
Revolution, perhaps with further temperings in the war of
1812 and the Civil War. True, constant and rapid change has
been recognized as a feature of American history. One could
hardly ignore such a point in a country whose population,
around 4 million in 1790, is now well over 200 million. But
this has been dealt with by including an appetite for innovation within the list of national characteristics. On the whole,
American historians have not concerned themselves with the
problem of whether 'permanent revolution' may not be a
contradiction in terms.

In part I think this is because they have also tended to
draw a contrast between dynamic America and static Europe.
In discussions of national behaviour Europe has served them
as an unchanging backcloth against which to pose the pageant
of an America on the move. This is apparent, for instance, in
Oscar Handlin's *The Uprooted*, which takes for granted that
there was an entity called 'Europe' all of whose component

nation-states have had essentially the same set of attitudes, changing very little in the past three or four hundred years. But has Europe ever been such an entity, except in the New World's imagination? And how could it be thought a static continent when, for good or ill, it has played so prominent a part in world history – colonizing, annexing, warring, industrializing?

In short, the concept of national character now seems not to have helped us very much in explaining the historic relationships between Old World and New. Instead of introducing fresh hypotheses it has built upon a traditional stock of assertions: America is 'new', America is 'different', America is 'American'. In recent years, as nationalism has lost favour among intellectuals in Western societies, so national character has come to appear a somewhat dubious proposition. For some, separatism has a livelier appeal, or at any rate allegiance to a unit not familiar in the geography of orthodox nationalism. In the United States, black spokesmen have insisted that Afro-Americans are more Afro than American; and militant women have resisted the idea that they share the same set of values as the American male.

It would be misleading to imply that historians' interpretations of the American past are in chaos. There is still a wide measure of agreement on broad propositions, such as that America grew out of and then away from Europe, under the pressure of new circumstances. Most historians, implicitly or explicitly, still believe there is such a thing as national character, even if we cannot define it with precision. Ideas about the special qualities of particular societies depend upon opinion rather than upon observable fact. In logic, every person, every town, every country is unique. Uniqueness is absolute. One cannot logically say that something is 'very unique', or that A is more unique than B. In ordinary discourse, however, such things are said; and belief in the exceptional nature of one's own society (cf. Milton on England: 'God hath not dealt so with any other nation') has been an important historical factor. So we have to reckon both with an accumulated mass of past thinking which is itself a historical datum, and with our present-day curiosity about how to understand the United States vis-à-vis ourselves.

2. *Comparison: how and with what?*

Another logical truism is that one ought to try to verify a
proposition that something is unique by examining other
things within the same realm. The statement that a particular society has a unique quality should involve looking at
other societies to be sure they really are different. Assertions
about the nature of America have always carried the corollary
that we are comparing it with some other area. A difference
must be a difference *from* something else.

But as historians have begun to move away from their previous concentration upon *national* history and culture – some
towards a recommendation that we should be studying *world*
history – comparison has enjoyed a new vogue. For example,
C. Vann Woodward has edited a group of essays entitled *The
Comparative Approach to American History*. There are ante-
cedent developments in other disciplines. Courses in comparative religion, or in comparative government and politics,
are well established. Political scientists have devoted a good
deal of effort to the concept of comparison. In literature too
there are journals and yearbooks of comparative studies, and
scholars accustomed to regarding themselves as 'comparatists'.

We might hope for guidance from these other disciplines
in refining our ways of looking at America. Yet on inspection,
they seem more aware of the snags than of the possibilities.
Harry Levin of Harvard University, one of the most eminent
literary comparatists, has conceded the difficulties in a number of candid essays. Levin tells the story of a colleague who

> enjoyed the precarious privilege of being introduced to
> Dylan Thomas, during one of that gifted poet's tours of
> American campuses. As soon as Thomas learned that my
> informant was a professor of comparative literature he
> asked: 'What do you compare it with?' And in his ... un-
> inhibited manner, he went on to offer a monosyllabic
> suggestion which we could not permit ourselves to enter-
> tain.

What do you compare, and how do you set about comparing? It is simplest to compare only two things at a time. We

can say that A resembles B or does not resemble B, or reveals more or less of certain features than does B. According to this criterion, most books on comparative religion or politics are not truly comparative. They simply furnish information about a number of different systems. They may provide ingenious taxonomies; but the scale of generalization is usually too large to satisfy anyone in search of a method that can be applied to close contexts. Comparative literature often suffers from the opposite defect. It involves, for example, looking at a couple of novels written in different languages and noting internal similarities. Even where taxonomies or classifications are instructive, as sometimes in comparative politics, they are too static to be of much help to historians. Historians operate in the time-dimension. They need to consider how ideas and institutions evolve. Certainly this is necessary for American history, where we have to explain how, from a European base, America generated 'unique' institutions, and how New and Old Worlds continued to interact upon one another.

True, there are some broad notions that try to accommodate such needs. There is, for instance, the 'convergence' theory, according to which all advanced societies, whatever their *political* form, are bound to go through the same stages of *economic* development. This experience, it is held, may lead to a more general convergence, since economic necessities and power obligations present similar problems of decision-making. But the attempt by S. P. Huntington and Z. Brzezinski to apply this theory some years ago to a comparative study of the United States and Soviet Russia, while intriguing, was unsuccessful. The theory was too large to fit the detailed case-studies offered in their book; and the idea that the two super-powers were actually converging, or coming to resemble one another, was going out of fashion by the time the book was finished. Equally disappointing were various attempts to devise a history of the whole American hemisphere, based on the premise that North and South America had both been shaped by unique common experiences (immigration, slavery, encounters with aborigines, frontier settlement). The large similarities could be conceded. But all the other differences seemed too considerable and too complex to be brought under one rubric; and their ties with northern and with His-

panic Europe respectively seemed to indicate that heritage
might count quite as much as environment in forming a
society.

The concept of comparison, like that of national character,
does not in itself solve anything. We are still left with the
questions of what is being compared, how it is done, and for
what purpose. Clearly, comparative studies involve an inquiry into aspects of two, possibly more, cultures. These must
allow comparison: there must be a reasonable symmetry,
even if of apparent opposites, or the task is hopeless. As to the
aim of comparison, at least where the United States is concerned, historians have quite often made up their minds before they start; they find what they are looking for.

Comparability may imply similarity. This is the sense in
which students in examinations are asked to 'compare and
contrast' historical material: in other words, draw up a
balance-sheet of resemblances and differences. The notion of
comparison-as-similarity may embrace a notion of *continuity
in time*: an emphasis on the stubbornness of *inheritance*.
That assumption underlies the 'germ' theory of institutions
expounded in the second half of the nineteenth century by
such Americans as Herbert Baxter Adams of Johns Hopkins
University, and by several European historians. In their view,
for example, the important thing about an institution like
the New England town meeting was its ancestry, which they
traced back to tribal gatherings in early German history.
Some of the intellectual historians among Adams's contemporaries likewise had no doubt that, in the history of ideas,
America and Europe were more or less one undifferentiated
civilization, moulded by a common heritage. And some of the
essays in C. Vann Woodward's symposium, *The Comparative
Approach to American History*, take similarity as their starting-point.

But some scholars on the other hand emphasise *dissimilarity*: *discontinuity in time*, the effect of environment.
According to the great French historian Marc Bloch (1928),
the main value of the comparative method is not in 'hunting
out resemblances' but in 'the observation of differences' between societies. This was the intent of the American historian
Frederick Jackson Turner, who was trained at Johns Hopkins

but rejected the germ theory. Turner's famous 'frontier thesis' (1893) maintained that the American character had been formed not by European origins but by the effects of the American wilderness upon successive waves of settlers. (We may note in passing that in asserting the fundamental dissimilarity of America and Europe, Turner avoids the problem of how Europe, itself once a frontier society, ceased to be one; and he seems to hint at a fundamental similarity between the United States and other frontier societies, though his concern was with American uniqueness.) Comparison for the sake of contrast is a basic principle in the writing of such present-day American historians as Daniel J. Boorstin. The assumption of dissimilarity is evident too in a number of the essays in Woodward, including that of Richard Hofstadter on political parties.

Here are two extreme positions. One enjoins us to look for resemblances. The other, generally more popular, says that the comparative approach heightens our awareness of the unique qualities of a particular society. The inheritance position presumes that people and institutions do not change a great deal once the original model has been established. The environmentalist position seems to suggest that people and institutions are infinitely plastic. There are intermediate interpretations, more sensible if less dramatic. None is finally provable, since history is an inextricable tangle of fact and opinion. But I should declare my own bias, as a European Americanist who has sometimes been irked by what he takes to be an American bias towards the proposition that the United States is 'incomparable' in more than one sense: not only different from elsewhere, but incomparably better than (or worse than) elsewhere. Dealing first with theories, which have a weight of their own, and then with facts, I intend to look at historical comparisons of the United States with Europe, and especially Britain, with a bias towards similarity. The reasons for this approach are simple:

America grew from Britain, and more generally Europe; other external influences have been relatively minor, at least until recently.

Historically, Europe was the area Americans nearly always

had in mind when they claimed to be different: they saw themselves as different *from Europe.*

Dissimilarity has been over-emphasized, in American patriotic discourse and in the writing of American history.

II. THEORIES

1. *The belief in American difference*

For several centuries, we must admit Europeans and Americans have often taken the two continents to be not only different but diametrically opposed, as two contrasting principles. Old World, New World: the very terms indicate the supposed polarity. For the past two centuries the United States has been regarded as the embodiment of everything 'American'. This usurpation has annoyed a lot of Latin Americans and Canadians. But it is a matter of historical record, so we need not feel any further hesitation in using 'America' and 'the United States' interchangeably.

The polarity has not necessarily been in America's favour. Many Europeans, as well as the self-critical Americans referred to earlier, have treated 'America' and 'Americanization' as dirty words, dire warnings of a fate likely to overtake Europe if it does not watch out. They have followed much the same lines ever since Buffon and other eighteenth-century European *philosophes* stated that America was an inferior continent, where animals and humans alike were deficient in size and sexuality, and steadily deteriorating. This approach obeys the same principle of polarity as the more frequent claim that America differed in being superior to Europe. In the standard antithesis, America has been associated with growth, space, futurity, democracy, virtue, innocence – and with the less admirable sides of these traits, such as boastfulness and naïvety. Europe has been characterized as moribund, limited, antique, class-ridden, depraved, worldly – and, of course, with more admirable traits such as delicacy and intellect.

Scores of examples of an Atlantic antithesis could be cited from sermons, political oratory, poems and novels. They show that each side of the Atlantic has historically served the other as a negative reference group: a mean of defining what one is by defining what one is not. Here is a small sample:

Europeans:

Corneille de Pauw (1770): 'We have depicted Americans as being a race of men who have all the faults of children, as a degenerate species, cowardly, impotent, without physical strength, without vitality, without elevation of mind.'

Charles Dickens (1842): 'I cannot change my secret opinion of this country – its follies, vices, grievous disappointments ... I believe the heaviest blow ever dealt at Liberty's head will be dealt by this nation in the ultimate failure of its example to the Earth.'

Knut Hamsun (*c.* 1890): 'By undermining all individual yearning for freedom in its citizens, America has finally managed to create that horde of fanatic freedom antomatons which make up American democracy.'

Sigmund Freud (*c.* 1925): 'America is a bad experiment conducted by Providence. At least, I think it must have been Providence. I ... should hate to be held responsible for it.'

Americans:

Thomas Jefferson (on European court-life, 1788): 'Their manners, could you ape them, would not make you beloved in your own country, nor would they improve it could you introduce them there to the exclusion of that honest simplicity now prevailing in America, and worthy of being cherished.'

Nathaniel Hawthorne (1863): 'We, in our dry atmosphere, are getting too nervous, haggard, dyspeptic, unsubstantial, theoretic, and need to be made grosser. John Bull, on the other hand, has grown bulbous ... heavy-witted, material, and, in a word, too intensely English. In a few more centuries he will be the earthliest creature that ever the earth saw.'

George Francis Train (1860): 'American character is not an imitation, but a creation – not a copy, but an original. Her power is not, in armies or armadas, but in railroad and schoolmaster....'

William James (1899): 'We must thank God for America; and hold fast to every advantage of our position. Talk about

our corruption! It is a mere fly-speck of superficiality compared with the rooted and permanent forces of corruption
that exist in the European states.'

All the criticism of America has not come from Europe,
nor all the criticism of Europe from America. Other examples, highly appreciative, could be given. But the greater
part of this transatlantic dialogue has drawn sharp contrasts.
It has tended to treat America as an ideal, even if an ideal lost
or perverted. It has entailed an American repudiation of the
Old World – Europe as the place to escape from. The claim
to American innocence, especially where couched in 'Adamic'
and primitivist metaphors, might appear hard to reconcile
with predictions that the United States would beat Europe at
its own game, by surpassing it in technology and the arts.
There has indeed been a shift of emphasis here. Yet the two
types of claim are not really incompatible. American visions
of an unpeopled wilderness were, at any rate in the nineteenth century, nearly always accompanied by visions of
transforming the wilderness into civilization. William Cullen
Bryant begins his poem 'The Prairies':

These are the gardens of the Desert, these
The unshorn fields, boundless and beautiful,
For which the speech of England has no name....

But by the end of the poem he imagines he can hear

The sound of that advancing multitude
Which soon shall fill these deserts....

The Old World was fixed: the New World was fluid, and so
symbolized change – *becoming* rather than *being*. America's
rapid and successful industrialization, which enabled it to
outmatch British productivity by about 1890, was explained
at the time (and later, by historians) as a consequence of having a highly mobile and resourceful labour force, and a pre-
disposition to produce for a mass market: in short, of having
a democratic society. American historians have delighted in
the writings of the sculptor Horatio Greenough (1805–52),

finding in his doctrine 'Beauty is the promise of Function' a splendid epitome of no-nonsense, democratic pragmatism:

> The men who have reduced locomotion to its simplest elements, in the trotting wagon and the yacht *America*, are nearer to Athens at this moment than they who would bend the Greek temple to every use.

The yacht *America* (bearing so obvious and yet so grandiose a name – the same one chosen by the full-time rebel Abbie Hoffman for his infant daughter) beat the British contender for the *America*'s Cup in 1851; and its successors, remember, have kept the Cup in the United States ever since.

Since Europe and America have been states of mind as well as actual places, they have been expected to behave in appropriate ways. Americans in Europe have insisted on discovering Old World charm, with some assistance in recent years from tourist boards. Where they have come across a European who acted like an American, they have enrolled him as an honorary New Worlder, and on occasion deported people deemed to be un-American, all this to keep the contrast tidy. An endearing example is Whitman's tribute to the works of Hegel:

> There is that about them which only the vastness and multiplicity and the vitality of America would seem able to comprehend. . . . It is strange to me that they were born in Germany, or in the old world at all. While a Carlyle, I should say, is quite the legitimate European product to be expected.

In reverse, Europeans have insisted that Americans should be different and inhabit a recognizably different continent. Reyner Banham's essay in this book mentions a complaint from a European visitor that the American skyscraper was too small. An earlier instance is the response of the English novelist Mrs Gaskell, when an American friend sent her some photographs of native scenery. She 'thought America would have been odder and more original; the underwood and tangle is just like England'. She had got a more satisfactory idea from a painting done by another Englishwoman, 'in some wild luxuriant terrific part of Virginia? [actually Louisiana] in a gorge full of rich rank tropical vegetation, – her husband keeping watch over her with loaded pistols because of the alligators infesting the stream. – Well! that picture did look like my idea of America'. Or there is the ironic explanation offered by the American writer John Jay Chapman for the interest conventional English critics showed in the 'barbaric' poetry of Whitman. He conveyed 'the unpleasant and rampant wildness' of America as the English imagined it: 'Mormonism and car factories, steamboat explosions, strikes, repudiation, and whiskey.' So 'the discovery of Whitman as a poet caused many a hard-thinking Oxford man to sleep quietly at night. America was solved'.

2. *Advantages of the contrast principle*

It is our habit to think in dualisms: male and female, *yin* and *yang*, body and soul. Some indeed are descriptions of reality, and others strike us as 'real' because they are so clear and bold. They seem indispensable as ways of organizing our thought, even when – as with the U and non-U game of Nancy Mitford, or C. P. Snow's 'two cultures' – they may be exasperatingly over-simplified. For much of their appeal lies in simplicity.

The America–Europe dualism has a stylized clarity that helps to account for its enduring appeal. It has been essential to Americans ever since the United States became an independent nation, as a means of defining identity; and before 1776 the polarity was already well established through legends of the earthly paradise, Puritan theories of God's New World providences, European dreams of the noble savage and the virtuous husbandman, and so on. As an ex-colonial nation the United States needed to repudiate the mother country; as a fragment or offshoot of Europe it felt obliged to deny that it was merely derivative. History and geography appeared to confirm the providential theme. 'Manifest destiny' presented the United States with an immense western domain; immigration bore out the idea of a universal 'nation of nations'. The nineteenth-century wars fought by the United States against England (1812–15), Mexico (1846–8) and Spain (1898) brought astounding triumphs as if God were emphatically on the side of Andrew Jackson, Winfield Scott and Commodore Dewey at New Orleans, Cerro Gordo and Manila Bay. The Civil War (1861–5) was a terrible setback, but the Northerner was able to see it in retrospect as yet another predestined triumph for the American Union, which in ending slavery removed the one remaining anomaly of the land of freedom.

For some observers the American Dream has been the American Nightmare. In either case it has supplied an extraordinary drama (or melodrama) peopled with scouts and trappers, Yankees and Cavaliers, cowboys and Indians, sheriffs and badmen, Huck Finns and Nigger Jims, Abe Lincolns and Huey Longs, preachers and robber barons, do-gooders and con-men, Al Capones and J. Edgar Hoovers, hoboes and work-bosses, loners and Babbitts. No other nation has produced so rich a cast of symbolic characters for modern times. There are South American epics in prose and poetry celebrating the heroic gaucho. For all I know they are finer than anything written about the United States. But they have not made a mark on the world's imagination. Perhaps Canadian history is full of wonderful stories waiting to be told. But I suspect they would require too many footnotes to get much beyond the walls of—academe. The Mounties are picturesque, yet too trim and decent to linger in one's fantasies. Territorially, Canada and Brazil are as big as the United States; but their historical folklore has seemed far smaller.

The contrast principle supplies leverage for many purposes. Scores of interpretative works have made use of it, implicitly or explicitly. It has pervaded the writing of American historians, from George Bancroft down to Daniel Boorstin and Louis Hartz in our generation. It is central to a number of interpretations of American art, architecture and literature. Again and again in their titles the word *America* refers to much more than actual latitude and longitude: it is meant to have a mythic resonance. Here are a few examples of books on literature: *The American Adam, Love and Death in the American Novel, Symbolism and American Literature, The American Novel and its Tradition, The Continuity of American Poetry, A World Elsewhere: The Place of Style in American Literature.* All these assume an essential Ameri-

canness and seek to define it as contrary to European literary
tradition. The same contrast is expressed by Europeans writ-
ing on American literature: for example, D. H. Lawrence's
Studies in Classic American Literature and Tony Tanner's
*The Reign of Wonder: Naïvety and Reality in American
Literature*. It is invoked in other European books, such as
Cyrille Arnavon's *L'Américanisme et Nous* and Jean-Jacques
Servan-Schreiber's *Le Défi Américain*. How could we manage
without it?

3. Disadvantages of the similarity principle

Arguments that America and Europe are closely related have
often appeared lame or prissy or propagandist. Geoffrey Bar-
raclough has attacked the notion of an 'Atlantic Community'
as being only an extended version of the tendency to Europe-
centred historical scholarship. He sees it as primarily a political or strategic idea, projected backwards from the Atlantic
Charter of 1941, and then embodied in the formation of
NATO. There was, he concedes, a historical Atlantic *economy*; but according to him these economic ties began to
loosen a century and a half ago.

An alternative notion is that of what the French call *le
monde anglo-saxon*: in other words, a close historical link between Britain and America. This can be objected to as a
Gaullist formula, expressing both anglophobia and anti-
Americanism. Or in its historical context the notion can be
regarded as an instance of French parochialism, for French
scholars are notoriously casual in their allusions to non-
Frenchmen. (A reputable French volume on world history
describes the great Scottish surgeon Joseph Lister as an
American.) In the United States it has unpleasant 'WASP'
connotations, snobbish and racist. In Britain too it is associated with late nineteenth-century visions of an imperial
union, a 'Greater Britain' of English-speaking peoples who
would run the world between them – with perhaps Anglo-
Saxon Germany thrown in, as with Cecil Rhodes's plan for
Oxford scholarships. It has a ceremonial, post-prandial, Sul-
grave-and-Runnymede quality, and as such is perhaps more a
theme for oratory than a satisfactory way of organizing a serious discussion of Atlantic problems.

If you try as a scholar to develop the similarity principle, you find that it appears to overstress inheritance, to limit influences on America to those emanating from Western Europe (what of black Americans? Chinese? Japanese? Puerto Ricans?) and to fly in the face of a mass of beliefs and facts about the sheer Americanness of the United States. Instead of a sharp formulation, the similarity principle seems to substitute a series of blurred qualifications. The frontier thesis may be unsound; at least it gives you something to hang on to when you begin to study American history. What is there to put in its place that appears to wrap things up so comprehensively?

III. 'FACTS'

1. *Similarity assertions and evidence*

Even if the prospect looks unpromising, I believe we should persist in questioning the validity of the contrast principle. There are three chief reasons:

(*a*) A good deal of writing about America has claimed as uniquely American phenomena that are manifestly not so, or has made assertions without supplying confirming evidence.

(*b*) A good deal of writing about the American past, especially in the twentieth century, is misleadingly selective: it focuses upon instances of or declarations of uniqueness but leaves out contrary material relating to similarity.

(*c*) A good deal of earlier commentary does not in fact insist upon American 'incomparability', or treats the theme ambiguously, conceding the importance of heritage, or the continuing parallels with British or 'Anglo-Saxon' attitudes.

A couple of illustrations may show what I mean by the first point. Tocqueville's *Democracy in America* is in more ways than one a classic piece of theorizing about the New World. But often it is a diagram of contrasting *theoretical* distinctions between 'democracy' and 'aristocracy', instead of an actual analysis of conditions in America and Europe. Tocque-

ville's Europe is Continental Europe; he finds Britain difficult to bring into the scheme, as we may see from his habit of
referring to the Americans as 'Anglo-Saxons'. His America is
the model of what a 'democratic' society ought to be like.
Thus, what he says about the role of the military and of war-
fare in abstractly contrasting societies is brilliant. But it is not
an accurate picture of the situation of the United States of his
day, nor of the situation in Britain – whose feelings about
standing armies, conscription and the like strongly influenced
the Americans.[1] If Britain is not for Tocqueville's purposes
part of Europe, how should it be schematically presented: as
the mother-country, moulding the United States, or as a quasi-
democracy obeying some of the inevitable rules that govern
such a society?

The other illustration relates to a more recent work, Leslie
Fiedler's *Love and Death in the American Novel* (1960).
Here we are offered fascinating theories about the evolution
of a peculiarly American psyche, given to morbid fantasies.
Overt sexuality is missing, Fiedler claims, from nineteenth-
century American literature. What we have instead, in some
of the tales of Edgar Allan Poe, in Harriet Beecher Stowe's
Uncle Tom's Cabin, or in Herman Melville's novel *Pierre*,
are bizarre sentimentalities, hints of incest, tears shed at the
deathbeds of young girls. This is true enough. But it is not an
atmosphere confined to American literature. Think of the
sentimental-prurient tone of English novelists like Dickens,
enormously popular in the United States, or of the French
excitement over *L'Inconnue de la Seine* – the beautiful,
unidentified, drowned girl, lying on a slab in the Paris
morgue, whose death-mask was once a popular item in sou-
venir shops.[2]

As for misleading selectivity, we might begin by noting
that one of the current sacred texts of 'Americanity', Crèvecœur's *Letters from an American Farmer* (1782), the first to
depict America as a wondrous melting-pot, was out of print
and almost forgotten for most of the nineteenth century.

---

[1] The point is developed in Marcus Cunliffe, *Soldiers and Civilians: The
Martial Spirit in America, 1775–1865* (1968).

[2] The morbidity of the European imagination is abundantly documented in
Mario Praz, *The Romantic Agony*, 2nd ed. (1951).

Crèvecœur was revived early in the twentieth century to furnish quotations for the controversy over whether immigration should be restricted. The American frontier West held a rather more prominent place in the nineteenth-century national imagination. But until the latter part of the century, as Frederick Jackson Turner, the Middle Westerner, well knew, many Americans tended to think of it as an open-air slum. Turner himself as an ambitious young scholar decided he must devote his life to some great theme of modern history. He concluded that the most significant were the growth of cities and the settlement of virgin lands. He fastened upon the latter because it was unique to America, or rather not a feature of Europe, though he was perfectly aware that urbanization was of enormous importance to the United States. His concern with uniqueness made him shut his eyes to a phenomenon because it was merely *in* America, not peculiarly *of* it.

There were American 'originals' whose words catch our attention today. Horatio Greenough was one of these, with his plea for functionalism and his dislike of 'embellishment'. But in his own day Greenough's doctrines won no following in the United States; American taste in architecture and the fine arts was more or less identical to that of London and Paris. Whitman was another original. John Jay Chapman pokes fun at English critics for praising Whitman, but on the curious grounds that Whitman, while a great poet, was completely out of the mainstream of contemporary American culture. Much more representative of this 'respectable mediocrity' were poets like Whittier and Longfellow – 'read by mill-hands and clerks and school-teachers, by lawyers and doctors and divines, ... whose ideals they truly spoke for, whose yearnings and spiritual life they truly expressed'.

In short, twentieth-century scholarship has tended to conceal the extent to which the United States was 'Victorian' in outlook. Victorianism co-existed with an American rhetoric of emulation and superior virtue. Yet even this rhetoric was somewhat Victorian in flavour, in calling for work, thrift, perseverance and piety. 'The longer I lived in the States', the Englishman Edward Dicey said of a journey made in 1862, 'the more I became convinced that America was ... the com-

plement of England. The national failings, as well as the
national virtues of the New World, are very much those of
the mother country, developed on a different and a broader
scale.' An American contributor to the *Atlantic Monthly*, just
a few months earlier, insisted that 'the features of society in
Great Britain and in all our Northern regions are almost
identically the same, or run in parallelisms, by which we
might match every ... incident, prejudice, and folly, every
good and every bad trait ... in the one place with something
exactly like it in the other'. George Francis Train, flamboy-
ant American patriot and entrepreneur, declared that his
country was *sui generis*. But he was also fond of announcing
that Americans were of English stock, and that the two
nations were travelling the same road, well in advance of the
rest of mankind. Perhaps Anglo-Saxondom was a less feeble
idea than was implied a few pages earlier.

2. *Origins and continuity*

So we come back to the argument that the United States has a
great deal in common with Europe, and especially Britain. If
that proposition formerly had a whiff of Pilgrims' banquets or
of NATO about it, it has come to life again in new guises.
Third World spokesmen like Frantz Fanon automatically
align the United States with the other 'have' nations of the
northern hemisphere, plus such 'European' zones as South
Africa and Australia in the southern hemisphere. It has been
given another twist in a book by Louis Hartz and others
called *The Founding of New Societies* (1965). Hartz sees the
United States as a fragment-nation, broken off from Europe.
His argument is that each fragment (Latin America, French
Canada, South Africa, etc.) has become quite separate from
Europe but is characterized by the dominant fragment of
ideology taken from Europe at the formative period. Ideology
in Europe has continued to be rich and to evolve through the
clash of rival systems. The United States, like the other frag-
ment-cultures, has remained stuck with its fragment, unable
to move significantly beyond it because the fragment has had
nothing to contend with. The United States is therefore
ideologically still caught in the late eighteenth century, although *materially* there has been great change.

There are some obvious weaknesses in this theory. It does, however, show that we are not obliged to opt for *either* the contrast *or* the similarity principle: various combinations are possible. Thus, we might suggest that there were several British heritages and that the young United States embodied one of these – the non-aristocratic, Nonconformist, tradesman's and skilled artisan's Britain, largely North Country and Scottish – and then extended it in a favourable environment with the aid of successive waves of like-minded immigrants. Another elementary but useful observation is that national societies embrace a number of institutions – political and governmental, educational, religious, legal, economic, military, cultural – and that each of these has a certain autonomy. Each may move at its own pace, within limits. Indeed, one would expect this to happen in an ex-colonial nation. So indigenous political forms could emerge much more easily than with literature and the arts, which were to remain derivative until the twentieth century.

Comparisons ought to specify which Europe (or which Britain) is being compared. They should not assume that what holds good for one type of institution necessarily holds good for others. Nor should they assume that similarity necessarily means amity, or that mutual hostility is a sign of dissimilarity. The majority of violent crimes, after all, are committed not against strangers but against close relatives. Also, it does not follow that people who have inherited features of another culture remain conscious of the inheritance. Often they annex these to what they perceive to be their own culture. The leaders of the Taiping rebellion in mid-nineteenth-century China absorbed a certain amount of Christian doctrine. The Northern King of the Taipings, giving audience to an English official, began to discuss religion with him:

He stated that as children and worshippers of one God we were all brethren; and after receiving my assurance that such had long been our view also, inquired if I knew the 'Heavenly Rules'. I replied that I was most likely acquainted with them, though unable to recognize them under that name; and, after a moment's thought, asked if they were ten in number. He answered eagerly in the

affirmative. I then began repeating the substance of the
first of the Ten Commandments, but had not proceeded
far before he laid his hand on my shoulder ... and ex-
claimed, 'The same as ourselves! The same as ourselves!'

Many Americans, like the Northern King, have no doubt
professed European notions in the secure conviction that they
were expounding native American articles of faith. Conversely, many Europeans have forgotten or never known that
some everyday idiom or artefact, utterly habitual to them,
originated in the United States. It is a nice question to decide
at what moment an inheritance becomes indigenous.

What we can say is that there was remarkably little sign of
native institutions in America at the time of the Revolution.
Every religious sect or denomination had come from Europe.
Only a handful of Americanisms had crept into the language,
which otherwise remained entirely 'English'. In his *White
over Black*, Winthrop Jordan shows that American racial prejudice was in some ways a carry-over from the attitudes
formed in northern Europe.

During the nineteenth century the United States developed a fairly distinct *political* culture. How distinct is a matter for debate. Robert Kelley's *The Transatlantic Persuasion*
(1969) contends that Gladstonian liberalism was common to
Britain and North America. Others might maintain that a
stable two-party system, resting on minimal ideological dis-
agreement, was among the outcomes of a British political
heritage. Except for the Mormons (many of whose recruits
were immigrants converted in northern Europe) and for
Christian Science (which soon got a foothold in Europe), the
American *religious* culture remained 'European', though
more varied and more composite than in any one European
country. A possible conclusion from this is that *American
uniqueness largely consisted in being eclectically European*:
in the borrowed mix rather than in American innovation,
though the resultant mix was peculiarly American. As for *arts
and letters*, these were still in 1900 heavily European in feel.
For the first twenty years of this century the role of the
American man of letters (Ezra Pound or T. S. Eliot) was to
orchestrate European culture by means of detached cosmo-

politanism. He was a continentalist where many European literati were nationalists. He was still a European in this sense, though very few Europeans were like him: he was more European than they.

3. *Two-way influences*

One of the objections to Hartz's fragment theory is that he supposes Europe and its offshoots to have had no significant effect upon one another after the separation. For Europe and America the facts seem otherwise. Immigration brought many millions of Europeans across the Atlantic; indeed the flow, though at its height on the eve of the 1914–18 war, has never ceased. The United States has not managed to remain neutral in any of the big European wars. Europe is still its best trading customer. The same is true of European exports to the United States. Technological, scientific and cultural exchanges have been close and continuous. Even before the steamship, Americans in droves visited Europe. European curiosity about the United States was less conspicuous; nevertheless, as we can see from published travel accounts, a varied and considerable company made the trip. There was an easy and incessant two-way traffic in fads, fears, music, fiction, poetry, inventions, reforms, theories. Because of language the Anglo-American links were especially close.

But how to evaluate the effects? One point is that early American assertions of independence took for granted that Europe was already superseded. The Old World was on its knees; the New World would take over at any moment. But these reports of Europe's demise proved premature. The cruder American flag-wavers continued to insist that Europe was dead. In fact, however, Britain was still the world's leading industrial–exporting–imperial power in 1914; and if America was contesting the leadership, so was another European power – Germany. The propaganda of nineteenth-century American nationalism understated the innovative vitality of Europe. The contrast principle still impels historians to overlook what was actually happening. The Europe they depict is the Europe of dynastic strife, of aristocracy and of class conflict, not that of city, factory and laboratory. The America they emphasize (see, e.g., Daniel Boorstin's *The*

Americans: The National Experience) is not the settled, 'European' East but the symbolic burgeoning West. In archi- tecture we hear about such American contributions as the balloon-frame to house-building, almost nothing about the novelty of Paxton's Crystal Palace. American art historians, used to take pride in the untutored originality of 'primitive' drawings and paintings – until it was discovered that some were copied from magazine engravings. In other words, the facts often contradict the theory of nineteenth-century Ameri- can uniqueness. Europeans did, as Americans complained, tend to be critical of the United States, sometimes ignorantly and superciliously. But a fair amount of apparent anti- Americanism may have been an understandable reaction to American distortions of what was happening in Europe.

In the nineteenth century the United States obviously evolved many special, un-European features. Political orga- nization is one example. In these ways it did, as James Bryce explained in *The American Commonwealth* (1888), stand as a separate society. Except among the intellectual and among the more socially pretentious classes, it did not feel like or behave like a European colony. On the other hand, as Turner's nostalgic appeal to the already fading frontier ex- perience reveals, there was a kind of 'convergence' during the latter years of the century. The United States then came up against the urban and industrial problems that Europe had been obliged to face earlier. So, at the moment when the United States was beginning to display its own characteris- tic, un-European combination of folkways, it was also para- doxically brought closer to the common Euro-American per- plexities engendered by so-called modern civilization. Some of the attempted American solutions, such as the Sherman Antitrust Act (1890), were peculiarly American. In other re- spects, many of America's reform expedients were borrowed from Europe: participatory devices like the initiative, refer- endum and recall from Switzerland, social welfare and town- planning schemes from Britain and Germany – not to men- tion the secret ballot from Australia.

Another way of putting this is to say that over the past cen- tury, whenever America has been in crisis it has tended to look abroad, especially to Europe, for curative ideas. And whenever Europe has been in crisis, this has tended to reinforce the old American conviction that Europe was iniquitous. So, in the American troubles of the Populist and Progressive era, from about 1890 to 1914, the perceived parallels were close. But then in 1914, as America had long predicted, Europe appeared finished, mired in its own suicidal folly, a horrid example of what not to do. The anticipated death of Europe, however, did not quite take place; and America's own dire social and economic predicaments in the 1930s made her look abroad once more for possible positive answers, whether from Marxism or from Keynesianism. In 1939 Europe seemed to have taken the ultimate step towards the destruction of its civilization and its empires. Once again the apparent contrast served to revive the Europe–America polarity, just when its outlines were blurred beyond use. For several years after 1945 theorists drew upon the old polarity, to the extent of assuming that Europe no longer counted in the world. This dismissal too has been falsified by events. In the 1970s Europe not only possesses considerable power and vitality; it is perhaps more of a genuine entity than was ever true when transatlantic commentators formerly spoke of it as such.

Has the New World–Old World antithesis outlived its purpose? In some ways Russia, Japan and China are of more concern to America than Europe is. An increasing number of Europeans regard the United States not as *the other* place, the repository of their hopes or fears, but simply as *another* place, among several regions of the world. Historians, probably without quite realizing why, are apt to respond to the thought-currents of their own day. We might therefore expect to find, as indeed we do, an increasing tendency to dwell upon what Europe and America have historically had in common, rather than upon what has differentiated them. Yet the old antithesis has not entirely lost its power. Even if they may be somewhat fallacious, or no longer relevant, historical assumptions take a long time to pass away.

IV. CONCLUSIONS

1. *Factors in comparisons*

We can never 'prove' the question of American uniqueness
one way or the other. Even if we can agree to restrict ourselves to 'facts' instead of 'theories' (a dubious hope: some
theories become facts), the answer we reach is shaped by the
kind of facts we deal with. On the largest scale, say that of a
Martian arriving on Planet Earth, all homunculi are much
alike. The bigger our scale of interpretation, the more similar
America and Europe are: mainly Christian, mainly white,
mainly affluent, mainly urban. The other extreme of scale,
millimetric instead of kilometric, indicates how unlike things
are. On the detailed scale, for example, Glasgow and Edin-
burgh not only pretend to be worlds apart but actually are
so.

In discussing American uniqueness we must obviously take
both inheritance and environment into account. But other
elements must also be brought in. Neither continent has remained static. Change (for instance, the growth of political
democracy in Europe), whether internally or externally
caused, has been a marked feature in both. It is even possible
that, ideologically, Europe has changed more than America.
So terms like 'heritage' and 'environment' can be misleading,
if the one is presumed to be wholly static and the other
wholly dynamic. Nor have the transatlantic societies ever
been mutually isolated. The two continents have evolved in
part through interaction, each modifying the other. There is
also an element that might be called logical momentum. By
this I mean that certain comparable decisions have faced all
European and American societies, such as the degree of
popular representation in government, or the priority to be
given to technological development. How these actually develop is affected by many considerations, not all of them
rational. But the problems themselves have an inner logic
and limited options, once a society is confronted by them.
America and Europe have travelled along these same routes,
whether or not they wished to. There may be something in
the idea that America is the same as Europe only more so.

2. Recapitulation

My argument has not been systematic. Here, though, in the somewhat random order in which they occurred, are the central comments:

(a) America grew mainly out of Europe, and Britain in particular.

(b) American claims of uniqueness have usually taken Europe as the measure.

(c) The belief in American uniqueness is ancient, persistent, and common to both Europe and America.

(d) The America–Europe contrast has an attractive symbolic boldness: it corresponds to a deep polarity in our thinking and supplies leverage for any amount of generalization.

(e) Assertions of Euro-American (or more particularly Anglo-American) similarity have tended to lack clarity and appeal, and to be used for unlikeable reasons.

(f) Nevertheless, many facts contradict the uniqueness claim: the two continents have continued to have a great deal in common, including mutual jealousy.

(g) A paradox: in the arts at any rate some Americans have been more cosmopolitan Europeans than the Europeans.

(h) Another paradox: in the second half of the nineteenth century the United States became simultaneously more sure of its distinct identity yet in socio-economic and cultural circumstances more like Europe.

(j) The two world wars of the twentieth century, apart from their many other effects, have helped to keep alive the uniqueness idea in America when one might have expected it to fade.

The question then is one of utility rather than truth. For certain purposes detailed comparison serves us best, for others broad comparison. Perhaps the conclusion can best be stated thus: *narrow comparison brings out dissimilarities, and broad comparison brings out similarities.*

2 The Relevance of Tocqueville

H. G. NICHOLAS

*Rhodes Professor of American History and Institutions,
Oxford University*

To anyone curious about America as a model for other societies, the appraisal which Alexis de Tocqueville made in his *Democracy in America* has more than a historic interest. The claims his work makes upon our attention are those of the true classic; it asks key questions and provides concepts to assist us in formulating our own answers. Tocqueville writes of his own time and place, but both his curiosities and his perception have a persisting relevance. A different America now confronts us, but it has its roots in the young nation that Tocqueville saw. The Britain that now looks across the Atlantic is one which is also just bridging the Straits of Dover; that ought, if anything, to sharpen the value of a philosophic Frenchman's view of what he habitually called 'the Anglo-Americans'.

The conjunction of stars that brought together young Tocqueville and Jacksonian America created, in the *Democracy*, something entirely new in socio-political inquiry. The book took shape as a result of a visit paid by two young liberally-minded French aristocrats, Gustave de Beaumont and Alexis de Tocqueville, to the United States in 1831, ostensibly to study the American penal system but actually, at least in Tocqueville's case, to see the new society that had arisen on American soil. The book published in France in 1835 under the title *De la Démocratie en Amérique* (Part II appeared in 1840) was immediately recognized as a *chef d'œuvre* both in France and in England. Proceeding simultaneously from two opposite poles – of induction from a wide range of observed and reported data, and of deduction from a fairly traditional set of moral and philosophical principles –

the *Democracy* presented for the first time a comprehensive assessment of a political system rooted in its own social attitudes and ethical assumptions. It had a moral base. It searched out and accepted 'natural' laws of social and political behaviour, but with equal assiduity and conviction it devised and recommended machinery for social and political regulation. It was descriptive, analytic and prescriptive.

Such a combination of techniques and purposes created problems and contradictions that critics then and since have been quick to seize upon. 'There were the makings of two works in his notes,' said Émile Faget, 'one on American life, the other on American democracy. He should have written on each separately.' '[His] descriptions of democracy as displayed in America,' said Bryce, '[are] no longer true in many points but ... in certain points they were never true. That is to say, some were true of America, but not of democracy in general, while others were true of democracy in general but not true of America.' Such criticisms have their validity, and disentangling such interweavings is a legitimate and continuing task of Tocquevillian scholarship. Yet such criticisms overlook the fact that it is precisely from this intermingling of the logically distinct (perhaps even the logically incompatible) that the peculiar potency and continuing fertility of Tocqueville's thought derives. This is precisely why he still speaks to us so much more pertinently than most political philosophers, so much more profoundly than all sociologists.

Logically, as well as to some extent chronologically, the *Democracy* comes at the end of a developing tradition of innovation and reform in European political thought. It is a tradition that began with the Utopias, models devised with complete freedom from an unlimited range of materials, not with serious expectations of any earthly realization but as points of reference for piecemeal reforms. The discovery and settlement of the New World provided an unexpected opportunity to attempt the translation of such models into actuality, as in Locke's Constitutions of Carolina or, more organically, the theocracy of Massachusetts. In proportion as these consciously contrived societies take root in their America, they provide in their turn objects of study, avoidance or emulation. In fact, of course, the Enlightenment was extraordinarily slow to use the comparative material at its disposal. It preferred to proceed from first principles and to hatch its own revolution and counter-revolution with the minimum of regard to what could be learned from the experience of other societies. Thus, when young Tocqueville and Beaumont set foot on American soil in 1831 they came historically quite late to learn what the democracy of the New World could teach them. Logically, however, they arrived at the culminating point of the process, when the limitations of merely deductive speculative theorizing had been amply exposed and when a fully articulated 'new society' was ripe for analysis and assessment.

While it is true that the study of American penal institutions was, in a sense, a cover for Tocqueville's real objective in visiting the United States, namely the examination of American democracy, yet it is not without significance that it was this which served as the official pretext for his and Beaumont's journey. The assumptions underlying the penal inquiry were closely akin to those which underpin the *Democracy*. Tocqueville and Beaumont's whole approach to penal reform proceeds, on good Benthamite lines, from the conviction that institutions are susceptible to change and improvement, however much, in the first instance, human nature is fixed and 'given'. It is from the datum of men as they are and institutions as they might be that the whole humanitarian approach to penal reform in the early nineteenth century proceeds. And this, no less, is the starting-point of the *Democracy*. The broad identity of human nature in both Europe and America is taken for granted. The revolutionary expectation of some swift generic change is wholly excluded. But the malleability of institutions, particularly political and legal institutions, is a firm conviction. This is why the study of the American system is worth while, not for its own sake, as an interesting or unique manifestation of human inventiveness and adaptability, but as something which may serve as a model to a Europe which, whether it realizes it or not, is being caught up in that same irresistible movement of democracy that the United States has experienced.

By 'Europe', however, whether he says so explicitly or not,

it is evident almost all the time that Tocqueville means France – the France which at the moment when he is writing seems to him in a particularly crucial phase of its development, having overthrown the *ancien régime* but being left still, after revolution and counter-revolution, without a political system that satisfies its needs. England, by contrast, not only has a less urgent claim on Doctor Tocqueville's diagnostic and therapeutic skills, but is indeed seen by him as only quasi-European, as being so different in evolution and condition as to be outside the applicability of most of what America has to teach. Indeed, as we shall see, England and America are to Tocqueville in many senses a unity, neither to be understood in isolation from the other, and both, despite the act of political separation, sustaining a large measure of social and intellectual symbiosis. So there is little in the *Democracy* which is directly addressed to England and English readers. The book's great success and influence in England owed much less to its prescriptions, which were seen to be mainly French in their application, than to its analysis, which was recognized as universal.

Here it is important to appreciate how Tocqueville views the American democracy. It is not just an American patent, something like Whitney's cotton gin, invented to meet American demands but exportable to serve an identical purpose wherever required. 'I confess that in America I saw more than America; I sought the image of democracy itself' – the celebrated admission raises more questions than it provides answers. In particular it draws attention to the existence, beneath the utilitarian and liberal belief in the malleability and transferability of institutions, of a certain fatalism or determinism in Tocqueville's approach to the phenomena of a democratic America. As he says in the preface to the *Democracy*: 'It appears to me beyond a doubt that sooner or later we shall arrive, like the Americans, at an almost complete equality of conditions.' This movement, a kind of social equivalent to the second law of thermodynamics, need not, of course, lead to democratic forms of government. This Tocqueville fully understands; indeed, some of his most graphic pages are those which point out the peculiar horrors of mass tyranny. But he is a good deal less than clear about where the boundary line between the inevitable equalization of conditions and the desirable institutions of democracy proper is to be found. Much of the inclination of his argument is a rebuttal, more or less explicit, of all those European diehards who equate American democracy with an indiscriminate debasement of standards – social, moral, aesthetic and intellectual. Chapter after chapter is devoted to demonstrating how, in America, popular rule can and does co-exist with respect for private and public rights, religion, property, scholarship, literature, chastity, poetry, etc. To the extent that this is shown, a good deal of Tocqueville's immediate polemical objective is achieved. Things can be so ordered in America; there is therefore no *a priori* reason why they could not be so ordered elsewhere. 'My aim has been to show, by the example of America, that laws, and especially manners, may exist which will allow a democratic people to remain free' (Part I, ch. xvii).

But Tocqueville's own honesty and curiosity do not allow him to stop there. His picture of the working of American institutions contains a wealth of material which can be used in rebuttal of this easy and central contention. He has seen the future in America and it works. But how much of that is due to the perpetuation of elements of the past? Furthermore, how much is due to the fact that it is in America that this future has been brought to pass? At moments he overlooks this, writing in his chapter on 'Democratic Government in America': 'In America democracy is given up to its own propensities; its course is natural and its activity is unrestrained; there, consequently, its real character must be judged.' But this almost romantic illusion of American democracy as some sort of a Mississippi without levees is repeatedly overtaken by a realization of American distinctiveness. 'The position of the Americans is ... quite exceptional, and it may be believed that no democratic people will ever be placed in a similar one.... Let us cease then to view all democratic nations under the mask of the American people and let us attempt to survey them at length with their own proper features' (Part II, book 1, ch. ix).

The first manifestation to Tocqueville of American distinctiveness lies in the nation's origins. As if in an honest, almost flaunted indifference to what his French critics may make of it, Tocqueville repeatedly resorts to the term 'the Anglo-Americans'. Indeed, he almost arrives at an anti-Crèvecœur paradox, of asking: 'Who is this Anglo-American, this new man?' His answer certainly comes near to saying: 'He is someone who has the best of both worlds, of aristocracy and democracy.' Anticipating Louis Hartz's theory of the liberal tradition in America, he finds that 'The lot of the Americans is singular: they have derived from the aristocracy of England the notion of private rights and the taste for local freedom [as against bureaucratic centralization]; and they have been able to retain both the one and the other because they have had no aristocracy to combat'. 'The English who emigrated three centuries [*sic*]¹ ago to found a democratic commonwealth on the shores of the New World had all learned to take a part in public affairs in their mother country; they were conversant with trial by jury; they were accustomed to liberty of speech and of the press, to personal freedom, to the notion of rights, and the practice of asserting them. Thus among the Americans it is freedom which is old – equality is of comparatively modern date' (Part II, book IV, ch. iv). The admission might seem to go too far. It breaks down democracy into its egalitarian and liberal components and locates the liberal elements exclusively in the Old World, in seventeenth-century England in fact. Thus it seems at times as if Tocqueville is directing the attention of his French readers almost as much across the Channel as across the Atlantic. Indeed, having regard to his consistent predilection for the liberal components in the democratic mixture, ought he not perhaps to have written a *Démocratie en Angleterre*?

Tocqueville himself proclaimed England to be intellectually his 'second country'. He had an English wife and many close English friends. He travelled a good deal in England and Ireland and was a close student of English history and institutions. Like many Frenchmen of his period and later

¹ Tocqueville is a bit loose with his chronology here. It is obviously the English of the seventeenth century, of the assertion of Puritan and parliamentary claims and of the 1688 revolution, that he has in mind.

(cf. Élie Halévy writing three generations later, of the England of 1815 and after), he was fascinated by the question of English revolution – why England had escaped its own counterpart of the events of 1789 and whether the immunity it had so far enjoyed would continue, and if so, why? In France, as it seemed to him, there was and would be no end to revolutions in his time, as he explains in a celebrated conversation with Nassau Senior in 1850. When he paid his first visit to England in 1833, as he records in his manuscript 'Notes, Ideas and Observations Gathered in England',[2] he 'arrived under the impression that the country was on the point of being thrown into the troubles of a great revolution'. He soon changed his mind. 'If one understands by a revolution a violent and sudden change, then England does not seem ripe for such an event and I see many reasons for thinking that it will never be so.' Essentially this is because the English aristocracy is not a brittle caste, as it had been in France, but an assimilating and fluid class willing to share its privileges and dilute its power. But this does not mean that Britain can evade the irresistible tide of democracy. 'The immediate future of European society is completely democratic; this can in no way be doubted.'

It is tempting to speculate why, with such ideas in his mind, his wealth of information and his widespread intellectual connections, Tocqueville never subjected the processes of English democratization to the same scrutiny that he expended on the finished product in America. A letter he wrote to Count Molé on his return from his 1833 visit to England may supply some of the explanation:

I think I have picked up some ideas in England, which, for me, are new, and may be useful later on; but I have never thought of writing a book about the country I hurried through.... It would take a very fatuous philosopher to imagine that he could understand England in six months. A year has ever seemed to me too short a time for proper appreciation of the United States, and it is infinitely easier to form clear ideas and precise conceptions about America

[2] Edited and translated by J. P. Mayer in *Journeys to England and Ireland* (London, 1958).

than about Great Britain. In America all laws originate more or less from the same idea. The whole of society, so to say, is based on just one fact: everything follows from one underlying principle. One could compare America to a great forest cut through by a large number of roads which all end in the same place. Once you have found the central point, you can see the whole plan in one glance. But in England the roads cross, and you have to follow along each one of them to get a clear idea of the whole.[3]

In other words, though England is subject to the universal process of democratization, the modifying and complicating influences are so manifold and sinuous that they defy neat or quick intellectual analysis, and would only yield their secret to prolonged historical study. Thus Tocqueville's main object, to display a model of democracy pure and simple, is much better served by the United States. Yet even here, by a historical paradox, the picture is complicated by English influences, by the American heritage from England. There is no *tabula rasa*. Thus, when talking in Part II of 'The Influences of Democracy upon Science and the Arts', Tocqueville uses language which seems to imply a belief in a single 'Anglo-America' or an 'Atlantic Community' with its own international divison of intellectual labour. Describing the American concentration on applied rather than pure science, he remarks:

At the head of the enlightened nations of the Old World the inhabitants of the United States more particularly distinguished one, to which they were closely united by a common origin and kindred habits. Among this people they found distinguished men of science, artists of skill, writers of eminence, and they were enabled to enjoy the treasures of the intellect without requiring to labour in amassing them. I cannot consent to separate America from Europe ... I consider the people of the United States as that portion of the English people which is commissioned to explore the wilds of the New World; while the rest of the nation, enjoying more leisure and less harassed by the

[3] Quoted in Introduction by Mayer to *Journeys to England and Ireland*.

drudgery of life, may devote its energies to thought, and enlarge in all directions the empire of the mind.

The neatness of even the American model must be modified to take account of the English inheritance.

Certainly it is New England that he views as the cradle of American democracy. Sometimes he talks as if all the democratic elements of the mother country had been literally transferred to the new by some process of self-selection, the Puritans attracting to themselves all who shared their capacity for self-government and leaving behind all who acquiesced in the perpetuation of aristocratic and feudal institutions. The idealization of New England democracy, with its township self-government, etc., is in large measure an idealization of English local government and Protestant or Puritan claims for the rights of the individual conscience. What then does America, as such, contribute?

The circumstances of colonization impose, in the first place, a rough equality. 'The happy and the powerful do not go into exile, and there are no surer guarantees of equality among men than poverty and misfortune.' Moreover 'the soil of America was opposed to a territorial aristocracy' (book I, ch. ii, 'Origin of the Anglo-Americans and its Importance in Relation to their Future Condition'). Do we have here a germ of Frederick Jackson Turner's thesis as embodied in *The Frontier in American History*? One might be pardoned for thinking so, were Tocqueville not on record elsewhere as opposed to Turner sixty years before him. In fact he deploys something less than his usual philosophic rigour in his explanation of why English systems of land tenure were not established in the New World. 'It was realized that in order to clear this land, nothing less than the constant and self-interested efforts of the owner himself were essential; the ground prepared, it became evident that its produce was not sufficient to enrich at the same time both an owner and a farmer. The land was then naturally broken up into small portions, which the proprietor cultivated for himself.' New England democracy is then literally founded on Plymouth Rock? Penury + infertility = democracy? Tocqueville knows that 'south-west of the Hudson', as he puts it, there were great

landed proprietors. But these, he tells us, were not really aristocratic, because 'they possessed no privileges, and the cultivation of their estates being carried on by slaves, they had no
tenants on them and consequently no patronage' ('Social
Conditions of the Anglo-Americans'). Yet Tocqueville attaches great significance to the abolition, at the American
Revolution, of the law of entail; as a result, 'the last trace of
hereditary rank and distinctions is destroyed'. What then of
frontier democracy, of the equation 'Free land + fertility =
democracy'? Here some *Turnerismus* is allowed in, but by
the back door. In dealing with 'The Causes Which Tend to
Maintain Democracy' in the United States, Tocqueville dis-
cerns three components, of which the first is 'the peculiar and
accidental situation in which Providence has placed the
American people'. This situation involves partly the happy
accident of America's isolation from any warring neighbours,
partly the lack of any great capital city, which will serve as
a breeding-ground for popular and revolutionary passions.
(The denizens of modern New York City or Chicago may
well sigh for Tocqueville's lost Elysium.) But the

> chief circumstance which has favoured the establishment
> and the maintenance of a democratic republic in the
> United States is the nature of the territory that the Ameri-
> cans inhabit. Their ancestors gave them the love of equal-
> ity and of freedom, but God himself gave them the means
> of remaining equal and free, by placing them upon a
> boundless continent. General prosperity is favourable to
> stability of all governments, but more particularly of a
> democratic one, which depends upon the will of the major-
> ity and especially upon the will of that portion of the com-
> munity which is most exposed to want.... In the United
> States not only is legislation democratic, but Nature herself
> favours the cause of the people.... [The] continent still
> presents ... limitless fields which the ploughshare of the
> husbandman has never turned.... At this very time thir-
> teen million of civilized Europeans are peaceably spread-
> ing over those fertile plains.... The stranger as well as the
> native is unacquainted with want. New wants are not to be
> feared..., since they can be satisfied without difficulty; the

growth of human passions need not be dreaded, since all passions may find an easy and a legitimate object; nor can men there be made too free, since they are scarcely ever tempted to misuse their liberty.

This, of course, is far from being the pure milk of Turner. The free land of the frontier contributed crucially to the maintenance of American democracy not because it was on the frontier, but because it was free and fertile. To Tocqueville the frontier itself, for all its romantic charm (in itself a very un-Turnerian concept), is an undemocratic, even anti-democratic agent. Like any good conservative, he deplores a condition of society in which all men are equal, not before the law, but before the six-shooter or the bowie-knife.

> It is in the Eastern states that the Anglo-Americans have been longest accustomed to the government of democracy and have adopted the habits and conceived the opinions most favourable to its maintenance. Democracy has gradually penetrated into their customs, their opinions, and their forms of social intercourse; it is to be found in all the details of daily life as well as in the laws.... In the Western states, on the contrary, a portion of the same advantages is still wanting. Many of the Americans of the West were born in the woods, and they mix the ideas and customs of savage life with the civilization of their fathers.... The inhabitants exercise no sort of control over their fellow citizens, for they are scarcely acquainted with one another.... Society seems to be ruled by chance.... Public business is conducted with an irregularity and a passionate, almost feverish excitement which does not announce a long or sure duration.
>
> (Part I, ch. xvii, 'Causes Which Tend to Maintain Democracy.)

What the frontier is is potential abundance. It is this David Potter aspect of its role,[4] its function as an agency of plenty, that Tocqueville regards as underpinning democracy – and this, not by stimulating democratic demands but by curbing

---

[4] See David Potter, *A People of Plenty* (Chicago, 1954).

democratic excesses. Free land makes conservatives because it makes every man a potential, if not an actual property-owner, like the émigré Frenchman whom Tocqueville encountered in 'one of the most remote districts of Pennsylvania', who, having been 'a great leveller and ardent demagogue' at home, now discoursed eloquently on the rights of property and the necessity of gradations in society.

Yet despite his prescient perception of the links between American plenty and American democracy, Tocqueville makes no serious attempt to work out what implications, if any, this has for his inescapably about-to-be-equalized societies of Europe. Towards the end of his long chapter on 'The Causes Which Tend to Maintain Democracy' in the United States, Tocqueville does ask whether laws and customs are sufficient to maintain democratic institutions in countries other than America. He returns a somewhat cautious answer: that no other nations outside America have the same laws and customs, and that one can therefore only hazard an opinion. But since human nature is the same everywhere, and since it is on legislation and the cultivation of appropriate behaviour rather than on 'the nature of the country and the favour of circumstances' that Americans have relied for the preservation of their democracy, so other countries with identical human nature but different circumstances may *mutatis mutandis* hope to do the same.

If we could put Tocqueville in the witness-box and cross-question him, this is the point at which we should ask him to resolve the elements of contradiction between his assertion about the primacy of laws and customs over circumstances and his earlier insistence that 'the nature of the territory that the Americans inhabit' is 'the chief circumstance' which has favoured the establishment and maintenance 'of American democracy'. Take away space and plenty, and would it still work? Was Jefferson right to think that the Republic could not survive the day when a stop has to be put to the diffusion of property and Americans pile up on each other in cities as they do in Europe? Would Marx be right to accord America no exception from the rule that a propertyless proletariat would struggle with a bourgeoisie owning the means of production and, of course, win? Surely, our cross-examiner

would insist, Tocqueville must have read Madison in the
Tenth *Federalist* Paper and formed some opinion about
Madison's thesis that the dominant struggle in society was always between those who own property and those who do not?
Surely he must have reached his own conclusion about how,
in American democracy, this struggle was to be contained
within manageable limits by the Constitution, by the institutions, social and political, or by access to a plenty so inex-
haustible that productivity would always seem more important than apportionment? Surely he would have a clear direc-
tive for his European readers based on these conclusions?

Unfortunately one cannot hector the dead. Tocqueville
escapes question; all we can do is scratch about for hints in a
book which is not primarily interested in the question we
pose. The question exists all right, but on the confines of
Tocqueville's thought – whenever, for example, he talks
about 'restless propensities' or 'opposing the idea of right to
the feelings of envy'. But the celebrated account of 'The Unlimited Power of the Majority and its Consequences' does not
include any reference to the most familiar assertion of the
claims of the many against the few – the use of taxation as an
instrument of equalization; attention is almost exclusively
focused on the realm of opinion. A similar silence pervades
the chapter in Part II devoted to 'The Desire for Wealth and
for Physical Prosperity'. Tocqueville's treatment of American
parties shows little trace of Madisonian awareness; 'the secret
propensities' of the parties are what they have always been in
free societies, to limit or extend 'the authority of the people'.
But there is little or no suggestion that this may take the form
of a claim by the poor on the resources of the rich; it is aristocracy versus democracy in a socio-political, not an economic
conflict that dominates Tocqueville's treatment. Only in that
arresting chapter on 'Occupations and Business Callings',
with its graphic forecast of the rise of mass production and
the consequent debasement of the labourer and the elevation
of the capitalist, are we given a glimpse of the road which an
industrialized America might travel. But even here the link
between the developments in technology and economics on
the one hand and their consequences for politics on the other
is not explored. In place of any adumbration of a Marxist

revolution, we are told that at the end of such a development 'though there are rich men, the class of rich men does not exist; ... these rich individuals have no feelings or purposes in common'. The *aperçu* has a certain distinctive validity for the way in which American industrial society was to evolve, but it does not provide a basis for any political projection, beyond the warning that 'the friends of democracy should keep their eyes anxiously fixed in this direction; for if ever a permanent inequality of conditions and aristocracy again penetrate into the world, it may be predicted that this is the channel by which they will enter'.

If the frontier is ruled out as a creator and preserver of American democracy, and diffused plenty, its enveloping nimbus, is accorded at best an uncertain pre-eminence in such a capacity, what about the claims of that most American of tutelary deities, the Revolution? Alas, any attempt to secure Tocqueville's endorsement for the celebrations of 1776 is doomed to failure. So far from regarding the Declaration of Independence and its accompanying phenomena as crucial to the establishment of American democracy, Tocqueville often writes as if unaware that any such revolutionary episode had occurred. Talking of the scars left on societies by protracted social struggles, he affirms that 'the great advantage of the Americans is that they have arrived at a state of democracy without having to endure a democratic revolution; and that they are born equal, instead of becoming so'. Again, apropos of Napoleon's centralization of French administration: 'No necessity of this kind has ever been felt by the Americans who, having passed through no revolution, and having governed themselves from the first, never had to call upon the State to act for a time as their guardian.' In fairness it must be said that both these quotations are taken from a context in which the French Revolution and its excesses form the point of departure. (Tocqueville's father saw six members of his family tried and executed in one afternoon under the Terror. By French standards the American Revolution had been a pretty tame affair.)

Yet, bloodshed and violence apart, it is obvious that Tocqueville did not regard the American Revolution as having constituted any great traumatic experience. 'There is one

country in the world where the great social transformation of
which I am speaking [the movement towards democracy]
seems to have nearly reached its natural limits. It has been
effected with ease and simplicity; say rather that this country
is reaping the fruits of the democratic revolution which we
are undergoing, without having had the revolution itself.'
The sentiment, thus first enunciated in the preface, recurs at
other points in the *Democracy*, and indeed such a contention
underlies Tocqueville's continuous emphasis on the English
origins of American democracy. The problem indeed is quite
other: to establish, having regard to Tocqueville's high estimate of the democratic levels attained in colonial America,
particularly New England, what he imagined the causes and
consequences of the American Revolution to have been. To
give an account of this chapter of American history is by no
means central to his purpose. From incidental remarks (e.g.
apropos of 'The Sovereignty of the People in the U.S.A., Part
I, ch. iv) one gathers the impression that he thought the Revolution merely accelerated certain democratic developments
already fairly far advanced, such as extension of the franchise
and the direct election of public officials. The one revolutionary reform which he explicitly singles out for mention is, as
we have seen, the abolition of entail. Even the disestablish-
ment of religion, which excites Tocqueville's warmest appro-
bation, is not explicitly related to the events of 1776. The
universalist pretensions of the Declaration of Independence
and the Bills of Rights in the federal and state constitutions
are passed over in virtual silence, as if the philosopher who
had seen the bloodshed that followed in the wake of the proc-
lamation of the *Droits de l'Homme* had judged it safer to
avoid the nemesis that might attend the invocation of such
glittering generalities on the American scene. More seriously,
we know that in general he regarded the political principles of
the revolutionary settlement as essentially Anglo-American.
Above all, it was not the assertion of general principles that
excited his respect. What he sought and admired was a right
which got itself established as an institution, like trial by
jury, or in a habit of mind, such as the right of association. In
relation to such rights, all the American Revolution could do
was to transfer responsibility for their observance exclusively

into American hands. Nor, when it came to the application of the American model, could these be exported by invoking a revolution or proclaiming a declaration; they were rooted, like the laws, in 'the manners and customs of the people'.

What then is left of America's utility as a model for European builders of democracy? They cannot hope, at least on Tocqueville's side of the Channel, to borrow the national and racial origins of the 'Anglo-Americans'. They cannot indeed in France hope to draw much on the democratizing legacy of Protestant Puritanism, though Tocqueville is at pains, at one point, to demonstrate from American experience that there is nothing in Roman Catholicism which is necessarily incompatible with political democracy – provided only that the American separation of church and state be adopted as well. Nor can the long-settled communities of Europe, where 'frontiers' are merely legal boundaries separating one national territory from another, be born again as pioneering equals, or enjoy, at a subsequent stage of evolution, the sense of the infinite abundance of unsettled land which protects the acquisition of property from exciting either the pangs of envy or the illusions of grandeur. Theoretically, since both France and England were, even in Tocqueville's time, relatively rich countries, he might have envisaged expanding productivity as providing, in another form, that cushion of plenty which David Potter claims has been available to American democracy at all stages in its development. In fact Tocqueville seems to entertain no such expectation; where the physical and economic context is concerned, he contents himself with asserting that democracy can adapt itself to an environment as different from America as Europe is. There remains one American experience that Europe can, only too easily, copy – has indeed done so: the Revolution – not, of course, against a mother country, but against father-figures, monarchs, aristocracies, bureaucracies. But this, as we have seen, Tocqueville regards, in its original American form, as supererogatory and, in its European adaptation, as catastrophic.

What then remains? There is, first and foremost, the whole political and constitutional structure that forms the bulk of Part I of the *Democracy*. Yet it is important to remember that Tocqueville's main purpose – as elsewhere in the *Democracy*, but particularly here – is not to hold up a model for emulation, but to demonstrate by an analysis of a democratic government at work that such a system is both feasible and tolerable. He repeatedly tells us, as in the chapter on 'The Real Advantages that American Society Derives from Democratic Government', that he does not 'regard the American constitution as the best, or as the only one, that a democratic people may establish. In showing the advantages which the Americans derive from the government of democracy, I am therefore very far from affirming, or believing, that similar advantages can be obtained only from the same laws.'[5]

None the less, one has to be a purblind reader of Tocqueville not to be aware that there are certain features of the American system which excite his especial admiration and which he would dearly like to see emulated in any other state seeking to make itself safe through democracy. Federalism as such he regards as a response to scale[6] and not therefore a necessary article of export. But the way in which American government, as he sees it, is decentralized, with each unit as responsive as possible to local needs and promoting the development of local participation – this he obviously regards as lying near the heart of the matter. The panegyric on the New England township as the schoolroom of national democracy, the arena in which true democratic habits are bred – this is in evident and continuous contrast to the strangling centralization of government and administration that the *ancien régime* bequeathed to post-revolutionary France, there to be nursed and intensified. How such a crucial feature is to be emulated, when the roots of this American style of government lie so deep in the English parish (or even, as many of Tocqueville's contemporaries believed, in the German forest), is never examined, but it is obvious that without it, any

---

[5] Cf. 'The Constitution of the United States resembles those fine creations of human industry which ensure wealth and renown to their inventors, but which are profitless in other hands.' ('The Federal Constitution', Part I, ch. viii.)

[6] Though not to diversity. 'I do not know of any European nation, however small, that does not present less uniformity in its different provinces than the American people, which occupy a territory as extensive as one half of Europe, (loc. cit.).

European democracy, in Tocqueville's view, would be starting life maimed and enfeebled. Although an admirer of English local administration, Tocqueville thought that its preservation owed more to aristocratic particularism than to locally
rooted democracy; he felt it necessary, in conversation with
Mill, to issue a warning that as the British aristocracy lost
their control of locally elected bodies, they might seek to impose centralization in its place. Analogous to the energizing
effect of American local government is the benefit in the legal
system which flows from the spread of the jury system, particularly its extension to civil suits. Here again it is the
educative effect of such participation in attaching the citizen
to his society that Tocqueville finds particularly important in
both America and England.

Such emphases reflect very clearly the bias of a liberal from
an *étatiste* homeland. Such a bias no doubt explains why
Tocqueville feels no obligation, as many students of American democracy have, to extol the great office of the Presidency, or the representative role of Congress. France had already had unfortunate counterparts to these. Indeed, it is the
curb rather than the spurs that Tocqueville recommends in
both contexts, especially since democracy cannot, for him any
more than subsequently for Bryce, be relied upon to select
the best men to govern it. So he favours less, rather than
more, direct election and thinks, apropos of the comparative
merits of House and Senate, that 'the time must come when
the American republics will be obliged more frequently to
introduce the plan of election by an elected body into their
system of representation or run the risk of perishing miserably among the shoals of democracy'.

Bearing in mind this consistent Tocquevillian preference
for freedom over equality and constitutionality over repre-
sentativeness, one might have expected to find, in his American model, a greater enthusiasm for judicial review, the device that has so regularly served as the governor on the engine
of American politics. Yet, greatly as he extols the ingenuity of
the Constitution's framers in devising their judicial system
and the statesmanship of the Supreme Court Justices who
preside over it, he shows little prescience about the functioning of judicial review as a brake upon what he would un-

doubtedly regard as the excesses of democracy.[7] Of course, he is writing before the Court has yet assumed much of a guardianship for the personal rights and liberties enshrined in the first ten amendments. At the same time, one can readily discern in Tocqueville's admiration for the American law, and his implicit approval of the lawyers as constituting a crypto-aristocracy for America, a modification of the naked principle of majority rule that he whole-heartedly endorses. Does he regard judicial review as capable of emulation? Hardly, since he sees it as essentially a by-product of federalism, with its divided and potentially conflicting sovereignties – and in any case as almost too complex for description, still less imitation. Later, when he visited England in 1835, and discovered how large a part the courts played in the administrative process, he saw that he had not previously fully appreciated the power of the English judiciary. But in the *Democracy* he rests on the clear distinction between the role of the judges in a system with a superior, written constitution and their much more limited role where Parliament, in effect, makes the constitution as it goes along. Tocqueville makes quite clear that, in his opinion, there is no scope for introducing – as for example some people have recently been advocating – a dash of judicial review into the English system.

The role of lawyers in general might be another matter. It is true that, as he himself points out, this is linked to the functioning of the English common law and, as such, is not readily reproduced in a Continental Roman law context. Nevertheless, in a more general sense, in his deep conviction of the importance for a democracy of there being a rule of law and of the necessity of having a priesthood to preserve it, Tocqueville is pretty clearly holding up America not merely to envy but also to emulation. In the very last pages of his

[7] Though it is, no doubt, with a concern about the clash between Jacksonian majoritarianism and Marshallian constitutionalism that he warns against the 'secret tendency to diminish the judicial power' by the popular election or recall of judges. 'I venture to predict that these innovations will sooner or later be attended with fatal consequences, and that it will be found out at some future period that the attack which is made upon the judicial power has affected the democratic republic itself' ('The Tyranny of the Majority', Part I, ch. xvi).

book (Vol. II, part IV, ch. vii) he reminds his readers that 'The strength of the courts of law has ever been the greatest security which can be offered to personal liberty; but this is more especially the case in democratic ages: private rights and interests are in constant danger, if the judicial power does not grow more extensive and more strong to keep pace with the growing equality of conditions'.

The law and its operations form then at once a link and a barrier between the workings of majoritarian government and the private citizen, uniting the two in areas of legitimate public concern, and preserving for each its own sphere where the aggression of either would be harmful to the other. To Tocqueville, who combined a liberal's concern for the public weal with an aristocratic regard for the individual, nothing could be more important than to preserve, in their full vigour, their dual identities. Here, more perhaps than anywhere else, the experience of America excited him both to admiration and concern. Here, more than in any single institution or practice, he finds matter for the instruction of his European readers. In the end what he is writing is not a set of instructions for democratic constitution-making, not even a description of how they order things in America with the implicit injunction 'go and do thou likewise'. It is a delineation of the many forms that democracy may take, of its multiple and insidious ramifications, of its remarkable and often unexpected potencies, of the range of devices available for its modification and control, of its compatibility with the highest and the lowest manifestations of the individual personality. Tocqueville looks at American democracy rather as the Tolstoy of *War and Peace* looked at Russia. He is both hedgehog and fox; he sees one big thing and many little things. The big thing is the universal movement towards an equality of social conditions; the little things are in fact as diverse in scale as the phenomena of North America itself. In the *Democracy* they are all to be found. The reader may help himself. Some are to be admired. Some are to be deplored. But, most important of all, they co-exist.

NOTE ON READING

Tocqueville's classic is available in many versions. From many points of view the original translation by Henry Reeve remains the best, but a more accurate and complete text is to be found in the version by Phillips Bradley (New York: Knopf, 1945). A convenient, somewhat abbreviated edition appears in the World's Classics edited by Henry Steele Commager (Oxford, 1946). George Pierson's *Tocqueville and Beaumont in America* (New York: Oxford U.P., 1938) is indispensable for the background of the *Democracy*, while Tocqueville's notebooks are available separately in an English translation by George Lawrence under the title *Alexis de Tocqueville: Journey to America* (London, 1959).

3 Europe and American Design

Reyner Banham

Professor of the History of Architecture, University College, London

I. DESIGNERS NEED AMERICA

Design – the design of anything from a nut-and-bolt to a New Town for 100,000 people – is an art of the possible just as much as is the art of politics. Moreover, the failure of design in a physical product will become more immediately and painfully apparent than the failure of a policy or an alliance, so the designer's work must involve as many known factors as possible. Designers therefore tend to work by example and to emulate successes: even when they claim high originality they are usually modest enough to admit that they stand upon the shoulders of other men; even when they aim by design to improve the condition of society, they must be able to point at other societies that have demonstrably benefited by designers' work.

Discussion of design – especially among designers – therefore requires a large intellectual stock of handy, striking, reliable, appalling, reassuring, etc., exemplars. Some are immediately to hand – awful warnings seem to be all around us – but examples of the morally sound, the hopefully humane, the ingeniously simple, the future indicative, seem always to be further away and harder to find. To some extent there is a psychological necessity in this. If something is to be held up as an ideal, it shouldn't be held close enough for sceptical onlookers to notice the oil dripping from the underside of the crankcase, or the scratches where the lid has had to be prised off with a kitchen knife. Examples of the good have therefore tended to come from the dead past (the Middle Ages, ancient Greece and Rome), from the exotically remote (Greenland,

Polynesia) or from the culturally underprivileged (peasant crafts from all over, and 'untutored' engineers in advanced cultures).

Missing from such an index of sources of inspiration must obviously be the future, since it doesn't exist as a physical fact anywhere. Yet design is always about futures, even if it thinks it is only about a better present, so that almost any kind of reasonable facsimile of a future is welcome, especially if it produces concrete objects that designers can admire. Since 1917 successive socialist countries have partially fulfilled this difficult role for some part of the world's design community, but none can rival the very long and persuasive run that America has had in the part. As a model of the future, America has been around longer and is more diverse, not only in its parts but also in the kind of design those parts have been able to offer to the Old World. Not only has America been some sort of future, but it has also seemed exotic and culturally underprivileged. To educated Europeans, the pale-faces who built the first Chicago skyscrapers seem to have been just as much noble savages as the redskins who built the pueblos. The fact that they were nothing of the sort – both William le Baron Jenney (1832–1907) and Louis Sullivan (1856–1924), to name two conspicuous examples, were Paris-trained – meant that the view of America and its artefacts taken by European polemicists had to be at least selective, and in some cases so selective as to be practically mythical. Where a political observer like Tocqueville had the wit, leisure and motivation to see America whole in order to hold it up as a working model of a democratic future, few design theorists have ever had the opportunity or inclination to emulate either his comprehensiveness or his fair-mindedness. America's long and useful life as a lesson to designers has been enjoyed only at the cost of being seen in extremely par-tial views. Sometimes the partiality has been that of de-liberate concealment; sometimes the polemicist has frankly warned his readers what not to heed, to look on this picture but *not* on that, and thus to create a kind of split image of America.

II. THE DIVIDED IMAGE

This problem of America as a model for European design is clearly epitomized by Le Corbusier's stern warning in *Vers une Architecture* (1923): 'Let us listen to the counsels of American engineers. But let us beware of American architects....' The immediately preceding pages had featured six illustrations of United States factories to make a point about the importance of surface (as against only one European example) and eight United States grain elevators (as against no European) to make a point about volume. So vital were these pictures to the rising Modern Movement in European architecture that they had already acquired almost totemic standing; the same pictures turn up again and again, and they are literally the same pictures. One particular packet of photographs appears to have circulated traceably through the Corbusier–Gropius network for almost a decade.

For them, these industrial structures were visible proof that engineers, above all North American engineers, were noble savages of technology, unconscious classicists who 'not in pursuit of an architectural idea, but guided simply by the necessities of an imperative demand ... show us the way and create plastic facts, clear and limpid, giving rest to our eyes and to the mind the pleasure of geometric forms'. Thus Le Corbusier again, but Walter Gropius as early as 1911 had asserted that 'the newest work halls of the North American industrial trusts can bear comparison, in their overwhelming monumental power, with the buildings of ancient Egypt'. The father of this vision of American design was, effectively, the turbulent Viennese architect and *laide-lettriste* Adolf Loos, who had visited America in 1893–6, and been vouchsafed something of a revelation – of a clean, well-ordered society unaffected by social pomp or unwarranted stylistic décor. If that revelation has an all-too-familiar aspect, it should still be remembered that Loos was specifically responsible for some of its most familiar details. He recounts, in an essay of 1902, how an American lady, when asked about the most striking difference between America and Austria, immediately cited the superiority of American plumbing, which launches Loos into a panegyric to 'the plumber ... the quartermaster of civilization, the civilization that really counts today'. He praised, as have generations since, the rationality of United States work-clothes, but professed to admire even more the fact that *der Mann im Overall* did not have to change into more formal gear for anything less portentous than a funeral. The arguments of his epoch-making squib *Ornament und Verbrechen* (*Ornament and Crime*, 1908) do not make a special point of any United States examples of good unaffected design, but echoes of his American experiences reverberate throughout the text.

As do they also in the words of others who admired American designers such as Frank Lloyd Wright. Statements by Wright that the surfaces of walls 'should be let alone from base to cornice' (1908), though more honoured in the breach than the observance, seemed to confirm the impression that Wright did indeed see design in terms at least analogous to Loos's moral stand against ornament, and made him one of the heroes of the purifying faction in European design.

That faction, disciplined, stern, rationalizing, classicist, saw these noble savages of United States engineering as the creators of an unconscious architecture that was spare, tidy, regular, unadorned, gifted with 'nobility and strength' (Gropius again). Against this, the school-trained architects of North America were seen as producing works of even greater and more florid depravity than their most unreformed European contemporaries. For someone like Le Corbusier, bent on extirpating the classically styled frivolities of the École des Beaux-Arts, the almost total dominance of the Beaux-Arts style in the United States in the early 1920s was particularly galling; so was the application of traditional ornament to skyscrapers, an illustration of which was used to justify the warning given at the head of this section.

For these reasons, any United States architects who, like Wright, overtly rejected academic formulae and appeared to cleave to the 'native genius in United States architecture' (the title much later of one of Sibyl Moholy-Nagy's books of noble savagery) were received with enthusiasm when and as their work became known. The Chicago School of commercial skyscraper design was viewed in a shortened historical perspective that ignored the ornamental preoccupations of Louis

Sullivan, and gave greater weight to his famous dictum that 'Form follows function'. This was clearly the kind of sentiment that was expected from a pure and unspoiled noble savage. The apparent collapse of the Chicago School almost before Europe discovered it as a right and hopeful preview of the future could be explained only as the work of evil forces. The pious myth of the 'ruination' of the Chicago School and of Louis Sullivan by East Coast classicists at the Chicago World's Fair of 1893 was accepted uncritically in Europe and within less than a decade by, e.g., Hermann Muthesius, who saw it in 1902 as further testimony of the decadence of United States architecture. This myth was largely of Wright's creation. As of 1910, no United States architect had a higher reputation than Wright among the European avant-garde, and he was to maintain that position long after his career had gone into its first eclipse in the United States. Much of that reputation depended on European-grown myths about the appropriateness of his work to a technological culture. Thus, the Dutch modernist J. J. P. Oud said of Wright's Robie house, which he knew at the time (1917) only in photographs: 'All the parts of this building, including the furnishings, were developed along mechanistic lines ...' – a proposition that would doubtless have shocked Wright. It would certainly have been anathema to his later European admirers like Bruno Zevi who, in *Towards an Organic Architecture* (1947), used Wright's post-1930 works to combat the mechanistic style that Mainstream European design had derived, in part, from American models.

III. SOMETHING ELSE

Although this apparent dichotomy between supposedly honest simplicity and supposedly corrupt sophistication has provided the most continuous theme for European attitudes to United States design for half a century, throughout the whole of this period there has been a confusing third term in the argument – the image, variously constructed, of 'the American city'. More precisely, one should say the image of New York (with an occasional assist from the Chicago Loop) because that image is of close-clustered skyscrapers and elevated

railroads. The power of this image is not only intrinsic, it is
also a consequence of the manner in which it was first presented to Europe – through magazine illustrations and the
beginnings of the visual mass media.

So, when the young Laszlo Moholy-Nagy (later to be head
of the Institute of Design in Chicago) wept in 1905 to discover that there were no skyscrapers in Szeged, the nearest
large town to his birthplace in Hungary, his disappointment
could only be measured against magazine pictures of New
York. The same process, with local variants, helped to stamp
the same skyscraper image on the minds of every provincial
intellectual of Europe, forming, ultimately, the standard ikon
of the City of the Future.

Thus Paolo Buzzi, Italian Futurist poet, to Umberto Boc-
cioni, Italian Futurist sculptor and painter, in 1909:

Érige les constructions massives pour la Ville future
Qu'elle s'élève dans le ciel libre des aviateurs

and the designs of their contemporary, Antonio Sant'Elia,
show Milan transformed into a city of skyscrapers. But these
same sketches are also the first to show the skyscraper city re-
made as a conscious work of art, which has also been a European rather than American ambition, with an ultimately
contradictory consequence which will appear later. What appears immediately is that round the top of Sant'Elia's vision-
ary towers runs something calling itself *Reclam-luminosa*.
Views of Times Square by night are not common in the
architectural literature until later, so this early manifestation
of illuminated advertising in the skyscraper context is not
only remarkable in itself, but also suggests that the skyscraper
image always had romantic overtones of the glamour of hardsell capitalism. When Le Corbusier takes up the theme, in a
projected *Ville Contemporaine pour Trois Millions d'Habi-
tants* (1922) that was deeply indebted to Sant'Elia, the skyscrapers are quite clearly to be regarded as glamorous symbols
of power which will 'contain the city's brains, the brains of
the whole nation. Everything is concentrated in them; apparatus for abolishing time and space, telephone, cables,
wireless; the banks, business affairs and the control of in-

dustry, finance, commerce and specialization'. It was almost his only excursion into *grattes-ciel à l'Américaine,* but his comment on finally arriving in New York in 1935, that the real skyscrapers were 'too small', suggests that the romantic image still held him in thrall.

However, it was among the German Modernists (especially the Expressionists) that the romantic attitude to skyscrapers really flourished. In the 1920s it spills over from the unexecuted projects of Mies van der Rohe and the illustrated books of Bruno Taut and Eric Mendelsohn into classic movies like *Metropolis,* and then into English epics like *The Shape of Things to Come* (which was even more thoroughly overrun by Middle Europeans than other English films of the high Korda period: Moholy-Nagy was a consultant on the visuals).

The romanticism shows in other ways. One German line, as in the writings of Richard Neutra or the *obiter dicta* of Mies van der Rohe, was to prefer skyscrapers 'in a state of becoming', the bare steel skeleton before the 'architecture' had been added. The other was to turn the classicist/purifying images literally back to front, and to revel pictorially, as in Mendelsohn's books of 1928 and 1929, in the untidy pipe runs, access stairs and ancillaries that had not appeared in the original Corbusier–Gropius pictures of their neat and regular fronts. Sometimes the Futurist romance of technology is heightened by direct fakery, the dodging-in of supernumerary aircraft in the skies over already complex multi-level traffic.

Such visions of the glamour of high technology, affluence and aggressive commercialism still persist and colour European apprehensions of America, but often with their meanings reversed when they are actually implemented. The 'contradictory consequence' of the skyscraper as a work of European art, referred to above, is that it often emerges as a social welfare residential block, not a commercial tower. From the time of the Cité de la Muette by Baudouin and Lods outside Paris in 1933, to the literal collapse of this image at Ronan Point, London, the European skyscraper has been at least intended as a symbol of better housing for the people. There are economic and technical justifications for such a form of construction, even where there is less pressure on land than in Manhattan, but they have proved so feeble over the years in Britain that one can only surmise that the 'City of the Future' image is the main motivation. In that case, this most deliberate following of an American model in design is also one of the most perverse.

IV. DICHOTOMY, ROUND 2

In the discussion reviewed so far, discussion of product design is almost completely absent. This may be due to the fact that, Tiffany-ware aside, few United States products physically known to Europeans would come within the category of 'applied art' which still framed most discussions of design aesthetics. While objects like small tools, typewriters and plumbers' hardware were increasingly well known, only a few extreme radicals like Loos and Le Corbusier felt the need to cite them in argument. Indeed, if they needed examples of neat, unadorned products they rarely needed to look further offshore than Britain at that time. In 1920, when Le Corbusier needed a gimmick-name for his projected prefabricated house, he punned on Citroën, not Ford. By the 1930s, however, the movies were making the minutiae of United States domestic life, its objects and their surrounding life-style, increasingly familiar to Europeans ('Andy Hardy' still labels a life-style and domestic environment to which many of my generation covertly aspire), but the systematic evaluation of United States product design really depends on a combination of other factors, viz.:

(*a*) The formulation by Herbert Read (1936) and others of theories of 'Good Design' based on the notion of the well-made, unadorned functional object.

(*b*) The emergence of a body of professional United States industrial designers like Norman Bel Geddes and Walter Dorwin Teague in the wake of the Depression.

(*c*) The physical uprooting and transfer to the United States of many of the leading Continental designers, architects and theorists during the political upheavals of the mid-1930s.

Having arrived in North America, most of these migrants tried to realize their progressive dreams of American culture, identifying themselves with aspects of America that had been traditionally admired by European intellectuals: Gropius was reportedly deeply flattered to find himself in moral and intellectual sympathy with his first New England clients. Professionally, however, most of them – especially those from the Bauhaus circle – tended to find homes in United States design education, often with the active support of well-meaning local magnates (like the Armours in Chicago) whose motives are uncommonly difficult to distinguish from those of earlier well-meaning magnates who had imported the now despised Beaux-Arts tradition. Both generations believed they were improving and beautifying the United States scene; both can now be seen to have simply bought a style while – as David Gebhard pointed out in 1968 – mislaying the social and moral ideology that gave the style life and strength.

On this occasion, it is true, the ideologues were imported with the ideology, and stayed around to give moral force to their concepts much longer than in any previous case. Moholy-Nagy and Gropius were to die in harness in America, and German remained the second language of United States design education until deep into the 1960s. Even so, the long-term effect of all this was so strikingly slight in terms of quality or style of design that the jesting question 'What did the Bauhaus ever do for America?' is very difficult to answer except with 'Not much, except give it a bad conscience!'

One of the most striking manifestations of this bad conscience was the emergence of a new formulation of the old dichotomy between good and bad in American design. The author of this new and encyclopedic formulation was one of the imported ideologues, Sigfried Giedion, in two books that have polarized discussion of the subject for almost three decades. An art historian and a professing disciple of the methodology of the great Heinrich Wölfflin, Giedion set himself up to write the history of the Modern Movement while it was actually happening, establishing himself as the confidant of its leading exponents, as an expounder and elaborator of its theories, and as the secretary of its organizational arm, CIAM (*les Congrès Internationaux d'Architecture Moderne*).

Though a Swiss resident and not under direct political threat, he nevertheless followed the exiled Modernists to the United States, first as Charles Eliot Norton lecturer in 1938–9, returning to Harvard for a longer teaching stint in 1941–5. From the first period came his compendious *Space, Time and Architecture* (1941, endlessly revised and enlarged) and from the second, *Mechanization Takes Command* (1948). The first is a classic, the second a legend; between them they have fixed the image of American design.

Giedion resumes the noble savage theme, but the native genius now comes into more detailed focus. He is spare and economical, producing clapboard houses and the balloon frame, Shaker domestic design and Windsor chairs, leading ultimately to the plain surfaces and framed construction of the Chicago School. He is rational and analytical; the 'reshaping of tools and the mechanization of hand processes' are presented as peculiarly American achievements, even when their European origins are chronicled. He exhibits Yankee ingenuity; Linus Yale, Jr, of cylinder-lock fame is presented as a kind of inventor-Thoreau (pity he wasn't making mousetraps!) and is the hero of a long section on 'The Means of Mechanization' in *Mechanization Takes Command,* outranking even the progenitors of the 'American system' of standardized and interchangeable mechanical components. Above all, the native genius is 'just plain folks' and *Mechanization,* a work devoted overwhelmingly to United States technology, is subtitled 'A Contribution to Anonymous History'.

But, having defined the native genius, Giedion has to point out that his descendants have gone astray. Technology is neutral and can – and has been – misused. The mechanization of baking has led to flabby sliced supermarket bread (not a word about Pepperidge Farms, which had already started); the mechanization of death in the slaughterhouse of Chicago triggers pre-echoes of Hannah Arendt concerning the mass slaughter of human beings in the Second World War. Above all, the mechanization of common products has led to a new kind of bad design which, unlike the older type of bad design, is not an imported antiquarian fancy from Europe, but a down-home

modern popular fantasy. Giedion in *Mechanization* (and almost simultaneously Edgar Kauffman, Jr, of the Museum of
Modern Art) was the first to identify this 'wrong' style which
he called 'Streamline'. Kauffman, who must have had connections with the Grand Rapids furniture trade, called it
'Borax'; most of us now simply call it 'Styling', to distinguish
its superficiality from the (alleged) depth of Good Design.

The recognition of this American modern, mechanistic but
'false' style produced a shock of betrayal; American design
was discovered to be its own enemy. Giedion handles his disappointment with a certain stoicism, recognizing that even
his own friends in the reforming European Modern Movement had some responsibility for the outcome. Kauffman
took up a more embattled stance and offered to educate the
public out of accepting this bad design. But some Europeans
responded in a tone of sheer cultural paranoia. Thus Max
Bill, ex-Bauhaus designer-critic, and Swiss like Giedion, declared of United States car-styling in 1954 that if this sort
of thing was not brought to a halt, 'the final collapse of our
civilization could not be averted much longer'.

V. ALL RIGHT; WHAT IS AMERICAN DESIGN?

Max Bill's observation is bound to sound hysterical nowadays.
Western civilization has survived worse, even if his own designer's universe was profoundly threatened. Nevertheless, it
illustrates sharply enough the ingenuousness with which both
design and America were approached twenty years ago – and
still are, for his tone is still persistently echoed. For serious
design theorists, down to and including Bill's *protégé révolté*,
the Argentinian Tomás Maldonado, bad design has become
evidence of Americanization; the doomed folly of capitalism
is seen to be almost axiomatically demonstrated by the depravity and vulgarity of American car-styling. If America has
triggered any *crise de conscience* in the world of design comparable to that of Vietnam in politics, it was precipitated by
the rising tail-fins of early-fifties Cadillacs and the abundant
chromium of all Detroit products of that vintage.

The sense of shock was worse for its suddenness, its utter
reversal of the dream of good Uncle FDR in which Euro-

peans tended still to bask in the early 1950s under the Marshall Plan. But if it required a profound reversal of emotional stance, it revealed a very shallow reversal intellectually. If various starry-eyed admirers of the dream-image of a universal American future had thought more deeply in matters economic and sociological, they must surely have seen that the Protestant ethic that had produced the sparse economies of New England technology would also sanctify the ravaging profit-seeking that stimulated the stylists' streamlined hardsell; and that the interchangeable standardized components found admirable in mail-order catalogues of the 1860s, and the proliferation of purely ornamental options in the General Motors catalogues of the 1960s, were both concerned, first and last, with turning a faster buck.

There is negative evidence abounding that the specifics of United States design had never been fully considered; the whole scene was regarded, substantially, as a continuation of Europe by other means, and the unique strangeness of the position of white men in the North American continent was but rarely brought into focus. The strangeness came through slowly: young architects visiting the United States after the Second World War and reporting a culture more alien than any part of the world they had encountered in their war service; the *Architectural Review* reporting on 'Man-Made America' in December 1950 and discovering that the American city – archetypically Los Angeles – was now so alien in its form as to be totally repugnant.

Yet it still waited (within the design context at least) for an American to spell out the differences in words of more than one syllable so that even intellectuals could understand. It was in *American Building: The Historical Forces that Shaped It* (1966 edition) that the Columbia architectural historian James Marston Fitch laid it finally on the line: 'It is still not generally recognized that if the Pilgrims had landed on a nearby planet instead of the New England coast, they could scarcely have made a more abrupt switch in ... environments.' Fitch specified thermal environments, but his point can be generalized to most other aspects of the North American environment. Elsewhere Fitch comments on another profound difference that has been noted by others: the shortage of labour in all but the slave-owning colonies, and the shortage of skilled labour everywhere.

Giedion and others had noted how the shortage of skilled labour had made it necessary to mass-reproduce and mechanize the craftsman's output, but one can also cite the sparseness of inhabitants in this strange environment to illuminate a related point that is still too little considered. Let us put the matter thus, by multiplying the noble savage into the frontier family, whose world was open, untamed (sometimes hostile, which is not the same thing) and deficient in the support provided by other people. The environment could only be manipulated by the resources to be found within the household, and the house had to become infinitely more resourceful as a consequence. Where the inhabitants of earlier, closer-packed communities had been able to call on one another for social aid and helpful skills, the frontier family in its isolation could call only on its own generalized skills and the contents of the mail-order catalogue.

The consequent devolution of quasi-skills throughout society, the expectation of many Americans to be part-master of two or three trades as well as jack of several, may prove in later analysis to have had as much significance in American history as any of those more grandiose themes attributed to the frontier by Frederick Jackson Turner. It seems almost too obvious a truism to locate the origins of do-it-yourself in the back-porch technologies of the frontier family, and yet it is worth noting that only in England of all European countries has DIY had much success in creating a domestic market for power-tools and the like. Elsewhere, especially in Germany, the DIY market 'has been a complete frost', to quote one frustrated exporter. This being so, it might be as well to look again at the relations between tools, skills and United States culture as they developed together in the years when the North American population was expanding into the free land of Turner's Great West. Out of the dearth of specially skilled labour and the enormous distances over which goods had to be transported, there clearly arose one very characteristic type of designed-in-America object; it is highly portable, usable by untrained hands, sophisticated in itself, and capital-intensive. It is a tool if it isn't a weapon. It is the bowie-knife, the

Winchester repeater, the Thompson submachine-gun, the
atom bomb. Or it is the die-cast axe, the sewing machine, the
McCormick reaper, the Fordson tractor, the Lunar Excursion
Module.

Each of these devices aims to help physically and socially
isolated men survive in untamed environments, without aid
from other people. They are not so much anti-social, which
would be bad enough, but asocial, which is worse in the eyes
of most European intellectuals whose *Weltanschauung* is
social if not specifically Marxist. They led to Galbraith's 'private affluence and public squalor' – a phrase much more often
used in Europe than in the United States. They help lead to a
domestic life-style of low-density private homesteading even in
major conurbations, a situation identified by Le Corbusier as
tolerable as one man's dream but '*du chaos*' when multiplied
by the population of a metropolis, with the exanple of Los
Angeles always to hand as demonstrable proof that this independent privatism leads to the destruction of cities as Europeans understand them.

But the tools and implements that have encouraged this
ideal of privatism also exhibit another characteristic that has
clearly been felt rather than discussed, and felt to be vaguely
hostile. Each of these devices is usually, in a phrase much
used by United States designers and misunderstood in
Europe, a 'neat engineering solution'. Expressed another
way, it is a 'problem-solving device'. The concept of design as
problem-solving is something the world has learned from
America, even though the belief that a properly posed problem brings its own solution is old and widespread. What
American experience points up, however, is that the neatness
of the engineering solution usually depends on phrasing the
problem in such a way that most of its context is omitted, or at
least enough of the contingent circumstances are set aside for
a 'solution' to be proposed using available technology, albeit
combined in a new and original form.

The growing nation had neither time nor resources to
spare for more subtle approaches, but usually had space to
spare to dispose of its mistakes. The ability to walk away from
the wreckage with a shrug 'Oh well; back to the drawing-
board' is a luxury European cultures have not enjoyed for

centuries. The availability of this escape route seems to have encouraged American engineers to define their tasks as narrow problems to be solved, and to leave the side-effects for others to clear up.

This has always been the engineer's way anywhere in the world: concentrate on the soluble and – Shazam! – a solution! Yet the proverbial neatness of United States engineering solutions at their most extreme can be radical enough to command real intellectual respect: for instance, Ole Evinrude's realization that if you hung the means of propulsion *outside* the boat, you could avoid having to drill awkward holes for propeller or paddle shafts, could remove the engine for servicing and storage in more convenient environments, could mate it to any number of boats or other floating objects at will, easily fit two of it to larger boats, etc.

But another example has to be the hand-gun as the universal instrument of law and order, which involves narrowing the context to the level of something like 'The only good Indian/nigra/Commie/hippy/rattlesnake is a dead one'. On the scale of world politics it involves narrowing the context of the Vietnam 'problem' to the point where it can be defined in terms of kill-ratio, and then applying enough weaponry to kill everything in sight. American faith in the efficacy of such 'solutions' is most pathetically shown in rhetorical tropes beginning 'Now that we can put a man on the Moon, how come we can do nothing about the problems of ...', which always fail to recognize that the problems invoked – ghettoes, drugs, pollution, campus disorders – have too much complex context (as opposed to the Moon programme's blissfully simple context) to be solved by 'one-shot' engineering solutions like gutting an apartment slum from top to bottom and dropping in a complete new multi-storey sanitary core of kitchens and bathrooms. Indeed, it now becomes doubtful if even the much-vaunted management techniques triumphantly devised by the Moon programme will ultimately be applicable to anything but putting men on moons.

Any European pundit worth his salt who knows that 'optimization' is now a philosophically dirty word can point this out now, and most are doing it, in American universities, for pleasure and profit, but they have been a very long time get-

ting round to it. And few, even now, seem to understand how
integral a product of United States culture the neat engineering solution really is. Without it the plough would never
have broken the plains, the West never been won, nor the
nation united from sea to shining sea. Therefore, one can say
that the capital-intensive, portable, handy and sophisticated
problem-solving device is the basis and crowning achievement of American civilization, and Adolf Loos was right
about plumbers.

VI. ORDINARY IS NOT ANONYMOUS

All those who have declared no faith in United States design
cannot be accused of superficiality. Maldonado, already mentioned, looked long and hard at American philosophy and
management theories in the hope that somewhere they might
yield clues to the delivery of European design from its growing sterility and mental aridity. He even dickered with Pop-
art as a way out of its elitist and Neoplatonic impasse, though
in the end his dialectical approach would not permit him to
take it seriously. It was characteristic of the generation that
grew up in the shadow of Giedion's two monumental tomes
that, sooner or later, they would bypass his rejection of Styling and try to come to terms, cautiously or enthusiastically,
with American pop. The reasons for this reversible attitude
towards Pop styling are numerous; however, they all seem to
be concerned with an increasing level of sophistication on the
part of America-watchers. It was possible – if you were a
member of the right generation with the right background –
to be totally disillusioned with United States policy during
the Cold War period and yet admire the show-biz qualities of
American product-styling, and this was not just simple-mind-
edness. The frankness of the commercial sales pitch in Madison Avenue advertising could be found a refreshing change
after the mealy-mouthed obscurantism of American political
rhetoric, especially during the Eisenhower years; the exuber-
ance of the vintage Marilyn Monroe movies was a welcome
and life-affirming change from the great tombstone face of
John Foster Dulles.

So, a painter like Richard Hamilton, father of European

Pop-painting, was either execrated by older critics for his persistent and erudite use of United States commercial imagery, or believed by others to be using this material to satirize the affluent society, because neither party could believe that a man of his known progressive beliefs could make such loving use of such imagery and remain true to his principles. Yet he was not alone – particularly among the British art community – in contriving to grow out of the earlier single-value, black/white, on/off attitude to America and adopt what would later be called a pluralistic view of the 'nation of contrasts'.

One of the most interesting cases was that of Ian McCallum, now the director of that unique institution, the American Museum in Britain, at Claverton Manor. Long an editor of the *Architectural Review*, he worked on the 'Man-Made America' issue already mentioned and then went back to America in 1955–6 to work on a further issue which, as 'Machine-Made America' (May 1957), almost reversed the message. It had a Pop-art cover by John McHale, who also contributed two pages of introductory material devoted to Pop and Styling without a word of censoriousness, but its main thrust was on the topic of the glass-and-metal 'curtain walling' then coming in as the standard cladding for urban business buildings.

Reverting to the noble-savagery approach, McCallum praises curtain walling as a truly anonymous idiom, which is familiar rhetoric, but an entirely new level of historical awareness appears in his detailed comparison of curtain walling with the rational standardization of the details of classical architecture; he knows exactly what European echoes he is evoking. Later he makes it perfectly clear that he is invoking the design of the New World to redress that of the Old. After praising United States architecture for its flexibility, variety and originality, he perorates:

Here, then, is an American experience of immediate relevance to other countries ... and that is perhaps the decisive factor in choosing the curtain wall for examination, for this special issue is designed to give Europeans, rather than

Americans, an insight into American architecture, and to present problems that are common to both.

In many ways McCallum's approach bridges two decisively different attitudes to 'America as a model' which are difficult to condense into simple verbal formulae. He praises a class of neat engineering solutions and holds them up for admiration, but like the fancies of Styling and other aspects of Pop culture, he recognizes that they are not necessarily Simon Pure and without fault. Especially in various follow-up discussions after 'Machine-Made America' had appeared, he made it clear that the curtain wall was not faultless: by reducing the concept of 'wall' to a simple weatherproof membrane, and discarding the rest of the context in which walls were traditionally conceived – privacy, permanence, monumentality – it had made it possible to wrap buildings cheaply and neatly in a skin of great elegance, but usually left the building's occupier to pick up the tab for increased heating and air-conditioning bills, and his staff to make their own visible and unsightly provisions for privacy.

Yet to a European observer there was a fascinating ruthlessness about the thinking that had pared the wall down to less than its essentials, and there was an equal fascination – picking up the old purifying tradition – in the way in which curtain walling offered to make a truly anonymous background architecture available for ordinary everyday buildings.

This theme, subtly transformed, has persisted; the sheer ordinariness, not to say ornery-ness, of day-to-day United States design continues to fascinate Europeans: tract-houses, mobile homes, gas stations, diners, U-haul trailers, the reassuring sameness of airport buildings, motels, rented cars, radio programmes. It is among designers more than anyone else that one hears the tag 'The function of Howard Johnson is not to serve good food so much as reliable food'. But a moment's reflection on Howard Johnson will reveal that standardization and ordinariness do not necessarily bring anonymity, nor is it the intention of Howard Johnson (or Holiday Inns, or Great Western Motels, or McDonald's Hamburgers, or Mobil Oil, or Thrifty Mart) to produce an architecture that retires into the background.

One of the hardest things for European art-lovers and intellectuals to swallow about American design – and therefore something that rejoices the hearts of some radical factions in the European art world – is the sheer visual assertiveness of all sorts of products and services which, in the original scenario for the Modern Movement, were to be as deft and unfancy as grain silos. This cuts deeper than just 'bad design'; the assertiveness of common products gives witness of the inversion of a previously unquestioned hierarchy of taste, in which the educated were to hand standards down a well-ordered social pyramid. The up-ending of this pyramid, with the pointy heads of the leisured classes being driven into the ground by the broadening masses of lower-class taste above, has been best celebrated by Tom Wolfe in *The Kandy Kolored Tangerine Flake Streamline Baby* (1965).

Wolfe's celebration of the extravagances of Pop style proceeds by overt contrast to standards of taste derived from Europe (the noble savage looking in the mirror?) and the point has not been lost on Europeans, for many of whom (especially dissident students in design schools) the discovery that banal objects in the United States are often the most conspicuously designed (e.g. the Coca-Cola bottle) has been liberating news. Partly this over-response, which led also to the rise of European Pop-art, is simple cultural *Schadenfreude* (to the extent that even some knockabout Marxists can use Pop-art idioms), but part is due to sheer acclimatization to commonplace United States design via the mass media.

The effect of magazine pictures of New York on Moholy-Nagy, mentioned earlier, is something that can be multiplied in both depth and extent for later generations. For millions of Britons, for instance, vicarious visual experience of the United States via the media completely outweighs vicarious, let alone real, visual experience of other European countries. We know what America looks like; and just as jazz-fans of my own generation who got their ear in and dug the sound in the 1930s were never fazed by the bopster argot of the 1950s and never found hippies incomprehensible beyond about like the middle of the second ugh-sentence, man, so something like three generations of the kind of grammar-school boys who grew up into industrial designers and architects have been at home with visual America in a way that their elders and university-trained betters often are not. They can take anything that America can produce; and they don't feel required to break down the product into good and bad.

This does not imply blanket approval. To understand all is not necessarily to forgive all, but understanding is bound to appear very different from instant accept/reject responses, and to feel very uncomfortable to those accustomed to neat black/white categorization. The divide which McCallum bridges is, in part, between an age group that found only American noble savagery justifiable, and younger groups who find many different aspects of American design justifiable.

VII. AS THE FUTURE SINKS SLOWLY IN THE WEST

Yet within the mental set of this more relaxed attitude there still seems to persist one area of America and one area of design where the old style still persists. For town-planners it seems that the future follows the sunset and is now, for better or worse, established on the shores of the Pacific Ocean, extending southwards from the Golden Gate. The reasons are complex and not always fully scrutable. First and most obviously, the imagery of the future still adheres to the myths of California, even if it has deserted other parts of the United States; Michael Davie can still call his book on California *In the Future Now*, and nearly get away with it. Again, the state still houses the largest communities of professional futurists, even though Herman Kahn has gone East, and further again its extremism – of liberalism and violence, of sophistication and crudity, of beauty and horror, of affluence and poverty – seems to suggest terminal conditions towards which European cities are assumed to be heading. More important, perhaps, is the fact that as an active importer of academic talent for two hectic decades, California has shown a number of European and particularly English academics the promise of a life-style they can never emulate back home. And the prestige of the West Coast universities can be almost crippling: 'I don't want to show you anything yet; the tapes aren't back from Berkeley.'

When Richard Llewelyn-Davies explained the plans for Washington and Milton Keynes New Towns as being based 'on a modified Los Angeles system', he was offering LA less as a model than as a term of comparison. However much the plans may seem to resemble parts of Los Angeles, they were arrived at by analytical methods which did not involve copying anything – but they were methods largely derived from American (mostly University of California) studies of urban problems and planning techniques, coloured by active involvement in the Model Cities work on Watts.

But in invoking Los Angeles in this way he knew perfectly well that he was making a loaded comparison that would trigger waves of recognition, alarm or excitement that would never be evoked by the names of Albuquerque, Kansas City or Tulsa. In the same way, advocates of improved public transport persistently cite the example of the Bay Area Rapid Transit system in San Francisco–Oakland, in spite of its well-publicized false starts and technical shortcomings and the fact that local politics have almost crippled its good intentions. If it's in California it must be of consequence; some of the old magic still attaches, even though it has long departed, in planners' eyes, from New York, whose problems are more comparable and solutions more relevant to those of the high-density cities of Europe.

The idea that New York is out of fashion may seem belied by the success of Jane Jacobs's book *The Death and Life of Great American Cities* (1961), since the core and strength of her argument is her knowledge of the fabric of New York. However, both she and her enthusiastic European readers can be seen as uniting to defend their kind of city against 'the fate of Los Angeles' – the motorized, centre-less, low-density urbanization of California is still the point of reference. Also, when defenders of the present state of Piccadilly Circus invoke Times Square and its illuminated signs, the reference to New York is still a negative one: high-density urbanism is being defended, if not actually embalmed, against prairie planning and the automobile.

If the attitude to illuminated advertising had been positive rather than defensive, then New York would not have been invoked; Las Vegas would, since it is now recognized as the

spiritual home of the neon sign. This legend (myth, rather,
since hardly any of the illuminated signs are in fact neon) has
now been established since the end of the 1950s. The better-
known signs along the Strip and Fremont Street are as much
part of the mental furniture of young architects today as were
the monuments of ancient Rome to their predecessors two
hundred years ago – a comparison easier to make since the
Roman-style 'Caesar's Palace' was built on the Strip. But unlike the monuments of Rome, the signs of Las Vegas are not
unquestioned models for emulation. They are highly debatable, and the debate brings together so many of the themes
discussed above that Las Vegas is a kind of summary recapitu-
lation of the whole problem of America as a model for designers.

Not only was Sant'Elia's dream of *Reclam-luminosa* fulfilled, but in the beginning there was no problem. The Pop-
art generation discovered in Las Vegas a self-sufficient phenomenon needing no discussion; all you had to do was point,
as one would have done at the Manhattan skyline two decades
earlier. However, it was also obviously the biggest ever exhi-
bition of unalloyed Pop-art, on which visiting aesthetes could
exercise fancy stylistic discriminations – until Tom Wolfe up-
staged the whole game by pointing out that the designers of
the signs were horse-opera characters in string ties who knew
nothing of modern art. This return to noble savage myth-
ology introduced a welcome moral note: could this be a true
art of the people? If so, was its absence from Europe due to
elitist suppression by a cultural Establishment? Or was it an
exploitative art imposed on the people by cultureless commercial interests, and weren't we better off without it?

VIII. LEARN ENGINEERING IN LAS VEGAS

At this point the argument begins to diversify. While Maldonado, say, in Europe took issue with Robert Venturi in
America about the signs themselves, and their meaning, the
argument constantly advanced by Venturi and his South
African wife, Denise Scott-Brown, was that what we should be
'Learning from Las Vegas' (the title of their famous article of
1968) was a lesson in town planning: that the loose spacing of

indifferent buildings along the Strip, with residual desert left between them, represented (this is a very crude paraphrase) a natural American way of making towns. They proposed that it had more to teach Americans than the formal planning imported from Europe in terms of usable pragmatics (the present author, Peter Hall, and others suggested in 1969 that a similar type of 'non-plan' could be tried in some parts of Britain, on the noble savage proposition of giving the people their heads). At all events, the Wolfe–Venturi view of Las Vegas is now well established in European thinking, even among those who disapprove.

Among those who disapprove there may well be a suspicion that another aspect of American design that is even more corrosive reaches its apothesis there. Maldonado, for instance, objected in 1970 that the signs 'are not alive but mummified, they are sign-emblems that serve only as stimulating décor to the pseudocommunicative farce of the age in which we live...', but he might easily have gone further and objected to the divorce of 'meaning', however banal, from 'building', however ephemeral. If architecture is meaningful construction, there is practically no architecture in Las Vegas, where a typical construction is a completely neutral shed with eight storeys of 'meaning' balanced on its roof or even standing separately alongside. Lacking the integrative probity looked for in European architecture, the Vegas juxtaposition of shed and sign does, however, have the American probity of the neat engineering solution. The problem – of providing a combination of functional space and compelling symbolism – is one that no casino promoter could afford to solve by using conventional architecture. The neat engineering solution – not unlike Evinrude's outboard – is to create the two separately and clip one to the other.

If this argument seems to turn too much on engineering, and not enough on cultural and environmental factors, it is because it seems to me that the cult of the neat engineering solution arises precisely from the problems of European culture finding itself adrift in a strange environment. In that environment it became necessary to abandon the caste system by which European culture has kept its engineers firmly on a short rein: an engineer should stay fixed and remain a calculator, etc. (Le Corbusier). In Europe engineers are normally let off the lead – like Barnes Wallis with his bouncing bombs – only in times of dire emergency, usually military. Radical engineering products, however admirable, tend to arise only from culturally unacceptable situations – like the Volkswagen's origin as a giant Nazi swindle. Yet without too much noble savagery one could claim that engineering has persistently led the way in nearly all branches of American life, and that Americans have usually understood that for them technology has always set the pace for culture. Is *Understanding Media* a book that a Roman Catholic professor of English could have written in Europe?

North America also has an honourable and honoured roster of thinkers like Henry Adams, who questioned the supremacy of engineering and the doubtless facile conception of material progress that justified it. Yet the fact remains that if European designers of anything from bread to bridges, telephones to towns, look across the Atlantic for something their own culture could not have given them, it will usually be an engineering solution: neat, radical and apparently devoid of cultural references. Our own European terms of cultural references teach us to regard great rivers as stern father-figures whose ever-flowing streams we interrupt at our peril, and we are accordingly condemnatory of the apparent determination of the United States Corps of Engineers to dam every river in sight as often as possible. But might not this be preferable in human terms to erecting an endless series of well-designed memorials to the victims of annual floods?

IX. A MODEL NO MORE?

The example of America can still force Europeans to ask awkward questions about themselves and about the engrained habits of thought that encrust a culture grown old in its own native landscape. It seems to demand more searching questions and less comfortable answers now that we can no longer pretend that what exists across the Atlantic is an exported European Utopia planted in virgin soil, but must accept it as a different culture with problems and possibilities that are not our fault and not our responsibility, a nation that has long since ceased to be the dependency of any European power.

This acceptance attitude must mark the end of an epoch in designers' attitudes to the United States. It means accepting America as it is, so that even anti-Americanism now wears an American face (and an American T-shirt, an ex-U.S. Army fatigue hat, basketball shoes, jeans, Indian beads, Bob Dylan shades and a 'Free Angela Davis' pin). Its wearer is probably deep into the community action thing, a rare example of a non-neat non-engineering non-solution that America has been able to offer Europe as an alternative to Europe's most ineffective and most treasured one-shot problem-solving device, town planning.

The acceptance attitude also means, most significantly, accepting America as part of the landscape of today, rather than as a great nation of the future. The strength of the concept of the United States as a model for almost everything, as well as design, stemmed largely from the idea of inevitable progress in the direction in which the United States was headed, so that American design was an automatic preview of the future of the man-made environment. As long as such a proposition was in any way accepted, designers were clearly obligated (*a*) to emulate United States design because it was the coming good, or (*b*) reject United States design because Western civilization was going to hell in a handbasket.

If, on the other hand, you accept that some things (Wimpy bars, hard rock, teach-ins, drag-racing, Kennedy-style politics, ecological doomsaying) are here already because conditions are comparable, and that other things (the Grand Canyon, the towers of Manhattan, photochemical smog, Mayor Daley, the length of East Colfax Avenue in Denver) will never happen here because conditions are not repeatable ... accept that and the need to make messianic generalizations about America disappears. Unscramble the romantic vision of the Age of Enlightenment into the diverse and pluralistic developments that have happened since the Declaration of Independence, and America becomes less a prophecy, less of a model, and more of a compendium of examples against which to compare our European experiences, experiments and ambitions.

4 'You Too Can Have Statistics Like Mine': Some Economic Comparisons

JIM POTTER

Reader in Economic History, London School of Economics

A few years after the Second World War a book appeared in England with the promising title *We Too Can Prosper*.[1] It emerged from inquiries undertaken by the Anglo-American Council on Productivity into American methods of industrial production, seeking ways and means to improve British economic efficiency. The proposition of the book was explicit: the post-war British economy was seriously ill; the prescriptions for recovery were to come from the United States. If we in Britain failed to take the medicine, the author foresaw 'an accelerating, and ultimately catastrophic, fall in our standards of living'.

The catastrophe has not occurred, at any rate not yet. Is this because Englishmen did indeed learn the lessons from America suggested in 1952? Is there still more to be learned? Has Britain prospered? If so, was it because our economy became more like the American? Could we have done better? If so, is that because of the still remaining gulf between America's best and our own performance? Or have the Americans become more like us? If so, in what respects? The questions to be raised in this chapter will be more general and the answers less prescriptive than those of the Anglo-American Council on Productivity.

But first let us note that it is less likely today than in 1952 to be accepted as self-evident that Britain should turn to the

---

[1] Graham Hutton, *We Too Can Prosper* (London: Allen & Unwin, for the British Productivity Council, 1952). Graham Hutton wrote in collaboration with the late Geoffrey Crowther and an advisory panel. Together they attempted to analyse the main recommendations of the sixty-six separate productivity reports drawn up by the panels of the Council on Productivity.

United States for a model. The massive loss of self-confidence by Americans in themselves in the last few years has infected the thinking of outsiders. We are kept more aware of American shortcomings (e.g. unemployment, pollution, continuing poverty) than of American achievements. Even the value of those achievements is called into question: *should* the maximization of gross national product (GNP) be the object of endeavour? Is the affluent, effluent or flatulent society, the acquisitive society, the rat-race society, the coronary thrombosis society, so much to be admired after all? The words of abuse come readily to the tongue, and all are to be blamed on the 'system'. Such strictures provide the social critic, in America and Britain alike, but especially in the latter, with the double satisfaction of allowing him to denounce the 'system' for its failure to deliver the goods, while at the same time protesting that he does not really want the goods anyway.

It is beyond the intentions of this chapter to discuss the legitimacy of these denunciations, or the nature of the alternatives, if any are suggested. From the statistical evidence available, with all its shortcomings and difficulties of interpretation, the United States still appears at the top of the league table for economic efficiency, with a considerable lead over the next in line. In 1970 there were twelve countries in the world in which GNP per head of population, measured at current prices and exchange rates, exceeded $2,000. The divergence among these 'high performance economies' is best demonstrated graphically, as in Fig. 1.

Since this volume deals mainly with British–American comparisons, what concerns us here is the gulf between the first and the last of these twelve countries, i.e. between America's $4,800 per head and Britain's $2,000 per head. But it might be observed in passing that the twelve countries which appear in the graph do not, *a priori*, appear to have very much in common, except that in a vague sense they have 'developed' economies. Size, whether in numbers or in area, appears irrelevant. In population the range is from Norway's 4 million to America's 200 million plus; four are under 10 million, three between 10 and 20 million and three in the range 50–60 million. In density they range from Canada and

Australia with a mere 5 persons per square mile to Belgium and the Netherlands with over 800 persons per square mile.

By other criteria too, the twelve leaders do not conform to any single pattern. Are we then to conclude that all economies are in a sense unique, and that therefore the United States has no monopoly of uniqueness? A popular, impressionistic view would surely be different, even if statistically

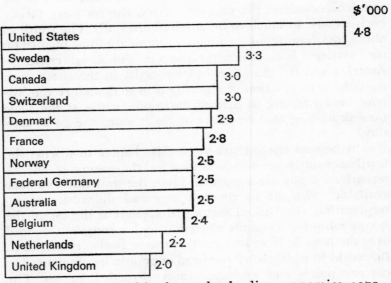

$'000

United States	4·8
Sweden	3·3
Canada	3·0
Switzerland	3·0
Denmark	2·9
France	2·8
Norway	2·5
Federal Germany	2·5
Australia	2·5
Belgium	2·4
Netherlands	2·2
United Kingdom	2·0

FIG. 1. GNP per head in the twelve leading economies, 1970

uninformative. The word 'Americanization' is an implied comment on *economic* behaviour and there is no similar verbal noun for any other country on the list.

The economic statistics, however, are only one piece in the jigsaw puzzle of change that has characterized American economic growth since the late nineteenth century. If one searches for uniqueness, it is surely to be found in America's experience as the country in which everything happened, and happened all at once. The speed was such that there was not time for human beings to adjust themselves to one major change in their lives before the next major change (or changes) occurred. Immigration brought millions of aliens to

American shores; at the same time the population was moving with growing, not lessening, restlessness; towns mush-
roomed and spread outwards; the population mix was complicated by the northward, westward and townward movement of the black population and, since 1940, by its more
rapid growth rate than the white population. No sooner had
railroads reached their peak in 1920 than they went into a
decline, displaced first by automobiles, then by aeroplanes.
Aircraft design never had the need to build in artificial obsolescence, since this occurred willy-nilly. When all the arguments about the respective contributions of turnpikes, canals,
railroads and automobiles to the American economy have
died down, we shall probably be left with the simple fact that
the most revolutionary change in transport was from the propeller aeroplane to the jet. Industrial methods of production
have changed, and changed again, beyond recognition.

All these things, to be sure, have happened elsewhere.
Modern technology is itself a denial of uniqueness, imposing
a common imprint throughout the world. But where outside
America does one find the same kaleidoscope of change, in
which the economic, and the social, and the demographic,
and the political, and the educational, and the religious, and
the emotional cannot be dealt with in separate categories, but
all impinge one upon the other? Where has such a continuing complexity of change occurred on such a scale, so rapidly
and so all-pervasively?

But, the sceptic will object, these are absurd generalizations. Many American products have now been with us for
over a century; a motor-car, that quintessential American
product, is basically the same today as half a century ago, four
wheels and an internal combustion engine. Have the small
tobacco-growers of some Southern states changed at all? Or
those New England townships where the white church still
stands placidly on the green amid the dogwood blossom in
spring and the russet colours of the Fall. The urban slums
still remain. Violence has been a constant feature over time
and the gun manufacturers still flourish.

Of course, such objections are valid. The average American
is non-existent. Aggregate figures reveal little of the com-
plexities of reality. Paradoxically, this tends to reinforce the

general argument: one cannot even assume that the elements and the speed of change are themselves universal; the complete picture includes the fact of minimal change in such areas as Appalachia.

The main argument is, however, that human adjustment has not kept pace with the speed of technological change; in this America is certainly not unique. The adjustment of public opinion has lagged far behind the intellectual leadership of Dewey, Freud, Keynes and Einstein, and behind the implications of automation and computerization. The elements in this 'culture-lag' necessitate a consideration of the historical background to present economic circumstances.

The present receives from the past two main legacies which influence contemporary behaviour and conditions. These are, first, the specific institutions (e.g. the Bank of England or the Federal Reserve System), with their own special histories and *raisons d'être*, which we have at our disposal for dealing with present conditions in our respective countries; and second, the national 'collective memory' which determines our attitudes to current problems through the beliefs and assumptions we hold about the past (e.g. that the Industrial Revolution 'created' poverty in Britain, or that there always has been and still is opportunity for everyone on the American frontier). There is no reason to assume that this heritage will be the same in any two countries, though such an assumption is all too often made; it is usually less misleading to expect difference rather than similarity.

The first section therefore examines briefly some of the contrasts in historical experience which are relevant to the circumstances of the British and American economies today.

I. HISTORICAL BACKGROUND

1. *Speed of change*

Economic progress came slowly to England through centuries of change. When America achieved independence, the former mother country was economically far in advance of her former colonies. Political independence did not bring economic independence to the new nation. For half a century or more after nationhood, the United States still remained in a colonial relationship with Britain, exporting raw materials, importing the more advanced industrial products she could not yet manufacture for herself, the capital her economy was not yet generating, and the skills she had not yet developed. The American potential was enormous, but the greatest obstacle was the lack of transport; this could not be built until capital had accumulated. Without this the potential could not be realized, since the raw materials of wealth, while abundant, were inaccessible.

Yet starting so far behind, within the next half-century (1850–1900) the American economy first overhauled and then surpassed the British. Already in 1901 Europeans were speaking of 'the American invasion of Europe' and one might have read the following passage:

> What are the chief new features in London life? They are ... the telephone, the portable camera, the phonograph, the electric street car, the automobile, the typewriter, passenger lifts in houses and the multiplication of machine tools. ... In every one of these, save the petroleum automobile, the American maker is supreme; in several he is monopolist.[2]

The pace of American growth in the second half of the nineteenth century was maintained in the twentieth, with the exception of the 1930s, and accelerated once again after the Second World War.

2. Technology

The American Industrial Revolution was not, like the British, based on coal. Wood and water were still America's main source of energy and remained so until about 1880. By the 1920s coal had been ousted as the main source of energy by oil and natural gas. The brevity of coal's dominance is one manifestation of the fact that American industry never settled

[2] Three publications appeared in London in 1901–2 entitled *The American Invasion*, *The American Invaders* and *The Americanization of the World*. 'The invasion goes on unceasingly ... in five hundred industries at once. From shaving soap to electric motors, and from shirt waists to telephones, the American is clearing the field.' See Mira Wilkins, *The Emergence of Multinational Enterprise* (1970).

into routine, habitual methods of production. American technology in the nineteenth century was essentially problem-solving ('engineering' in the sense used by Reyner Banham): how to make the best use of a limited labour supply; how to adapt techniques developed in Europe, and especially in Britain, to American resources and needs; how to make do with the materials to hand until eventually it would be possible to gain access to superior ones; how to take the toil out of human labour; how to produce cheaply; how to distribute bulky products over vast distances. No step was regarded as final, but rather as an interim measure until a better solution came to hand. The motto was: find something that works; get it working quickly and cheaply; improve on it later; scrap it when it is rendered obsolete by newer developments, but all the time keep things moving. Charles Dickens remarked that the most overused word in the American vocabulary was the verb 'to fix' (and that was long before it conjured up thoughts either of bribery or of drugs).[3] If you wanted something done, you either fixed it yourself or called on somebody to fix it for you. 'Fixing' meant finding a means of doing a job – and doing it.

Implicit in this approach were several attitudes of mind that remain influential today. Firstly, it is assumed that no problems exist which cannot be solved by human ingenuity and application (resulting in petulance and frustration when the human and social problems of the mid-twentieth century have proved themselves less susceptible to solution by 'social engineering'). Secondly, obsolescence is taken for granted: the *status quo* is not sacrosanct; no technique, no solution is permanent; when better is found, what exists at the time has to change (resulting in hardship for those who are called on to change, e.g. farmers, textile workers, coal producers). Thirdly, the purpose of solving a problem is to satisfy an observed want, i.e. to respond to the demands of the market.

3. *Home versus foreign markets*

Historically the British economy has been outward-looking, the American inward-looking. The British Industrial Revo-

[3] Charles Dickens, *American Notes* (1842) ch. 10.

lution depended on imported raw materials and her work-force eventually on imported food; markets were found abroad as well as at home. Industrialization in America was largely an internal process, with resources domestically available; sales in foreign markets were of only marginal interest and until the beginning of the twentieth century the United States was a net importer of manufactured goods.

Britain's vulnerability to fluctuations in foreign trade, and the critical role of her balance of payments, are not new phenomena. Her visible trade was always in deficit after 1820 with rare exceptions (1970 and 1971 were among the very few years in which Britain exported a greater value of goods than she imported). The improvement of living standards in the 1870s was associated with an enormous rise in imports,[4] a stagnation of exports and a doubling of the foreign trade deficit from about £60 million annually to about £120 million. From that decade we can date the recurring paradox that every substantial rise in British living standards and increase in industrial activity has been accompanied by balance-of-payments difficulties owing to the resultant upward surge in imports of food and raw materials. So long as invisible exports were buoyant, the deficit could be ignored, and the contribution of invisible exports is still of crucial importance. One such invisible, shipping services, can no longer be relied upon as much as in the period before the First World War. The replacement of the Cunard Line ships by American-built 707 and 747 aeroplanes as the main means of transatlantic transport has an economic as well as a symbolic significance.

Because American markets were internal, they were more homogeneous and more standardized than the multiplicity of fragmented foreign markets which British industrialists supplied. The British firm had to specialize; the American firm could produce a single, uniform product and widen its sales simply through successful marketing. The nature of the market, especially at the frontier, was such that simple products, as long as they did the job, would suffice. The mass

[4] A simple example is the rise in York of factory production of cocoa, chocolate and confectionery in the last quarter of the nineteenth century; the industry depended on imported raw materials.

production of standardized items was therefore possible, indeed requisite, in American conditions. The British producer was selling to a large number of small foreign markets, all with different needs, or for the smaller and less uniform domestic market. Such circumstances encouraged British firms to remain small and specialist, while they encouraged American firms to become large and to produce *en masse*. Technology assisted this growth in America by the development of interchangeable part production, leading to assembly-line mass production and eventually to automation.

Because of its independence of foreign markets, American industry has had less need to be cost-conscious. Ford merely rationalized what had been implicit in the American high-wage economy for a century, when he raised automobile workers' wages to enable them to buy automobiles. Finally, because of her ability to supply most of her needs for food and raw materials from internal resources, America's balance of trade does not react so directly and immediately to increases in economic activity.

In recent times, therefore, the threat of inflation is always potentially more dangerous to Britain than to America, because of the delicacy of Britain's balance of foreign payments, on which depends her ability to import food and raw materials to keep industries working. Paradoxically the United States, able to tolerate inflation with fewer fears than Britain, has taken the problem more seriously and has on the whole dealt with it more successfully.

4. *Land abundance and agricultural productivity*

America's near self-sufficiency in agricultural produce is in sharp contrast with Britain's partial dependence on foreign supplies. Developing economies may be divided historically into those with a frontier and those without. In the latter category (which includes most of Western Europe) the rule of pessimism, or Malthusian–Ricardian economics, prevailed. Where a nation's territory is fully settled, the law of diminishing returns in agriculture applies. Since the best land is cultivated first, any new land brought under cultivation is inferior land yielding ever-lower returns. Hence, agricultural improvements can occur only through more intensive cultivation, and as population grows the pressure on food supplies begins to be felt.

In a frontier economy, as in America (or Australia, Canada or Russia), there is at least a possibility that the new lands progressively brought into cultivation will not necessarily be inferior but may be of equal, or even of superior, quality. So long as America could continue to bring fresh land into cultivation (which occurred until about 1930, despite the 'official' closing of the frontier by the Census Bureau in 1890), the Ricardian law of diminishing returns was set in temporary abeyance. Thus, while England began to import foodstuffs on a growing scale from the time of the repeal of the Corn Laws in 1846, America developed as a food exporter. So far from population outstripping food productivity, food production outstripped population growth and agricultural over-production created (in low returns to farmers) a Malthusian crisis in reverse.

The area under cultivation in America today is roughly the same as in 1930 but, through intensive agriculture and great improvements in methods of production, the expansion of output has continued. Less than 5 per cent of the work-force is now employed in agriculture, but it produces more than enough to feed the rest of the population, often with a surplus left over for storage and export. The agreed export of 25 million tons of grain to the Soviet Union from America during the winter of 1972–3 would have required, if loaded into 60-ton juggernaut trucks of 15 metres length, a convoy stretching from New York to San Francisco and beyond.

America's ability not merely to feed herself, but also to produce exportable agricultural surpluses, has for well over a century created fundamental differences in the basic preconditions of economic life in the two countries.

5. Population growth

The high productivity of American agriculture has enabled the American population to grow at a very much faster rate than British or European population in every decade from 1790 to the present. In the nineteenth century the British decennial growth rate varied between 17 per cent (in 1811–21) and 12 per cent (1881–91); the American variation was

between 36 per cent (1800–10) and 21 per cent (1890–1900).
In the twentieth century the lowest American decennial figure was 8 per cent in the 1930s, but British growth has
fluctuated around 5 per cent in every decade since 1911. In
every decade before the Civil War the American population
grew by over one-third, i.e. at double the rate of British
growth at its most rapid; even the American slave population
(growing considerably more slowly than the white) had an
average decennial growth rate about double the British
average. After 1860 the American population growth rate fell
for three decades to 25 per cent, to 20 per cent in 1890–1910
and 15 per cent in 1910–30, but still remained very much
higher than Britain's nineteenth-century average.

The causes of American population growth were natural
increase and immigration, with the latter making greater and
greater contributions after the 1840s. By 1870 the foreign-
born element in the population exceeded the black. By the
late 1920s immigration restrictions were coming into effect
and during the inter-war years the black growth rate began to
exceed the white. Consequently, by 1940 the black population again exceeded the foreign-born, by over one million.
Thus, another important contrast with Britain is America's
extremely heterogeneous population.

6. *Mobility*

One consequence of the frontier – and the one most often
noticed by historians – is that the population moved regularly
and rapidly from place to place. The habit of mobility remained long after the frontier was closed. A higher percentage of the population was living outside their state of
birth in 1960 and 1970 than at any time in the nineteenth
century, even when westward movement to the frontier
seemed to be at its most active.

But the frontier had other significant consequences. Above
all, it allowed the Jeffersonian ideal of the yeoman farmer to
dominate American folk-mythology far into the twentieth
century. The view persisted that 'true' innocence, 'real'
values, honesty, integrity, justice, could exist only in the
rural life-style; urban life was seen as degenerate, vicious and
dehumanizing. Still today, American 'radical' and 'progres-

sive' movements echo the sentiments (and sometimes unknowingly use the language) of Jeffersonian 'agrarian fundamentalism'.[5] Those who turn their backs on urban industrial society and seek refuge in rural communes are preaching the same eighteenth-century Rousseauesque philosophy which motivated Jefferson, and copying the countless community experiments to be found throughout the nineteenth century. The American exemplar of civic virtue has never been the cloth-cap industrial wage-earner of European radical tradition, but the self-employed, small landowner. Rousseau rather than Marx has provided the folk-mythology.

With its high productivity reflected in the relative decline of agriculture as a source of employment, the movement into the cities has been intensified, and indeed necessitated if agriculture were to prosper. One of the greatest sources of economic imbalance in American history has been the demographic fact of life that from the very beginning of the nineteenth century, farm families have tended to be larger than urban families. This is the simplest illustration of the falsification in America of the Malthusian formula: farm families (the producers) continued to be large while their productivity also increased; town families (the consumers) were much smaller; equilibrium could be maintained only if some members of farm families changed from food-sellers into food-buyers. The First World War was a significant turning-point, for it was then that the farm population reached its peak. Since that date the viability of American agriculture has required a constant movement to the city of some members of every family. In a situation (as in the 1920s) where farm families had an average of about four children and town families an average of about two, it was economically essential that, at most, only one male out of every farm family of four children stayed on to be a farmer himself.

Since 1945 the buoyant industrial economy has created conditions which have permitted a massive movement out of agriculture, a movement which has been particularly marked since 1960. A new element in this recent rural–urban move-

---

[5] The expression was taken over by R. Hofstadter in *The Age of Reform* (New York, 1956) p. 31, from Joseph S. Davis, *On Agricultural Policy* (Stanford, 1939) pp. 24–43.

ment is that it has become multi-directional, not merely East–West. Moreover, since the Second World War this movement away from agriculture into towns has included a vast movement of the black population; the habit of mobility, so characteristic of white America during the nineteenth century, has now become a characteristic of black America.

Britain's frontier for migration has historically been external; the advice to her young men was not 'Go West!' but 'Emigrate'. The main period of urbanization was much earlier in British history than in American, but when it occurred it created problems analogous to those of American cities today. British internal mobility has tended to be on a much smaller scale, involving fewer numbers and far shorter distances. Society was more settled, communities more stable.

Since 1945 many factors have combined to increase British internal mobility, not least the shift of the economic nerve-centre away from the northern areas of the nineteenth-century staple industries, back again to the South-east. Moreover, the greater scale of immigration in recent years has given a mild taste of some of America's century-old ethnic problems. London in 1971 had an immigrant percentage in its population almost the same as the total foreign-born percentage in America throughout the late nineteenth century.

7. *The assumption of improvement*

When nineteenth-century European observers spoke of American 'optimism', what they usually meant was that everywhere they encountered the belief that next year would not be the same as this one but would be better, that son would do better than father who had already done better than grandfather. There was no simple acceptance of present circumstances, but a conviction that they would improve, and a determination to improve them. This reflects the belief that virtue, especially hard work, would bring reward and explains some of the disillusionment reflected in the agrarian movements when 'outside forces' appeared to prevent the fulfilment of that simple equation. The assumption that betterment was in the nature of things was encapsulated in Carroll D. Wright's phrase, the 'divine discontent of Americans with

the *status quo*.[6] The process of improvement might be associated with movement to greener pastures or to a better job,
with upward social mobility for native workers as immigrants
came in at the bottom of the ladder and, eventually, upward
mobility for these immigrants or for their children.

In the early phase of growth, improvement was more concerned with reducing life's toil than with increasing life's
pleasures. Once the initial, rudimentary necessities of life
were provided, improvement came to be equated with positive rewards rather than negative alleviation. The vast increase in the range of consumer goods, especially since the
1920s (though partially interrupted by the Depression), has
made possible a continual enlargement of goods and services,
and their diffusion to groups well down the social scale.[7] 'The
one really new gospel we have introduced', wrote André Sieg-
fried in the 1920s, 'is the revelation ... that man may at last
free himself of poverty and, most fantastic innovation of all,
that he may actually enjoy his existence.' The American economy *has* expanded – and still continues to expand – at a rate
which has enabled the assumption to be fulfilled that next
year will, in the normal run of events, be better than this
year.

Similar beliefs have been present in European economies, but with few exceptions the ambition has often been
limited to preventing real or imagined deterioration, rather
than to pursuing improvements as a matter of course. Yet
since the Second World War, the European attitude has
moved much closer to the American. The range of available
consumer goods here too has vastly expanded. Even more significantly, a whole new generation since the Second World
War has grown up with the American-type assumption that
next year I (not my neighbour, my boss, or just 'they', but my
very own self) have a right to, and will have, better food, better clothes, better housing, more household equipment,
longer and better holidays, more goods to give me pleasure

[6] Carroll D. Wright became the first Commissioner of the Bureau of Labor
in 1885 and held that office for twenty years.

[7] Automobiles are prominent in the novels of Erskine Caldwell about depressed farmers, and the Joad family in Steinbeck's *The Grapes of Wrath* had
a truck in which to drive to California, at a time when most English farmers
had neither car nor tractor.

and better services to meet my needs. Unsatisfied expectations, however, are a potent source of discontent and frustration. Not all European economies (and certainly not the British) have accompanied the change in attitude with an economic performance to match. Expectations have risen – but efficiency and production have lagged far behind: result, to adapt Mr Micawber, private misery and public inflation.

To be sure, the Great Depression of the 1930s was a traumatic experience for America – all the more so because of the assumption that the human destiny was to improve. The Depression in Britain was accepted with greater fatalism as part of the natural order of things. For a century or more, the American gross national product had doubled every ten or fifteen years; in the 1930s there was no growth; by 1939 the economy was just about getting back to the position of 1929.

Two points only need concern us here about the 1930s, but both have been of great importance since 1945. Firstly, when the American federal government and the British government did step in, the American reaction was to create work, the British to provide dole. Even in the Depression the gospel of salvation through hard work reasserted itself. 'Will the American people overcome the Depression?' asked F. D. Roosevelt in his 1933 inauguration speech – and answered quite simply: 'They will if they want to.' No human problems existed that human beings could not solve if they tried. Above all, work at it ('bold, persistent experimentation') rather than wait and see. This was in sharp contrast with the British motive of 'safety first' during these same years.

As an economic recovery programme the New Deal failed, but its public works undertakings left a legacy of roads, airports, schools, hospitals that made an immense contribution towards making up America's shortage of social capital, which had existed since first settlement. With a fraction of that legacy of road mileage and public buildings, Britain would have entered the post-war era with a much healthier economic basis.

The second point about the 1930s is that the experience was politically, socially and economically far less divisive in America than in Britain. The American nation was not sharply divided, as was Britain, into the prosperous section and the depressed section. True, some regions and sectors were worse hit than others, but by and large all regions in America, all states, all economic groups, all social classes, all occupations, all ages, suffered in some degree or another from conditions that were all-pervasive. The American Depression was a shared experience, unifying the nation in a common effort to solve a common problem. It did not, as in Britain, accentuate the social division between haves and have-nots, 'them' and 'us', South-east and North-west, car-owners and slum-dwellers. Despite the fanaticism of contemporary attacks on President Roosevelt, the 1930s left behind a far less acrimonious legacy than in Britain, where the experience of depression was so acutely divisive that not even the patriotism evoked by the Second World War served to heal the wounds.

Hence, the United States in 1945 faced her post-war problems with a society that was ideologically far less divided by class animosities and political embitterment than Britain. The fears of unemployment, of the dole, of exploitation, which have bedevilled the British economy since 1945 and played a major part in frustrating the attempts of successive governments (and those outside government) to come to grips with the weaknesses in that economy, have been less acute in the American scene.

Other socially divisive problems have troubled America since 1945. But much of the discussion, even of racial problems, for example, has proceeded from the American assumption that the Good is measured in goods, i.e. that all individuals should be enabled by the workings of the economy and society to gain more of the material benefits available to those people around them; the converse is that the denial of material benefits on grounds of colour is a denial of a fundamental American value.

8. *Government and economic life*

Potent among the historical myths is the view that American economic development was accomplished without governmental intervention, under a regime, or non-regime, known as *laissez-faire*. The view derives partly from a failure to distinguish between government intervention to promote economic development and intervention to achieve social welfare, partly from the success of business propaganda that 'alone we did it', and partly from the assumption that 'government' must mean 'federal government'.

The power of the federal government to intervene in economic affairs rests largely on the taxation and inter-state commerce clauses of the American Constitution of 1787. By denying the *state* governments the right to levy customs duties the Constitution established, in perhaps the only sense in which the expression can legitimately be used, internal conditions of *laissez-faire, laissez-passer*. States could *not* impede the free flow of goods within the United States by tariffs (or impede the free flow of the factors of production, labour and capital). New England states could not protect their farmers from cheap Western grains in the mid-nineteenth century or their textile manufacturers from cheap Southern cottons in the twentieth century. The new Alabama iron industry could not plead the 'infant industry argument' to keep out cheaper products from the well-established Pennsylvanian industry. West Virginia (and other) coal producers could not get protection from their state governments to suppress competition from oil in the 1920s.

But the federal government (not an abstraction, but the legislators who controlled Congress) embarked on a policy of high tariffs in the 1860s and protection continued to increase, apart from the brief episode of Wilson's 1913 Underwood Tariff, until after the Second World War. During the period of most rapid economic growth America enjoyed free trade within a vast home market sheltered by tariffs against the outside world. These conditions did not constitute *laissez-faire* as known to Adam Smith, Richard Cobden, Sir Robert Peel or Gladstone.

Until the Civil War most state governments were active, in some cases extremely active, in promoting economic expansion. British observers (e.g. Harriet Martineau, Richard Cobden, Charles Dickens) frequently commented on the involvement of state governments in the promotion of economic development (as well as in educational and other activities). Spurred on by inter-city and inter-state rivalries, the state governments became involved in a veritable mania for 'internal improvements' (and met with very mixed success in their enterprises). Above all, the incentives to railroad-building provided by government at every level, down to the small townships, greatly accelerated the opening of the West. The problem often came to be a definitional one of demarcating the areas of permissible action under the inter-state commerce clause. The question was not so much whether government should act but which government should act. From the time of Jackson's Presidency in the 1830s it was established that the federal government might not intervene in an enterprise entirely confined within the boundaries of one state. Thereafter, the question was to define under what circumstances a transaction did transcend a state's boundaries and thus become inter-state and a legitimate federal concern.

In the second half of the nineteenth century the two countries appeared to be moving in opposite directions. In external trade the 1860s saw Britain finally accept complete free trade just when the United States was moving to protection; but in internal affairs after the Civil War, government in America, at any rate at federal level, appeared to be moving away from active participation, while in Britain government was intervening more and more in ever-expanding areas of regulation.

In both countries the First World War brought government involvement on an unprecedented scale. Although the return of peace brought a rapid dismantling of the wartime apparatus of control, the precedents for massive intervention had been created and experienced personnel were at hand. When the Depression of the 1930s brought both governments back into action, the return to intervention was in significant respects merely a return to the wartime controlled economy.

In America particularly, the 1930s were of crucial importance. It was with the New Deal that the eighteenth-century Constitution was reinterpreted, in practice if not formally, to bring it into line with the realities of a modern economy, recognizing that railroads had been built (and gone into decline), that telegraphs hum, that aeroplanes fly; in other words, the political federation of the United States had at last become the integrated economic unity of America. Since the 1930s the Supreme Court has allowed the federal government to intervene in virtually any economic activity. The question has no longer been *whether* the federal government could and should act. By the end of the Roosevelt era, attention could be turned to the much more difficult questions of *how* and *to what purpose* the government should intervene.

II. CONVERGING COURSES? RECENT CONDITIONS AND PERFORM-
ANCE

The preceding section has stressed elements of difference rather than similarity. Yet from the early 1970s British commentators have assumed a set of common problems, equally insoluble, in both countries. Some bitter satisfaction has perhaps been derived by Englishmen from the thought that America too suffered from economic ills, some worse, some better than their own, and was apparently just as impotent to solve them: too many people were out of work; prices were rising too fast; and finally – who would have anticipated this twenty years ago? – the almighty dollar was threatened with devaluation.

Has the course of economic life in Britain and America therefore converged sufficiently to assume similarity rather than difference? We should observe that many developments in the twentieth century have brought changes and problems common to all industrial nations. Outstanding is the development of a common technology, imposing its own pattern on productive techniques throughout the world, so that a present-day American industrial plant resembles a present-day British (or Russian) plant far more than it does an American plant of a generation ago. This section will examine certain matters of common concern in British and American economic life during the past quarter-century.

1. *Economic growth*
We Too Can Prosper urged Britain to heed the lessons to be learned from the American economy. What, then, has happened since that book appeared? The data available do not always permit direct comparisons, and attempts at international statistical comparisons are fraught with hazards; but it is necessary to attempt some comparisons.

In 1950 the American GNP was (in constant dollars)

$350 billion; in 1972 it reached $790 billion.[8] Between those years, while the American population increased by about one-third, her GNP more than doubled. In roughly the same period the British GNP increased by two-thirds while population grew by about one-tenth. Measured in constant prices, the British GNP per head of population increased by about 50 per cent in the twenty years, while the American increased by about 45 per cent. Although the chart on p. 94 demonstrated the large gap still remaining between per capita GNP in Britain and America ($2,000 per head compared with $4,800 per head), the size of that gap has *narrowed* slightly since 1950; in this respect there has been some convergence. But much of that improvement (from Britain's point of view) is attributable to a slower rate of population growth.

On the American side the GNP has, on average, taken eleven years to increase by half and has more than doubled in every twenty-year period. This healthy growth has permitted a faster population growth to be accompanied by a sharp rise in family incomes. Measured in 1971 dollars, the median income of white families rose from about $5,500 in 1948-9 to $10,700 in 1970-1, and for non-white families from about $2,800 in 1948-9 to $6,800 in 1970-1. The number of families with incomes below the assumed poverty line of $3,000 (in 1971 prices) fell from 6·7 million white families in 1948 (19·1 per cent of all white families) to 3·3 million in 1971 (6·9 per cent); the number of non-white families below the same line fell dramatically from one-half of the total in 1948 to one-fifth in 1971.

The mid-1960s were years of continuous expansion for the American economy. In each of the five years 1962 to 1966 the increase of the GNP exceeded $20 billion, and reached $40 billion in 1966. The number of white families below the $3,000 poverty level fell by 1·5 million and the number of non-white families by half a million. It would be very difficult to find anywhere in previous American experience such a prolonged period of economic growth and social improvement, or such a rapid reduction of poverty. A setback oc-

[8] The word 'billion' is used in the American sense of one thousand million. The basic unit of the 'billibuck' is thus $1,000,000,000.

curred in 1970, when America's GNP actually fell (by $4 billion) and there was a slight increase in the number of families below the $3,000 line. The years 1971 and 1972 were somewhat equivocal with GNP growing by $20 billion and $48 billion respectively, but no further reduction in the number of families below $3,000.

2. *Population*

Despite the fact that the American population has grown considerably more rapidly than the British since 1945, American fears of over-population sound very strange indeed to European ears. The United States sets aside in national, state, county and municipal parks some 39 million acres of land for purely recreational uses, an area greater than the *total* area of England and Wales (37 million acres). The United States has a population density of about 58 persons per square mile, a figure which is considerably *below* the world average (about 68 persons per square mile). If Alaska and Hawaii are excluded, the figure for the remaining states is under 70 persons per square mile, still extremely low compared with countries of Western Europe: the Netherlands, 985 per square mile; England, 915; West Germany, 630; France, 240; or even Scotland, 170 persons per square mile. America's present-day density of 70 persons per square mile may be set in perspective by comparing it with that of England and Wales at the time of Charles II, three hundred years ago: about 100 persons per square mile.

It is misleading to speak of the 'average' American population density, because of the very great variations from state to state; four states have densities of over 600 persons per square mile, but eight states have under 10. California is the median state in terms of population density; approximately the same number of Americans live in states of higher and in lower densities. The present population density there is about 130 persons per square mile, far below that of Scotland. No American state reaches the population density of the Netherlands. Only one, New Jersey, with 7·2 million persons (a mere 3·5 per cent of the total American population), exceeds England's density; only 8 million Americans, residing in the two states of New Jersey and Rhode Island, live in a higher density than the people of England and Wales. About 164 million Americans, or four-fifths of the total population, live in an environment with a *lower* density of population than that of England and Wales in 1851, a time when Emerson had just written that all England was a 'garden'[9] – but a garden with 357 persons per square mile. Today 40 million Americans still live in states with under 50 persons per square mile.

It is very difficult to sustain the argument that America is over-populated, if density figures are the criterion. If 'usable' or 'productive' land only is considered, then America is far better endowed than most other countries of the world.[10] Nor is the present American population growth rate significantly higher than that of Western Europe. American population is growing at just over 1 per cent per annum (compared with Britain's 0·8 per cent, or Holland's 1·3 per cent); indeed, in 1970 there were 15 per cent *fewer* children in America under the age of five years than in 1960. Within the overall growth rate, there is a significant difference between the white and black population. Between 1960 and 1969 the white population increased by 11 per cent (17·7 million) from 159·4 million to 177·1 million; the black population increased by 19 per cent (3·6 million) from 19·0 million to 22·6 million. There is every indication that the white growth rate has declined very sharply since 1965 and has now reached zero growth.

One of the reasons for the low density of population in America is to be found in its uneven distribution. Far larger numbers than in Britain still live in rural, semi-rural or small-town conditions. As recently as 1940, nearly half the American population was either rural or living in small towns of under 5,000 persons; in the South almost two-thirds of the population was rural, living in communities of fewer than 2,500 persons. Of forty-eight states in 1940, twenty-eight were still over half rural, and four (Mississippi, North Dakota, South Carolina and Arkansas) more than three-quarters rural.

The fall in the rural sector between 1940 and 1970 is one of

---

[9] Ralph Waldo Emerson, *English Traits* (1849).

[10] For a geographer's estimate, see R. C. Estall, 'Population Growth and Environment: Some Aspects of the Problems in the United States and the Response', *Journal of American Studies* (Apr 1972).

the most important features of recent American social history. Even so, more than one-quarter of the total population is still classified as 'rural', and considerably more than one-half of the population (115 million, or 56 per cent) lives in places with fewer than 50,000 inhabitants. The corresponding figure for England and Wales is 18 million, or 40 per cent of total population.

At the other end of the scale, we find 80 million persons living in metropolitan areas of over a million inhabitants, together accounting for almost 40 per cent of the American population. The growth of these giants in the past half-century, and especially since the Second World War, has been a second demographic phenomenon with immense social consequences. In 1950 there were fifteen metropolitan areas of over one million inhabitants; twenty years later, in 1970, this number had more than doubled to thirty-three.

The contrast is such that while 80 million people are concentrated in giant metropolitan areas, at the other extreme 75 million are widely scattered in places with fewer than 10,000 inhabitants. The enormous differences of geographical environment make a direct comparison with Britain difficult. The characteristic British unit may be represented as the medium-sized town within one of the seven areas designated as conurbations. The latter account for just over one-third of the total population of England and Wales (17 million persons), but are composed of identifiable, though proximate, towns. About three-fifths of the population of industrial south-east Lancashire, for example, live in seventeen separate towns with an average size of about 170,000, ranging from Liverpool (606,000) to Bury (68,000). A representative example might be taken as the cotton-spinning town of Bolton, with about 160,000 inhabitants in 1961 and 1971.

What this evidence suggests is that to attribute many of America's present economic and social difficulties to over-population is to over-simplify and misidentify the problem. The thirty-three metropolitan areas which in 1970 had populations of over one million have increased by 27 million since 1950. Four main belts account for half of America's urban area: the north-east coast from Massachusetts to Maryland; the Great Lakes zone; the southern California coast; and northern and eastern Florida. In these concentrations, more than one-third of America's population inhabits some 5 per cent of the coterminous land area. Even there, however, the general density of population in those concentrations is below that of the Netherlands or of England.

Moreover, such problems as resource depletion and pollution cannot be wholly, or even mainly, attributed to population size. The level and style of consumption are equally important determinants of resource usage. Pollution, in all its many aspects, is not a function of population size or even of density (as some of the American environmentalists acknowledge when they pay tribute, for example, to the 'life-style' to be found in the Netherlands or in Britain). Moreover, British experiments (for example with 'smokeless zones') have suggested that part of the problem at least is susceptible to solution by means of strictly enforced legislation, when the will to act, and willingness to comply, are present.

One final demographic point. Unlike the normal European pattern (which is that populations show a female surplus), America has had, thanks mainly to immigration, a male surplus in every census until that of 1950 (in 1930 of 1·5 millions, in 1940 of half a million). Since 1950 there has been a growing female surplus reaching 5 million by 1970. This change is combined with a population 'bulge' in the age group between 15 and 30 years of age. These two components together amount to a marked change in the composition of the population: more women and more youths. Many economic and social consequences follow from this. There are at present more women of child-bearing age in the American population than ever before. Despite this, there were half a million fewer births in every year in the late 1960s than in the early years of the decade; in other words, the birth rate is not increasing. The fertility rate is now lower than ever before in American history (85 live births per 1,000 women aged 15–44 years). In the United Kingdom the fertility rate in 1971 was identical, 85 per 1,000, suggesting that the American growth rate of population may now have fallen to the British level.

3. *Employment and unemployment*

The phenomenon of convergence was well demonstrated at the end of the Second World War, when the British and the American governments both passed Acts pledging themselves to prevent a recurrence of unemployment on the scale of the 1930s. In its 1944 White Paper, the British government accepted responsibility for maintaining 'a high and stable level of employment' after the war; it defined 'full employment' as a 3 per cent unemployment rate. The American Employment Act of 1946 declared the intention of maintaining 'maximum' employment, but deliberately avoided the use of the term 'full employment' because of its British and socialist associations. In examining success in attaining these goals, we have to bear in mind that for technical reasons British and American unemployment statistics are not directly comparable: differences in the methods of data collection mean that American figures tend to overstate the incidence of unemployment, while British figures tend to understate; an American figure of 4 per cent is about equivalent to a British figure of 3 per cent.

The American record since 1946 shows a considerable measure of success in achieving the main aim of the Employment Act. Mass unemployment has been avoided. Unemployment has averaged 4·3 per cent over the twenty-five-year period 1948–72, ranging from 2·9 per cent in 1953 to 6·7 per cent in the recessions of 1958 and 1961 (compared with the lowest unemployment figure in the 1930s of 14·3 per cent in 1937). Unemployment fell steadily in the 1960s to 3·5 per cent in 1969, when the figure for married men was down to 1·5 per cent. The figures since then have fluctuated, rising to 5·9 per cent in 1971, but falling thereafter. Simultaneously, the civilian labour force was increasing from around 60 million in the late 1940s to 70 million by 1960 and 97 million at the end of 1972; the economy was thus able to absorb an increase of some 27 million in the work-force.

Unemployment averaged around 3 million in the 1960s, but reached the highest post-war figure of 5·5 million in June 1971. Certain groups, however, have regularly had unemployment rates above the average: blue-collar workers as a whole (5·6 per cent average, 1963–72), black workers (8·4 per cent average, 1963–72), school-leavers (14·7 per cent average, 1963–72); when the last two are put together, it is evident that unemployment among black youths aged 16–19 years has been particularly high. At the end of 1972 black unemployment was about 10 per cent and teenage unemployment 16 per cent.

While America's record since the Second World War represents an enormous improvement over the Depression years, her unemployment figures are regularly higher than the British. Between 1947 and 1966 the average monthly unemployment figure in Britain hardly ever exceeded the half-million mark; in percentage terms, unemployment was generally well below 3 per cent, and often below 2 per cent of the work-force. While the American figures continued to improve in the late 1960s, however, the British began to deteriorate: from 1·5 per cent (360,000 persons) in 1966 to 3·6 per cent (807,000 persons) in 1971. February 1972, however, saw the peak (one million) and the level dropped markedly in subsequent months. Even allowing for problems of direct comparison, these average figures suggest that Britain has been more successful in meeting its unemployment problem than America. The British economy, of course, has had a much smaller increase in the labour force; this has been reflected, for example, in the greater ease with which school-leavers have found employment.

Much less of American unemployment, however, appears to be long-term. Taking bad months for both countries, we find that in December 1971, of 5·1 million unemployed in America, 10 per cent had been unemployed for 27 weeks or over; in Britain on the other hand in January 1972, of 828,000 males unemployed, one-third had been unemployed for a similarly long period.[11] Hard-core unemployment (measured by any duration) is proportionately twice as great in Britain as in America. In 1971 hard-core unemployment (over 27 weeks) in Britain represented about 1 per cent of the

---

[11] The British data only show male unemployment by duration; if, in order to make the figures more comparable, it is assumed that *all* the American unemployment of over 26 weeks' duration is of males, then the American figure rises to 17 per cent.

total work-force, while in the United States it represented only 0·6 per cent; a difference of 0·4 per cent is large when one is dealing in millions.

The lower American percentage of long-term unemployment confirms the view expressed earlier that the habit of mobility still remains a feature of American economic behaviour today, and is found both in geographical and occupational mobility. The relatively high level of long-term unemployment in Britain is, in part at least, attributable to a continuing unwillingness of workers (or in some cases inability, e.g. because of housing shortages) to shift from place to place or from job to job even when unemployment has become chronic in particular localities: in the North the rate of long-term unemployment in January 1971 was two-thirds greater than in the South-east. Higher short-term unemployment and lower long-term unemployment in America reflects, in part at least, the greater mobility of the American labour force.

4. *Inflation*

Both in America and in Britain, concern with full employment has been challenged in recent years by the growing preoccupation with inflation. No explanation of inflation will suffice which considers only one or two countries, as the phenomenon has been international since the Second World War. Britain and America conform to a world-wide pattern, with some countries showing a better, and some a worse, record.

Nevertheless, the difference between the British and the American record is also of importance. Prices have risen much less sharply in America since the late 1940s. The contrast was perhaps the greatest in the mid-1960s. The years 1960–7 show an annual price rise of about 1·5 per cent, a particularly low figure for years of rapidly falling unemployment and buoyant economic expansion. In each of the periods shown in Table 1, British price rises were greater.

The new phenomenon which has confronted and confounded the Western world since 1968–9 is the combination of increasing unemployment with inflation. This has appeared to invalidate the former assumption (known to economists as the 'Phillips curve'[12]) that these two phenomena tend to move in opposite directions. In America from 1968, with unemployment at first rising sharply, prices also began to rise at a rate of about 5 per cent per annum; the rate of inflation was reduced in the United States in 1972 to around 3 per cent, but it is not possible to say with confidence that American inflation has been halted. The rate of inflation has been the same as in most Common Market countries, but British inflation, also starting in 1968, has been about 8 per cent per annum.[13]

TABLE I

AVERAGE ANNUAL PERCENTAGE INCREASES IN
CONSUMERS' PRICES, 1947–71

	U.K.	U.S.A.
1947–56	5·4	2·2
1956–62	2·0	1·8
1962–9	3·7	2·8
1969–71	7·9	5·1

Inflation is a shared experience. In both countries the government resorted to a wage and price freeze, with America taking the lead in this policy; both countries have experienced similar problems in the subsequent thaw. Looking at the post-1945 period as a whole, we see that the British response to inflation has been less successful, despite Britain's greater vulnerability to its consequences because of her greater dependence on foreign trade. There are many contributory factors; one must distinguish, for example, between fundamental causes and the mechanisms which propagate and perpetuate the conditions created by those causes.[14] At least two interesting features are shared by America and Britain. The first is the importance of consumer expectations. The second is that as living standards rise, consumption shifts

[12] From the article by A. W. Phillips, 'The Relation between Unemployment and the Rate of Money Wages in the United Kingdom, 1861–1957', *Economica* (Nov 1958).

[13] For a fuller discussion of many aspects of the problem, see D. Jackson, H. A. Turner and F. Wilkinson, *Do Trade Unions Cause Inflation?* (Cambridge U.P., 1972).

[14] Ibid., p. 16.

from industrial products (where mass-production techniques reduce costs of production, or at least keep increases to the minimum) towards satisfactions which are less susceptible to cost-reducing techniques, above all, personal services of all kinds.

The former Chairman of the President's Committee of Economic Advisers, Arthur Okun, once suggested, in a semi-serious way, that one might compile an Index of Social Discontent by adding together the percentage rate of unemployment and the percentage rate of inflation. If this is done, then both Britain and America show a sharp rise in that index in 1968–71, years marked in both countries by the problems created by the harnessing together of the stubborn mule of unemployment with the unstoppable racehorse of inflation.

5. *Trade unions*

Among the institutional inheritances from the past, the forms, strength and the ideology of the labour movement are of immense significance to a nation's economy. Trade unionism developed much later as a force in economic life in America and followed its own distinctive paths. One is well advised to start from assumptions of difference between Britain and America. Even apart from institutional differences, industrial wage-earners are a much smaller percentage of the total labour force in America than in Britain, and a much smaller proportion of them are members of a trade union. It was not until the Wagner Act of 1935 that American trade unions achieved effective legal recognition; the Taft–Hartley Act of 1947, and subsequent amendments, have set up fairly strict rules of conduct. The eventual acceptance of the regulatory legislation by American labour is in sharp contrast with the militant opposition of British unions to similar attempts at control.

In the late 1930s, while British trade unions remained weak through the Depression, the period saw a very rapid growth of American trade union strength and militancy, despite continuing unemployment figures of well over 10 per cent. More recent years have seen another example of divergence. Professor Turner and his associates[15] have drawn atten-

[15] Ibid., p. 86.

tion to the surprising fact that in Britain since the mid-1960s the number of unemployed and trade union militancy, as measured in the number of strikes and days lost through strike action, have consistently moved upwards together, contrary to the former assumption that strikes decline as unemployment increases. The American data, however, usually show movements in opposite directions, in accordance with former assumptions (see Table 2).

TABLE 2

UNEMPLOYMENT AND STRIKES IN THE U.K. AND THE U.S.A., 1961–9

| | U.K. | | U.S.A. | |
	Total number unemployed ('000)	Total days lost through strikes (million)	Total number unemployed ('000)	Total days lost through strikes (million)
1964–5	2·5	355	23·1	3·6
1966–7	2·6 (+)	(+) 460	33·8 (+)	(−) 3·0
1968–9	5·8 (+)	(+) 561	50·0 (+)	(−) 2·8
1970	11·0 (+)	(+) 603	66·4 (+)	(+) 4·1
1971	13·6 (+)	(+) 807	47·4 (−)	(+) 5·0

(Direction of change indicated in brackets.)

The answer to the apparent paradoxes must surely lie in the role of leadership in the trade union movement and in the attitudes of membership. To regard trade union activity merely as a reflection of general (or even particular) economic conditions must be inadequate. The difference would appear to lie in the personalities and policies of trade union leaders in the two countries at different periods of time, and in the loyalties to the movement and attitudes to the economic 'system' of trade union members. The roles of John L. Lewis and his associates in America in the 1930s and of British trade union leaders in the early 1970s are crucial in giving unions dynamism (or militancy), even when general conditions are unfavourable.

Although industrial wage-earners constitute the largest single category of employment in America, they are still very much a minority group (consistently about one in four of all workers between 1940 and 1970). 'Middle-class' occupational categories include the vast majority, two out of three employed persons. In this respect there is convergence, since the number of industrial wage-earners (and thus of potential trade unionists) is also in relative decline in Britain (accounting for about one-third of employed persons in 1970).

Partly for reasons of political arithmetic, America has not experienced a direct alliance of trade unions with a single political party as in the British Labour Party. American society has historically lacked a strong sense of working-class consciousness, partly because of the diverse origins of the immigrants who entered the factories during the main period of industrial development. In addition, upward social mobility, or at any rate the *aspiration* to middle-class status, has been, and still is (now, particularly, for most of the black population), more important than class solidarity and identification with fellow-workers. The myth of the independent yeoman farmer still continues even in an urban setting. Above all, American unions have never been ideologically committed to socialism, and thus by implication to the destruction of capitalism. Far from being hostile to the 'private enterprise system', they see their best interest in making the system work efficiently, then extracting from it the best possible bargain for their members. Many British union leaders and members are, to say the least, ambivalent in their attitude. In a society in which pressure groups are a normal method of political activity, American trade unions see themselves, and are seen, merely as one more special-interest pressure group rather than as the predestined instruments of an inevitable Marxist revolution.

6. *From dollar shortage to dollar problem*

The most striking recent similarity in the performance of the British and American economies – and at the same time the most complex – is the role of the pound and the dollar as international currencies, and the mounting strains of this role. Because pounds and dollars are, together with gold, the main media in which the markets of the world reckon and settle their international payments, the past, present and future price of all three is of crucial importance to international financial transactions. All of them are susceptible to hoarding and speculation.

A generation ago the first dollar crisis meant a dollar *shortage*: everybody wanted dollars; few people had enough. The dollar appeared to be as impregnable as the vaults of Fort Knox itself. For twenty years sterling was at risk and underwent two devaluations. More recently the impossible has become reality. The second dollar crisis has become a dollar glut; people are selling, not seeking, dollars and the dollar itself has been mildly devalued.

Just as Britain's excess of imports over exports was at the root of sterling weakness, so also the transformation in America's balance-of-trade position accounts in part for the present dollar weakness. In the early 1960s America exported annually some $5 billion worth more merchandise than she imported. This surplus had fallen to half a billion in 1968–9 and the account went into deficit in 1971; in 1972 the deficit was of about the same magnitude as the 1964 surplus. When all other transactions besides merchandise trade are taken into account, the United States is seen to have been in deficit in four of the five years 1968–72 (compared with only three significant deficits in the twenty-two years 1946–67). Meanwhile British and American reserve holdings moved in opposite directions, British increasing, American falling (see Table 3).

TABLE 3

U.S. AND U.K. INTERNATIONAL RESERVES, 1949–72

($ billion)

	1949	1953	1967	1970	1971	1972 (*Nov*)
U.S.A.	26·0	23·5	14·8	14·5	13·2	13·3
U.K.	1·8	2·7	2·7	2·8	8·8	5·9

Data from the *Economic Report of the President*, Jan 1973, p. 298.

The link between the external and the internal value of the dollar is less obvious than that with sterling. Foreign trade is still marginal in American economic activity, not central as in Britain. Total merchandise exported is a mere 4 per cent of GNP and that imported only 3 per cent (British percentage figures, and those for such countries as the Netherlands, are ten times greater). Nevertheless, American in-

ternal conditions greatly affect the rest of the world: her imports are 14 per cent of total world imports and 50 per cent of
certain items (e.g. coffee); whenever domestic conditions
cause America to reduce these imports, the consequences for
the suppliers can be very serious indeed.

III. ENDS AND MEANS

The broad economic aims of both British and American
society since the Second World War have been to prevent
mass unemployment; to induce stability and avoid large
cyclical disturbances; to bring about economic growth; to
eliminate poverty; to maintain the value of money. In the
long view, there has been considerable success in achieving
economic aims set up three decades ago. It has proved possible in both countries to achieve some of those aims some of
the time, but (with the possible exception of America in the
mid-1960s) not to achieve all the aims all the time. It has
proved particularly difficult in America to combine growth
with monetary stability and in Britain to combine growth
with a stable balance of payments, and later to combine a
reduction in unemployment with stable prices. The most recent years have brought to Britain and America alike the
troublesome combination of both higher unemployment and
inflation.

The principal means used by the central government in
both countries to achieve their economic ends have been
fiscal and monetary policy, with direct assistance to strategic
areas of the economy. Given American political institutions,
fiscal policy is still a very blunt weapon, since the United
States administration does not have the 'instant budget' as a
normal procedure, of the type available to British governments. Control over monetary mechanisms has been used,
through the Federal Reserve System, more regularly and successfully in America than in Britain.

All the weapons of government economic intervention
have involved centralization and an increase in government
power. Any sharp contrast between America as a private
enterprise economy and Britain as a controlled (or, to some
Americans, socialist) economy is now extremely blurred.

There is no adequate measure of the extent (still less of the nature) of government intervention. Governments in America take in taxes a somewhat smaller proportion of total national income than in Britain, but directly employ a greater proportion of the labour force.

The mood in both countries now is to question some of those aims: above all, to ask whether a fetish has been made of economic growth as a goal in itself, and whether sufficient attention has been paid to other desiderata, e.g. resource conservation, income equalization, environment, and improving the 'quality' of life. It is legitimate to point out that as GNP figures include inputs devoted to the reduction of pollution, some part of the recorded growth reflects the quantity of pollution and the consequent efforts to remove it. Anti-pollution has itself become a growth industry.

Some of these problems appear less urgent in Britain. Many Americans in fact look to Britain for models to copy in such matters as town planning or health services, and speak with envy of Britain's ability (in their eyes) to allow urban agglomeration to occur without the destruction of 'civilized' values. We British are perhaps less sure of our own achievements and capabilities, not least as we see ourselves increasingly troubled by the 'American' problem of strangulation by road traffic and by threats to supplies of essential resources.

Our own lack of concern also reflects the continued difference in per capita incomes. Britain is far enough away from American standards of affluence to give first priority still to the economic problem of raising living standards. The constant demand is for ever-higher incomes, with too little concern for consequent pressures on resources or for any resultant increase in environmental pollution. The few who voice their fears about such matters rarely accept the corollary that for remedies to become effective, economic growth (and thus such expectations as increased old-age pensions and higher real wages) might need to be held in check. It is perhaps ironical that the Anglo-French supersonic jet aeroplane Concorde was promoted by Anthony Wedgwood Benn, a left-wing Socialist, but is opposed by the United States Congress.

The time may well have come for a redefinition on both sides of the Atlantic of the aims of economic endeavour. If this is to be done, the onus lies on those who desire such a change to state clearly how they wish to reorder the priorities. If growth is to be de-emphasized, or more resources devoted to the improvement of the environment, what activities are to be contracted in order to release those resources? And what would be the secondary consequences of this redeployment?

Almost any sensible redefinition of economic objectives by Americans must involve a willingness to tax themselves more highly (whether for purpose of environment control, or of income redistribution). But merely to assume that higher taxes can buy solutions is to fall into the American trap of assuming that money will solve any problem. Some of the problems Americans would like to see solved are not susceptible to the quick, easy remedy of merely spending more money: such problems include socially caused poverty, race, the unemployables, urban decay, crime, violence and pollution itself, if one recalls the litter of Coke and beer cans, paper, etc., left behind on a university campus after an anti-pollution Earth Day rally.

Moreover, the assumption that government has a central role in economic processes is also being called into question once again. The New Deal crusading zeal has long passed. Since the 1930s the intervention of government has increased and still is increasing, but now, many are saying, ought to be diminished. Why? The arguments advanced against government intervention are similar to those advanced in the nineteenth century and to those which made Herbert Hoover so hostile to Congressional politicians. Governments are accused of being inefficient, corrupt, remote, uncontrollable and untrustworthy. The nostalgic hope of a simpler, more primitive society has its counterpart in the political and social cry for *laissez-faire* seen in Britain in the opposition to government attempts to enforce wage restraints, or translated more simply in America into the cry: 'Let me do my own thing.'

BIBLIOGRAPHY

P. Ehrlich, *The Population Bomb* (1968). The best-seller that persuaded many Americans that their country was overpopulated.

A. J. N. den Hollander and S. Skard, *American Civilization: An Introduction* (1968), esp. ch. 3 ('Economic Structure') and ch. 4 ('Social Structure').

D. Jackson, H. A. Turner and F. Wilkinson, *Do Trade Unions Cause Inflation?* (1972). A discussion of the problem from British and international viewpoints.

W. E. Rappard, *The Secret of American Prosperity* (1955). An assessment by a Swiss writer of the mainsprings of American economic success.

E. Stillman and others, *L'Envol de la France dans les Anneés 80* (1973). Published by the European Institute of the Hudson Institute, with introduction by Herman Kahn. A report predicting that by 1985 Britain's *per capita* GNP will be half that of France.

United Kingdom, Central Statistical Office, *Annual Abstract of Statistics; Monthly Digest of Statistics.*

United Nations, *Statistical Yearbook* (annual). Gives statistics of population, production, trade, etc., for most countries of the world.

United States, President, *Economic Report of the President together with the Annual Report of the Council of Economic Advisers* (annually in January for previous year). Invaluable for most recent American economic statistics and for discussion of economic performance and problems in preceding year.

United States, Bureau of the Census, *Statistical Abstract of the United States.* Annual volume of American statistics.

B. A. Weisbrod (ed.), *The Economics of Poverty: An American Paradox* (1966). Essays by leading economists on social and economic aspects of poverty, with discussion of suggested remedies.

E. S. Woytinsky, *Profile of the U.S. Economy* (1967). An examination of many aspects of the American economy, with maps, tables and charts.

Part Two

Lessons Drawn

5 A Model Democracy?

RICHARD ROSE

Professor of Politics, University of Strathclyde

> 'In the midst of it all the stranger, who sees so much that he hates and so much that he loves, hardly knows how to express himself.'
>
> Anthony Trollope, visiting Washington, 1868

America cannot claim to have invented the idea of government, but Americans can claim that they have invented many novel institutions of governance. With confidence born of continental isolation, Americans have come to assume that their institutions – the Presidency, Congress and the Supreme Court – are the prototype of what should be adopted elsewhere, once the world is made safe for democracy.

The British government against which the American colonists revolted was, according to Walter Bagehot, 'a sort of museum of the defects of a constitutional king'. But after the French Revolution it became outstanding in Europe for the adaptability and authority of its representative institutions. Just as Alexis de Tocqueville travelled to America to seek the secrets of democracy, so he could journey to England to seek the secrets of stable representative government.

In strictly quantitative terms, far more people today are governed by institutions modelled on British parliamentary forms than by an American-type presidential system. In addition to planting parliamentary institutions firmly in Canada and Australia, Britain also gifted parliamentary institutions to many African and Asian colonies at the moment of their independence; in India, the largest territory of the old Empire, these institutions have best taken root. If only by force of reaction, American government was itself modelled upon lessons drawn from English experience. As Bernard Bailyn notes: 'The pattern of political activity in the colonies was part of a more comprehensive British pattern and cannot be understood in isolation from that larger system."[1]

If British and American governments today appear inimitable, it may be for lack of imitators. Moreover, neither America nor Britain is now so sure that its form of government is the model for the world of tomorrow. The governments of Tito, Castro, Sadat or Syngman Rhee appear more suited to the troubled conditions of many countries in the world today.

The two oldest prototypes of representative government can none the less be analysed to see what lessons each can learn from the other. Some occupants of the White House have been heard to speak admiringly of the powers of a British Prime Minister relatively untroubled by legislative harassment. The inauguration of a youthful John F. Kennedy made the Presidency fashionable in English eyes. Britons have written since about the alleged 'Presidentializing' of the office of Prime Minister. It is unclear which President provides the model for imitation. For example, Harold Wilson lacked the style of a John F. Kennedy, or the great stature and tragic flaw of a Lyndon Johnson. To imitate Richard Nixon is a dubious claim to second-hand merit.

Comparing British and American models of government helps make clear what elements are common to both and what elements are distinct to one country. The existence of differences in government does not mean that one model must be superior to the other. But it does provide a basis for assessing their contrasting assumptions and consequences. The conclusions are unlikely to lead to the transfer of institutions across the Atlantic, for the machinery of government is very sensitive to national influences. Comparison leads to greater understanding of the political culture that inhibits institutional transfer.

Two problems crucial in every democracy are the subject of what follows. The first is the citizen's role in the political system. The second is the role of those who govern. The former emphasizes the liberties of the individual, and the latter the collective power of his government. Democratic government is concerned with both these issues. The idea of

[1] *The Origins of American Politics* (1967) p. ix.

popular rule not only emphasizes the views of the populace but also the need for institutions of government strong enough to rule.

I. THE GOVERNED AND GOVERNMENT

In America the doctrine of popular sovereignty places ultimate authority in the hands of the governed. Government is their creation. The opening words of the preamble of the American Constitution make this explicit: the government established therein is ordained by 'We the people'. This declaration of popular sovereignty has been followed in many lands. For example, the Constitution of the Fifth French Republic states: 'The French people solemnly proclaim ...', and the Federal German Republic: 'The German People in the *Länder*...'. The Constitution of India begins: 'We the people of India ...'. Even the constitutions of Communist China and the Soviet Union pay lip-service to popular sovereignty, while vesting power in practice in the party's soviets. The preamble to the Constitution of the Republic of Ireland marries Catholic tradition with secular American doctrines: 'In the name of the Most Holy Trinity, from whom is all authority and to whom, as our final end, all actions both of men and states must be referred, We the people of Eire...'

The American Constitution makes explicit the implication of popular sovereignty. The tenth and last article of the Bill of Rights of 1791 declares that all powers not delegated to the federal government are reserved to the states or, if denied the states, to the people. The concept is also given practical expression in the second article of the Bill of Rights, which declares 'the right of the people to keep and bear arms shall not be infringed'.

In England, by contrast, the Crown is the ultimate source of sovereignty. Bills that have been approved by Parliament become law because, in the Norman French formula still in use today, 'La Reyne le veult'. The outward and obsolete formula no longer expresses the whole of reality. England today is no more governed by the personal wishes of the Queen than America is governed by town meeting. But sovereignty is still not endowed in the populace. It rests instead with Parliament, a body representative of the nation yet not a body of popular delegates. The contrast with America is captured by L. S. Amery, a former Conservative minister, in his description of British government as 'government of the people, for the people, with but not by the people'.[2] If American government is ultimately based upon the people, the ultimate locus of authority in Britain is Parliament, governing in trust for the people.

The explanation for this contrast is easy to find. The existence of a written constitution makes explicit a citizen's place in government. In the New World there was no government sanctioned by tradition or dynastic legitimacy. The Constitution was drafted in the 1780s because revolution had voided pre-existing colonial charters, and something was needed in their place. Nearly every government in the contemporary world has followed the American example of establishing a written constitution, because at some point in the past – often, the not very distant past – a regime has been overthrown by force. The new governors require a document formally stating the rights of citizens and the source of sovereignty, whether the people, the nation or an economic class. England is anachronistic; its basic legal procedures have evolved through eight centuries. They are not sanctioned by a document drafted and ratified at one point in time, because England has never had a revolution successful at a stroke.

The implications of these contrasting views are multiple, and sometimes controversial. The question of popular control of government is approached from opposite extremes in America and Britain. In America the problem of governing is the need to aggregate powers dispersed among heterogeneous and sometimes jealous bodies, each claiming to speak for one part of a pluralistic populace. By contrast, in Britain the great historic problem was how to share power between Her Majesty's Government and the well-bred few in the House of Lords and House of Commons; it latterly became how to share power between the Government, Parliament and the mass of the people.

The rights of the individual citizen are given far greater legal protection in America than in England today. The

2 *Thoughts on the Constitution* (1953 ed.) p. 21.

American Constitution grants individuals rights superior to those of Acts of Congress or executive claims to authority. The Supreme Court hears suits in which individuals seek to protect their rights against the claimed authority of government. Until the 1930s, the Court so interpreted these rights as to declare unconstitutional many 'progressive' measures already familiar in Europe, such as the income tax and Acts regulating safe conditions in industry. Since then, the Supreme Court has been ready to declare legislation or government actions unconstitutional when they infringe individual claims to privacy, liberty of the person, or freedom from self-incrimination.

By contrast, Parliament is sovereign. In the classic phrase: 'Parliament can pass any law, except to make a man a woman.' Latterly, even this practical inhibition no longer seems binding. The courts do not consider themselves arbiters of what government may or may not do. English courts explicitly reject the claim that they should declare an Act of Parliament unconstitutional, nor will they consider that an Act should be set aside because it conflicts with a previous Act of Parliament, or what claimants describe as natural rights. English judges believe that 'an unwritten constitution must be constantly made and unmade, but they want no part of the job. That is for Parliament and the electorate.'[3]

The American Bill of Rights is a far different document in wording and contemporary application from its English homonym of a century earlier. The English Bill of Rights of 1689 justified deposing a Catholic and authoritarian monarch, and replacing him with a Protestant monarch subject to parliamentary influence. It was not a general attempt to entrench the liberties of every Englishman. There was no effort to give citizens rights that the courts would or could enforce against the Crown. The doctrine that 'The Queen can do no wrong' asserts a presumption that the officers of the Crown – civil servants, police and soldiers – will not act unlawfully. Individuals may sue the Crown for alleged wrongs by its servants only in restricted circumstances. By contrast, an American convicted on criminal charges can use the federal courts to quash a charge or a conviction, not on the grounds of his

---

[3] Louis L. Jaffe, *English and American Judges as Lawmakers* (1969) p. 4.

innocence but on the ground that in prosecuting the case against him the government has violated his rights to due process of law, as the judges infer these from the Constitution.

The existence of legally enforceable rights makes Americans turn to the courts to protect or advance causes as readily as an Englishman might turn to his MP, or write a letter to *The Times*. The evolution of American race relations in the past generation illustrates how the courts can help to regulate conflicts between citizens, and between citizens and government. The 1954 Supreme Court decision against school segregation, declaring segregated public facilities intrinsically unequal, was the climax of almost two decades of litigation in which black plaintiffs, often assisted by white lawyers, pressed for the court to enforce their rights against state laws and state constitutional provisions. Two decades later the courts can no longer claim to be the sole arena in which racial disputes are resolved. But the courts, through their decisions on behalf of blacks seeking rights, have done much to encourage civil rights leaders to trust to established political institutions to secure rights that private and governmental bodies had sought to deny them.

In England, by contrast, the courts do not give the citizen a handle that he can grasp in an attempt to defend himself against what he regards as a government action infringing his rights. In the words of one English Law Lord:

In the Constitution of this country there are no guaranteed or absolute rights. The safeguard of British liberty is in the good sense of the people and in the system of representative and responsible government which has been evolved.[4]

It is often argued that individual rights are better protected by the good sense of the citizenry than by formal statutes. In the 1950s, for example, it was said that England offered greater protection for its citizens, particularly people with unconventional political views, notwithstanding its lack of legal safeguards for the subject. Cultural attitudes were said

[4] Lord Wright, in Liversidge *v.* Anderson (1941). More generally, see Harry Street, *Freedom, the Individual and the Law* (1972).

to make it 'inconceivable' that Englishmen would act like American followers of Senator Joseph McCarthy or of a racist governor. The absence of a virulent anti-Communist movement was taken as full proof of this proposition. Just as Americans may be readier to countenance giving freedom to a few persons who have committed crimes in order to safeguard the Bill of Rights, so Englishmen were readier to countenance the risk of Communist spies in order to safeguard rights of public servants.

Luck provides an alternative explanation for the respect historically shown to individual rights in Britain. In the fortunate absence of Communist conspiracies, racial turmoil or armed gangs, English police and courts could afford to be nice. Libertarian attitudes have depended upon the absence of challenges to liberal values. Once these challenges arise, a British government may show as little regard for individual rights as its American counterpart, and have popular support in so doing.

An influx of coloured immigrants to Britain, beginning in the late 1950s, provides an apt test of the concept of rights in the two countries. The fact that Britain's coloured immigrants constitute less than 3 per cent of its population might be expected to make it all the easier to recognize the rights of people who, though black, often had legally valid claims to British nationality as an inheritance from the days of Empire and Commonwealth. Moreover, there was no tradition of segregation established by law, as in many American states.[5]

The initial response of the British government was 'benign neglect'. While noting racial tensions in America, the government assumed 'It can't happen here.' For example, a BBC interviewer was shocked when Alabama's Governor, George Wallace, pointed out that British people who go to places like Southern Rhodesia react even more strongly against the grant of political rights to blacks than do the white citizens of Alabama. The surprise victory of one racist candidate for Parliament in the 1964 British general election forced politicians to abandon their illusions. Since then, the government has sought to enact anti-discrimination legislation. The limited use made of the laws can be interpreted in contrasting ways.

[5] See, e.g., E. J. B. Rose *et al.*, *Colour and Citizenship* (1969).

The optimistic interpretation is that there are no instances of racial discrimination in Britain. The realistic interpretation is that the difficulty of establishing proof and the burden of pressing charges is such that few persons with grievances will employ the grievance machinery. The pessimistic interpretation is that blacks have already given up believing that grievances can be redressed by the due process of English courts.

There is far less faith today in the essential tolerance and fairness of British citizens, unsanctioned by law, than there was two decades ago. The reason is simple: Britain is now a multi-racial rather than a mono-racial society. Politicians believe that the easiest way to protect individuals from discrimination is to keep Britain as white as possible. This means passing laws intended to limit severely further immigration from non-white areas of the Commonwealth. In one respect Britain has even led America in segregationist measures. In 1968 Parliament passed an emergency measure denying right of entry to Britain to about 100,000 British subjects then living in Kenya, because they had brown rather than white skins. A member of the Labour Cabinet responsible for the Act, R. H. S. Crossman, later commented, with a transatlantic glance, that the measure 'would have been declared unconstitutional in any country with a written constitution and a Supreme Court'.[6]

The experience of Parliament in seeking to govern Northern Ireland – the smallest and most un-English part of the United Kingdom – illustrates clearly what can happen when citizens lack the opportunity to protect or advance their rights through the courts. When a government of Northern Ireland was established by Act of Parliament in 1920, it was explicitly stated that it could pass no laws sanctioning religious discrimination. But the numerical predominance of Protestants in Ulster sustained, in an Ulster Prime Minister's words, 'A Protestant Parliament for a Protestant people.' Civil rights groups found that there was no judicial remedy for discrimination in the administration of these laws.[7] The

[6] 'Understanding the Profusion of Shrinking Violets', *The Times* (London), 6 Sep 1972.

[7] For background, see Richard Rose, *Governing without Consensus: An Irish Perspective* (1971) esp. chs. 3–4, 15.

absence of any judicial recourse led Ulster Catholics to express dissidence by illegal means. Armed insurrection, led by the Irish Republican Army, proved futile on its own, for lack of widespread popular support. In 1968 Catholic demonstrators, drawing an explicit lesson from America, began conducting protest marches. When the marches were declared illegal, again following American examples, the marches continued. Peaceful demonstrations finally gave way to three-sided armed conflict between the British Army, the illegal Catholic-oriented IRA and the illegal Protestant-oriented Ulster Volunteer Force.

Faced with the threat of civil war in August 1971, the British government sought to secure order by interning hundreds of Ulster Catholics suspected of involvement with the IRA. The people interned were not satisfied when told that they were held prisoner by authority of an Act of Parliament, for the Act contravened habeas corpus and the European Convention on Human Rights. Denied hope of redress in the courts because judges cannot overrule an Act of Parliament, Republicans escalated violence. Upon one occasion, a non-violent protester, John Hume, a Catholic MP from Londonderry, did fight a case to the High Court and won. The courts ruled that a number of actions by the British Army, one of which had resulted in a £10 fine for Hume, were outside the Army's statutory authority. That afternoon the Home Secretary introduced a Bill in the House of Commons to give the Army statutory authority for the actions complained about and then some. The Bill was approved by both Houses of Parliament and became law the same day. As it was retrospective, it repudiated the advantage that Hume had won in the courts.[8] The violence escalated yet again.

The beginning of the 1970s was once forecast to be a time of great violence in American race relations. In the event, the greatest violence has occurred in Belfast, not Newark or Chicago. In the first four years of Ulster violence since 1969, more than 800 people have died in a part of the United Kingdom with the same size population as the city of Detroit. It can be argued that it is unfair to cite Ulster experience when making comparisons between America and the United King-

[8] See House of Commons *Debates*, vol. 831, cols. 1285–454, 23 Feb 1972.

dom, because Northern Ireland is not 'really' a part of the United Kingdom. If this plea of exceptionalism be allowed, then one might equally argue that Mississippi, Chicago or Newark is not really a part of America.

The conflict between an individual contending for his rights against the leviathan of the state is, by definition, atypical of problems of government. Government is usually about collective action, decisions made by a few on behalf of many whom they represent. America can undoubtedly claim to have pioneered many novel forms of representative government, ranging from the gerrymander to the Presidential primary. The electoral and party institutions through which Americans collectively express their views remain distinctive today. Whether they strengthen or weaken popular sovereignty is another point.

America is unique in the frequency with which its citizens are asked to vote, and in the number of political decisions taken by popular ballot. In England, as in most European countries, an individual votes for Members of Parliament and for local government councillors, but for no other official or policy. In America, by contrast, citizens elect representatives at three levels – federal, state and local. They elect administrators and often judges. In Britain, Cabinet ministers are the only elected persons paid to administer government at any level; other administrators are civil servants or appointed. In America no post, whether President or county coroner, is too high or too low to be outside the scope of popular election. An American finds nothing odd in a ballot several feet long, listing up to a hundred persons as candidates for dozens of public offices. The use of elective primaries to choose candidates for minor as well as major office permits Americans to vote about who shall be voted on in a general election.

The effect of the popular election of office-holders is compounded by the range of jurisdictions that elect governing councils. School boards and sewer districts as well as the United States Senate typically fill their ranks by popular election. Americans also vote bills by referendum, vote on the recall of elected officials, vote about property taxes and the issuance of bonds to finance capital investment in highways, bridges and other collective goods and services. These practices too are unheard of in Britain. If frequency of voting is one's measure of democracy, America is in a class by itself.

The consequence of great popular participation in the choice of governors can be confusion rather than clarity. Confusion arises in the first instance when different parties are elected to control different parts of government. In half the elections since 1946, the result has given one party control of the White House and the other party a majority in Congress. Similar patterns of opposition can be found between the White House and many governors, as well as governors and state legislatures. Individual voters show that they approve of dividing powers between the parties by splitting their ticket, voting for candidates from different parties as they mark down a long ballot offering choices for federal, state and local offices. For example, in one-third of all Congressional districts in 1968, voters favoured the Democratic choice for President and the Republican choice for Congress, or vice versa. In three-fifths of the states where a Governor and a Senator were elected on the same day, the voters elected men of opposing party loyalties.

The inconsistency of American voters at one election is complemented by their instability through time. From 1948 to 1972 America and Britain have each held seven national elections. In each country the two parties have been almost evenly divided in success: the Conservatives are one ahead of Labour and the Republicans are one ahead of the Democrats. But the votes of the American electorate have swung far more widely than in Britain. The vote for the Democratic candidate has ranged from 37·5 per cent to 61·1 per cent, and for Republicans from 38·5 to 60·7 per cent. By contrast, the range in the vote for the Conservative Party has been 10·1 per cent, and for Labour 5·7 per cent. A comparative analysis of party fortunes in nineteen Western nations finds America outstanding in the volatility of electoral support for the two major parties.[9]

One argument for a voter switching his choice between parties is that men of opposite parties may have more in common with each other than candidates of the same party. This

[9] See Richard Rose and Derek W. Urwin, 'Persistence and Change in Western Party Systems since 1945', *Political Studies*, XVIII, 3 (1970) p. 306.

can happen because at a single national election the Democratic Party will offer under one label candidates ranging across the whole ideological spectrum of the country's politics. Republicans will offer candidates who span the distance from extreme reaction through a liberalism that in all but name places them in the Democratic Party.

By comparison with America, British parties and elections offer the individual a much more clear-cut choice. In voting for his Member of Parliament, an individual is also stating his preference for the party he wishes to control the executive branch of government. Whichever party wins will dominate both the executive and legislature for up to five years. The sanctions of discipline within the parliamentary party, threatening expulsion and electoral defeat to any persistently recalcitrant MP, ensure the party leaders in the executive the continuing support of a majority in Parliament. The ideological spectrum covered by the British parties is about as wide as that covered by American parties. The content of views is not identical, but the Labour Party's left-wing Socialists are counterbalanced in America by right-wing Republicans. The centre of political gravity in Britain is to the left of that in America, assessed in terms of government intervention in the economy.

The most persisting distinction between the party systems is that there is greater cohesion – both organizationally and in policy terms – in Britain. The Conservative and Labour parties, notwithstanding internal differences do not each seek to cover as wide a spectrum of political views as do the Democrats and Republicans. Moreover, local politics in Britain does not provide the resources to compete for power outside Parliament. In Britain the voter has less choice and can choose less frequently than in America. But he has a clearer choice *between* parties. In America, at primary, local, state and federal elections, an American chooses *within* as well as between parties. The greater variety of choices offered makes it more likely that the cumulative collective preferences of Americans will not add up to anything resembling a coherent pattern.

One reason why the American party system is unique is the complexity of American government. Not only are political institutions and jurisdictions almost infinitely subdivided, but also the electorate is subdivided by religion, race and ethnic origin, as well as by class and region. The task of making a majority is difficult, because society is divided into so many different social sub-groups and each is relatively small in proportion to the whole. The two parties must aggregate citizens divided along lines of race, religion, class and urban–rural distinctions. The two largest groups in American society – working-class and middle-class white Protestant urban and suburban dwellers outside the South – constitute less than one-third of the electorate. By contrast, in Britain the two largest social groups – working-class and middle-class white Protestant English city-dwellers – constitute almost three-fifths of the electorate. The only European country that might claim to match America in social complexity is Switzerland. It too has uniquely complex political institutions. The Swiss sustain a multi-party system and a coalition government. America has coalition government too, for effective government requires a coalition of effort between the President and Congress, and within as well as between parties.

A second reason why the American party system is unique is that other countries do not wish to copy it. Critics of the American system charge that the dispersion of governmental powers among a variety of elected office-holders and the inability of the parties to discipline officials elected independently of each other undermines rather than accomplishes majority rule. Citizens cannot hold their governors responsible for what they do, for each can blame another for the frustrations of office. The party system has created what E. E. Schattschneider describes as *The Semi-Sovereign People*. In Britain, by contrast, the governing party has every incentive to make a good record while in office, because undivided responsibility gives it all the credit for success – just as it must bear all the blame if things go wrong.

II. THE GOVERNORS AND GOVERNMENT

The control of government is a problem for governors as well as the governed. The alternative to popular sovereignty is not necessarily elite domination; it may be that no one runs the shop. American fears of a strong, centralizing monarch made popular sovereignty an end in itself and a guarantee of liberty. If the best government is that which governs least, then the best governors are those who have least power to influence the lives of those whom they are meant to govern. By contrast, in Europe fears of anarchy or mob rule have made strong government valued as an end in itself and as a guarantee of order. Popular participation in government becomes one means to the end of legitimating strong central powers. The existence of centralized powers offers an incentive to popular participation, in that those who capture control of government find themselves with more effective authority than a newly elected American President, who finds popular election a stage in a long struggle; following inauguration, he must battle within the arena of federal government to assemble power to act in many fields.

In form the institutions of British government concentrate power just as much as the institutions of American government fragment it.[10] Whether the substance of government differs as much as the form is a different point. To note that Britain is a unitary state, while the United States has a federal form of government, does not mean that in one country all decisions are taken in London, and that in the other Washington is powerless to act without state and local cooperation. Reciprocally, to contrast the eminence of the President with the Prime Minister's role as chairman of a collegiate Cabinet does not mean that the Prime Minister cannot act without Cabinet consultation, or that the President can command where the Prime Minister can only confer. Comparing the process of government in the two countries can show to what extent problems of central control are generic or specific to Britain or America.

In form and as a matter of historical fact, British government is a 'top down' structure of authority; by contrast, American government is built from the bottom up. British government today is based upon the achievements of strong, centralizing monarchs who eliminated localized power bases centuries ago. American government, by contrast, often re-

---

[10] For the author's view in detail of British government, see *Politics in England Today* (1974).

sembles England in the time of Magna Carta, with the barons drawn up to humble the monarch by telling him the terms on which his authority is to be exercised. In America the states antedate the federal government. In England the monarchy preceded by centuries the authorities that it charters to provide local government. The place to be in Britain is in or near the Cabinet. In America, however high up one goes, a politician is expected to retain a power base in his own constituency. This is as true for a Kennedy, concerned with Massachusetts politics, as it is for a man like Senator William Fulbright, whose position in the Senate depends upon securing re-election from a constituency more concerned with cotton and rice than with foreign affairs.

In Britain the model of government resembles a pyramid. In this hierarchical structure, every official and institution has a place. The largest number of politicians and civil servants are at the base in local government, administering education, health, housing and environmental services. But the authority to take decisions comes from above. The *ultra vires* rule stipulates that it is outside the power of a local authority to undertake measures not explicitly authorized by Act of Parliament, if they involve expenditure of more than a tiny portion of its total income. Most of local government's funds come from the centre. This is not a form of revenue-sharing such as President Nixon might like, but rather revenue-contracting. Local authorities receive money to provide services authorized by central government. Their plans are subject to central review in advance of action, and expenditure is subject to audit by central government after the event. The lines of authority run uninterrupted from the base to the top of the pyramid, going through central government departments responsible for education, health and environment to the Cabinet. In principle, any action that a local authority wishes to take can be appealed to the Cabinet. A Cabinet can discuss such matters as the siting of a road in Oxford, or the reorganization of secondary schooling in a medium-sized English city. The decisions of central government can have the full force of commands. In extreme instances the central government can suspend or abolish a subordinate authority, as happened with the government of Northern Ireland in March

1972. No American President, no matter how much he sought power, would ever wish responsibility, say, for how New York City spent its budget. Nor would he ever hope to be able to suspend obstructionist governors or recalcitrant school boards opposed to racial integration.

The shape of government in America is neither so simple nor so tidy as in Britain. It can better be symbolized by the kind of landscape seen in the Far West: jagged peaks, deep depressions and arid land, all subject to sudden disruption or transformation by torrential floods or drought. States, counties, cities and villages have jurisdictions independent of federal government. School boards, transport and other functional agencies are often independent in financial and electoral terms too. The President may claim to be the man on the top of the tallest peak, but he cannot send orders from the White House to the lowest hamlet, expecting them to be obeyed. He must rely upon runners to carry the message through, and upon the friendliness of the natives who receive his addresses. Whereas a statement from Whitehall would sound like an authoritative request for action, a statement from the White House is likely to sound like a plea for help from someone whose troubles may be a source of local satisfaction rather than regret. The decanting of powers across the continent is matched by the dispersion of power within Washington, between President, Congress and the courts. Whereas a British Cabinet can almost always be sure of majority support for its initiatives in the House of Commons, an American President can hardly ever be sure of such support. The federal government is, in the words of Woodrow Wilson, 'a standing amicable contest among its several organized parts'.

Differences in the structure of government do not lead to absolute differences in practice. American politicians can get together to adopt national policies on some things, e.g. defence and foreign affairs. But it is significantly easier to secure a national policy about matters concerning the rest of the world than it is to adopt a national policy about issues within America, such as race relations, a minimum wage or persisting regional unemployment patterns. Federal, state and local officials do come together – co-operatively or warily – to devise schemes for improving the lot of American citizens. In this bargaining situation, politicians in Washington are much more weakly placed than members of a British Cabinet. They cannot issue directives; instead they must rely upon mutual self-interest reinforced with bribes, that is, federal funds paid to states and cities to undertake programmes that the federal government thinks worth while but cannot carry out itself.

In Britain the responsibilities of central government have become so great that central authority is 'subcontracted' in functional and spatial terms. The nationalized industries, employing almost one-tenth of the nation's labour force, are a well-known example of functional decentralization. Each industry is operated by a board independent of the Cabinet for its day-to-day operations, though ultimately relying upon the government for investment funds and for the appointment of board members. Local government builds houses, manages schools and carries out many other welfare tasks with significant administrative discretion. The ultimate power to review or reverse local decisions remains, however, with central government. The co-existence of many governmental jurisdictions within Britain permits conflict between them. For example, a nationalized industry and a local authority may be in dispute about whether the proposed site of a new factory or open-cast mine is in the public interest. When disputes do arise, the central government is able to act, albeit often hesitantly and reluctantly, as an umpire, deciding in a way binding upon all sides what course of action should be followed.

While there is a common need to strike a balance between centralization and decentralization, the balance struck differs in the two countries. In Britain the Crown remains dominant. Her Majesty's Government jealously protects established central authority against potential encroachments by the barons in nationalized industries or local government. In America, by contrast, the problem of the President is the opposite: how to break the stranglehold of the barons, entrenched not only in distant urban fiefdoms and in state capitals but also inside the walls of central government, in quasi-feudal strongholds in Congress and the bureaucracy.

One consequence of the differing degree of centralization is that there is greater territorial justice in the provision of wel-

fare services in Britain than in America. Because standards of
welfare services are set centrally, an individual Englishman
can expect to receive the same social security benefits wherever he lives, have the same rights to medical and hospital
care, and send his children to schools meeting national educational standards. The planning powers of central government
can also be used to compensate poorly endowed or declining
regions by making extra grants for public services or by directing expanding firms to locate in areas of high unemployment, thus tending to equalize economic advantages between
regions. In America, by contrast, education, land-use planning and police powers rest with state and local governments.
Many welfare programmes established under federal law,
such as aid to disabled workers or aid to dependent children,
allow benefits to be fixed by state government. The average
weekly benefit for an unemployed person in America varies
from $36 in Mississippi to $65 in Connecticut and $66 in
Hawaii. The rate of unemployment benefit is the same everywhere in Britain. In education, the average spent per pupil
ranges from $553 in Mississippi to $1,561 in New York State.
In England the difference between the highest- and lowest-
spending education authority is much less; 95 per cent of all
local authorities spend within 17.5 per cent of the national
average figure for primary education. In America, by contrast, only 30 per cent of the states are this close to the
national average. The English average reflects benefits that
nearly all children receive. The American average is but the
result of a substantial number of well-to-do and poor states
counteracting each other.

If centralization achieves equity in the treatment of citizens wherever they live, it also compels uniformity. By contrast, decentralization permits diversity in political responses
to social problems. The structure of federalism places effective centres of decision-making closer to the ordinary citizen.
In Britain the town hall is also closer to the citizen than
Whitehall, but it is the latter that holds most of the power. In
America the dispersion of powers creates multiple points of
access. The existence of local centres of power gives both
major American parties the chance to enjoy majority status in
some parts of the country. If neither party can ever sweep all

the reins of government into its hands, neither can it be deprived of authority to the extent of the minority party in the British House of Commons. The dispersion of powers also inhibits pressure groups from completely capturing governmental authority. For example, for two decades the agricultural lobby enjoyed a privileged position in Britain because both major parties supported its programme. Whichever party won a general election, the farmers were favoured. By contrast, in America disunited farming interests have had to compete with each other for influence in Congress and the executive.[11] Diversity can also show itself in ethnic or black-oriented political machines capturing control of government in many major cities, while middle-class WASP citizens settle in suburbs governed to suit their rather different political priorities.

Contemporary political trends face governors in both countries with the dilemmas implicit in centralization and decentralization; it is in the nature of a dilemma that there is much to be said for each alternative. Pressures for change are not leading each society to imitate the other, but rather simultaneously pulling each government in opposite directions. In America the demand for territorial justice led blacks to enter the courts to demand that the federal government guarantee each of its citizens equal rights within each state. These demands have been followed by pressure to reduce income inequalities between blacks and whites, between urban, suburban and rural groups and between the 'have' and the 'have-not' states. Each demand implies strengthening the authority of the federal government. Yet concurrently, underprivileged Americans have begun to demand the decentralization of some governmental functions, such as schools and health clinics, down to the neighbourhood level. This not only reflects a desire to turn gerrymandering to a group's own end, as in the creation of an all-black school district, but also to ensure that the bureaucrats and professionals required in programmes to aid the poor will be immediately responsive to local rather than distant centres of power.

In Britain local government was reorganized in 1972, by

[11] See J. Roland Pennock, 'Responsible Government, Separated Powers and Special Interests', *American Political Science Review*, LVI, 3 (1962).

measures which *increased* the distance between the individual citizen and his government; the total number of local authorities and elected office-holders was reduced. As is appropriate in a 'top down' political structure, the measure was taken because it was judged most suitable by central government. It provides larger (and hopefully, technically more efficient) centres for administering services on behalf of central government. It also creates far fewer units for central government to supervise and negotiate with. Yet concurrently, the growth of government responsibilities has concentrated so many responsibilities and demands in Westminster that there is a real danger of so overloading central government that it becomes incapable of responding promptly, intelligently or discriminatingly. The dangers of overload are most evident at the top. Cabinet ministers and, *a fortiori*, the Prime Minister can no longer know about everything for which they are formally responsible in constitutional theory. Yet the same constitutional theory makes it difficult for them to let go of authority which they hold but cannot use.

The choice between more or less centralized government is much more than a technical matter for students of public administration. British proponents of centralization emphasize the value of equity, resulting from uniformity of treatment. They argue that strong central government – the means of collective action – is a prerequisite for effective popular sovereignty. Americans respond that uniform regulation means remote and unresponsive government. Trusting government less (or trusting individual resources more), the proponents of the American form of government see decentralization as protecting the citizen best against incursions upon his liberty, as well as giving him more chance of influencing those who wield power in his locality. The contrasting choices in the two societies reflect contrasting values between them. British citizens (and, even more, their European neighbours) have always expected to be subject to some authority. The question thus becomes: who rules? Americans, by contrast, have historically had a greater suspicion of any centralized authority. For Americans the question is: how much rule?

Whatever the collective power of the barons, one man stands pre-eminent in British and American government.

This is not to say that the President and Prime Minister occupy an equal eminence. It is to note that the position of each relative to the other political actors helps characterize the nation's whole system of government.

The uniqueness of the President's office rests in the unchallenged executive power formally vested in his hands. The President need defer neither to monarch nor, as in Germany or Italy, to an elder statesman exercising a monarch's constitutional powers. The President likewise need not defer to any parliamentary sentiment as a condition of remaining in office. Last and not least, the President need fear no rivalry from his colleagues in the administration. In Britain the Chancellor of the Exchequer or the Foreign Secretary is a Prime Minister *in potens*. In America members of the Cabinet hold office at the pleasure of the President. They are *his* men – and those who lose his confidence lose both power and repute in a city in which everyone is uniquely sensitive to the mood of the President.

In Britain, by contrast, the Prime Minister is only one among several claimants to authority. The Queen remains the ceremonial head of state. The Prime Minister is head of the majority party in Parliament, as well as chairman of the Cabinet, effectively a committee composed of the directors of the executive departments of government. To describe the Prime Minister as *primus inter pares* is apt, for this Latin tag leaves ambiguous whether the stress falls on his position as first among ministers, or as spokesman for a body of men equal in a collectively responsible Cabinet.

In Washington the strongest phrase of command is 'The President wants this'. In Britain it is 'The Cabinet wishes this'. A President cannot be challenged by anyone else as the single spokesman for government. A Prime Minister can be challenged and even repudiated, if what he says is not acceptable to a majority of his Cabinet or party in Parliament.

While the President is more important than the Prime Minister as an individual, he is weaker as a governor. This is because the executive branch which he heads does not dominate the whole of government, as the Cabinet does in Britain. In Britain courts and local authorities accept subordination to the will of Parliament, and Parliament is bound to Cabinet by the ties of party discipline. An American President is hedged in by the autonomous powers of the courts, state and local government, and Congress. The American Congress stands almost alone as the last legislature in the world that is truly a law-making body. Congress is less like the British House of Commons than it is like the Finnish Eduskunta or the Italian Chamber of Deputies. In these Continental assemblies, legislators can create or depose coalition governments. In America the Congress is better armed to dispose of Presidential authority by frustrating his proposals than it is to take creative initiatives. Faced with competing centres of power, a President's significance varies with his political resources and resourcefulness. How many measures can he cajole out of Congress before exhausting all his political capital? The answer is: a lot less than what a British Cabinet can obtain. Its legislative powers are limited only by the amount of time there is to discuss legislation in the course of a lengthy annual session of Parliament.

In foreign affairs both President and Prime Minister are equal, in that each has vested in him the authority to represent the nation in diplomatic negotiations and to take decisions of great consequence in times of crisis. Both Chief Executives have usually enhanced their diplomatic role by appointing as their chief Cabinet officer in foreign affairs a man whose status is that of a subordinate. Yet when the Chief Executive can best claim to speak and act for the whole nation, his powers are most confined. In international affairs his government is not sovereign, but only one among many nations competing to influence events. The decline in Britain's standing in world affairs since 1945 has also meant a decline in the Prime Minister's status. The rise of American power in world affairs enhanced the President's status for two decades, until political opponents in South-east Asia made evident that there were political forces that no American President could control.

In domestic politics both President and Prime Minister can claim to speak for the nation. But their claims to be national spokesmen are necessarily challenged by those who lead the Opposition party. In America a President need not fear competition from his Cabinet. In Britain a Prime Minister must contend with his Cabinet colleagues, who have a personal interest in speaking for matters for which their departments are responsible. For example, while Presidential candidates receive the overwhelming amount of publicity devoted to American national campaigns, in Britain in 1970 Harold Wilson, the Prime Minister, received only 56 per cent of his party's broadcasting coverage, and Edward Heath, leader of the Opposition party, 60 per cent of the attention given to his party's spokesmen.[12] The publicity given the American President is not, however, proof of greater power; it is only proof of greater visibility. This is an advantage when a politician wishes to make a statement attracting attention. But it is not an asset when things start to go wrong. Then, the man who has stood in the spotlight collecting bouquets cannot dissociate himself from the resulting brickbats.

In both England and America the burdens of government have been growing greatly, in peacetime as well as wartime. In President Madison's time the American government had fewer than 10 million citizens to worry about, and the work of central government could be done with only 500 federal employees in Washington. Today the President must execute laws on behalf of more than 200 million Americans. He has more than 300,000 employees to assist him in Washington, and another 2·5 million civilian staff scattered throughout the country. Britain too has had a similar escalation of government activity. While Britain has 'only' 55 million people, the greater centralizaion of authority in Whitehall and the greater involvement of central government in the policies of a mixed-economy welfare state make the Prime Minister's burden comparably great.

To meet the burden of governing, neither President nor Prime Minister can expand his power simply by issuing orders to other members of the executive branch of government. An American President may find that his orders are ignored by lifetime officials in the federal bureaucracy, or even by members of his own Cabinet. The individualistic attitude of members of the federal executive led one member of John F. Kennedy's staff to complain: 'Everybody believes in

[12] See Martin Harrison's analysis in D. E. Butler and M. Pinto-Duschinsky, *The British General Election of 1970* (1971) pp. 207 ff.

democracy until he gets to the White House'.[13] Once there
he begins to see the advantages of a more hierarchical command structure. A Prime Minister does not enjoy this advantage because the Cabinet must enter into any formal governmental commitments. No member of the Cabinet expects
to work simply as the agent of the Prime Minister. The British government's annual statement to Parliament about
legislation (the Queen's Speech) is not a personal message, like
the President's State of the Union message; instead it is a
collective Cabinet document.

To increase their personal authority within government,
both Presidents and Prime Ministers have found themselves
in need of staff assistance. While the President remains a
single individual, the Presidency is an organization that now
employs thousands on the White House staff. In the same
time period and for the same reason, the Prime Minister has
established a Cabinet Secretariat to help him administer government. Downing Street has not grown in size like Pennsylvania Avenue. A few London town houses can still accommodate the personal staff of the Prime Minister and those
who collectively service the Cabinet; there is nothing like the
Plantation sprawling around the White House. Size is not an
unmixed blessing. The larger the staff, the more distant the
man at the apex is from the man on the ground, whether that
man is in the jungles of some warring overseas territory or in
the jungles of the capital's bureaucracy. While the staff man's
claim to authority depends upon his Chief Executive, the latter's ability to influence events depends upon the judgement
and initiative of his staff.

Both President and Prime Minister find their power limited by one common constraint: each must fit his week's
work into the same finite number of hours. The time available to deal with problems does not increase as the quantity
of problems increases. The introduction of new analytic techniques or organizational structures may improve the way in
which the Chief Executive learns about the nation's problems, but it does not give him more time to deal with them.
As the volume of government's work increases, the Chief Ex-

[13] The title of an article by Thomas E. Cronin in *Law and Contemporary
Problems*, xxxv, 3 (1970).

ecutive becomes more and more dependent upon staff who act as gatekeepers as well as windows on the world around him. A Chief Executive may not be told about matters deemed insignificant, like hints of scandal. In addition, he may be kept uninformed about matters considered too disturbing to merit repetition, like reports that the country is losing a war in Vietnam or a fight to prevent devaluation of the pound.

In such circumstances a Prime Minister may find himself emulating one of the less attractive features of the American Presidency: the inability to know about all that is done by 'his' government. The readiness of a President and, latterly, a Prime Minister to emphasize a 'preaching' and 'teaching' role may increase public knowledge of government and give the politician personal publicity. But it masks the Chief Executive's weakness in private. The classic autocrat had no need for the mass media, because he could enforce his commands privately. The modern Chief Executive may turn to the public for support because he is unable to control what goes on beneath him without mobilizing popular pressure. Charges of a credibility gap usually presuppose that the Chief Executive wilfully withholds knowledge of what is happening in his domain. The gap can also exist if both Chief Executive and populace are caught by surprise revelations of government activities that neither knew about.

Given the limits of what one man can do, neither a President nor a Prime Minister can concurrently exercise all his nominal powers. One might argue that the most powerful Chief Executive is the one who shows the least gap between expectations and capabilities. Since it is merely impossible to expand the number of working hours in a week, there is no chance for the White House incumbent to close the gap by doing more. He can only do so by attempting less. A British Prime Minister might argue that his office is relatively more powerful, because fewer demands are made upon him than upon the self-appointed leader of the free world.

In the final analysis, one must judge an institution by the men who have held office in it. Since 1945 six men have been President and six have been Prime Minister. In this period each country has had one Chief Executive whom historians

unanimously consider great in aspiration and achievement:
Franklin D. Roosevelt and Sir Winston Churchill. Churchill
(unlike his predecessor, David Lloyd George) needed the
opportunity of wartime to exercise great power; Roosevelt was
great in peacetime too. Of post-war leaders, two Presidents
and two Prime Ministers had high aspirations and accomplished much. Both Harry Truman and Lyndon Johnson had
an activist conception of the Presidency. Truman made his
mark in foreign affairs, but experienced difficulty in carrying
forward domestic 'Fair Deal' legislation. Johnson's reputation
rests upon his 'Great Society' achievements; foreign affairs
proved his undoing, and greatly so. Clement Attlee was far
more modest in mien than his American counterparts; with a
team of experienced senior ministers to aid him and a great
majority in the House of Commons, he did not need to speak
loudly. In six years his 1945–51 Labour government accomplished nearly all their very substantial intentions for domestic policy. As a Conservative, Harold Macmillan entered
Downing Street in 1957 representing a party demanding far
less change than would be expected of a Labour Prime Minister. Yet during his nearly seven years in office he established
himself as the dominant political figure in a Cabinet of strong
men, and he also took major initiatives in granting independence to African colonies, applying to enter the Common
Market and in efforts to stimulate economic growth.

By contrast, the remaining Presidents and Prime Ministers
cannot be classified as men of high aspirations and substantial
achievements. Dwight D. Eisenhower might be considered a
success in his own terms; he sought and succeeded in minimizing the role of the President, believing that less government
is better government. Sir Alec Douglas-Home, in his eleven-
month period of office as Prime Minister, also minimized the
influence of the Prime Minister, though not from intellectual
conviction. Richard Nixon's achievements, like much else
about the man, are ambiguous. In domestic politics he has
succeeded in the role of minimalist. In foreign affairs he has
at times taken active initiatives, as in his trip to China in
1972, and at times shown signs of delay and uncertainty, as in
the four-year period negotiating a settlement to end American involvement in the Vietnam war. Harold Wilson entered

Downing Street in 1964 with rhetorical commitments to leadership echoing those of John F. Kennedy. He survived in office for six years. In that time he identified himself with a number of major policy initiatives, abroad as well as at home. Most of these failed.

No complete judgement can be made of the achievements of John F. Kennedy and Sir Anthony Eden. Kennedy began as a cautious President in both domestic and foreign affairs. By the time of his assassination he had shown signs of becoming more activist and successful. Eden began with little interest in domestic policy. His one major initiative, the launching of the Suez war of 1956, was a great miscalculation. Eden's health broke under the strain, and his Cabinet colleagues had little hesitation in pronouncing him unfit to remain in office. Sir Winston Churchill's tenure of Downing Street in peacetime from 1951 to 1955 shows a record of achievement more nearly resembling that of Eisenhower than the wartime Churchill. Here again, health was a reason for inactivity.

The White House and Downing Street can accommodate very different types of political leaders. There is no indication that those with greater claims to personal authority govern longer. Dwight D. Eisenhower had as long a tenure of office as John F. Kennedy and Lyndon Johnson combined. The physically infirm Sir Winston Churchill and Sir Anthony Eden in total occupied Downing Street about as long as Clement Attlee. Since 1945 relatively weak Presidents have held office for about as long as relatively strong Presidents; the same is true of Prime Ministers. The power of Chief Executives varies more within America or within Britain than it does between the two countries.

III. HOW MUCH GOVERNMENT?

One theme running through each of the comparisons is the same: how much government is good government? The answers given are consistent, and consistently different, on each side of the Atlantic. The British political system favours more government. The courts give the government the power to decide what legally enforceable rights citizens may have, and the electoral and party system allows electors to choose their government. The hierarchical and integrated structure of government makes the election of the majority party in the House of Commons the single instance of popular control of government. By comparison, at each of these points American government inhibits a single strong central authority, enhancing the claims of individual citizens, individual politicians, individual state and local governments, the legislature and the courts.

In America the problem of government is an elemental problem of power: how can people who need collective action to forward their aims gain sufficient collective resources to get things done? Almost every case-study of a major American domestic political event is a long story of how the bits and pieces of influence – outside as well as inside government – were assembled together. The political broker, the man skilled at putting it all together, is often the hero of such narratives. In Britain, by contrast, the problem is the reverse: how can governors use wisely and well the formidable power that they enjoy? Many case-studies of domestic political events are accounts of how a formally omnipotent central government seeks to move cautiously in the world outside Whitehall, lest in throwing its elephantine weight about it inadvertently tramples down what is underfoot. The process of consultation with affected pressure groups, including pressure groups representing local authorities, often takes years; the need to consult within Whitehall is also great. The obstacles are no less real because prescribed by custom and convention rather than law.

Differences in the process of government reflect differences in political values between the two countries. One student of comparative local politics, L. J. Sharpe, has summed this up as 'a much greater willingness in Britain to accept government as a necessary and inevitable fact of life in modern society'. In addition, Sharpe notes a 'much greater public trust of government in Britain – a greater willingness to believe in the probity of government however disagreeable its actual policies'.[14] While Americans no longer live in a Wild

[14] 'American Democracy Reconsidered', *British Journal of Political Science*, III, 1–2 (1973) esp. p. 17.

West environment beyond reach of civil authority, many seem to hanker for the old days, good or bad. Freedom in America is typically considered freedom *from* government, e.g. minimizing taxes or maximizing the role of private rather than public institutions, as in the provision of hospital services. In Britain it is freedom *for* combining together to use the collective institutions of government to secure common purposes, such as a national health service or strict town and country land-use planning. American values are individualist, and British values collectivist.

One cannot say categorically that America or Britain is *the* model of democratic government, because so much depends upon conditions of choice. If one wishes to increase centralized political power, then clearly Britain is the preferred model. If one wishes to increase diversity and individual autonomy, then the American system is preferable.

If one asks which system of government is best at getting things done in aggregate, proponents of each system could point to substantial achievements. In Britain, central governments have developed extensive welfare programmes and sophisticated techniques for managing the economy. The more *laissez-faire* orientation of American government has certainly not produced any less successful an economy, but it has produced a different package of economic benefits for its citizenry. Politicians in each country have been able to mobilize resources for substantial political reforms about three times in this century. In Britain there was a period of Liberal reform just before the First World War, matched by the progressive reforms in America under Woodrow Wilson. In response to economic depression, a second cycle of reform began in America in 1933 under Franklin D. Roosevelt; it did not begin in Britain until after the outbreak of the Second World War, and was carried through by the first post-war Labour government. In the 1960s America went through another cycle of domestic reform, affecting welfare policies as well as civil rights for blacks. In Britain, government's role in the economy began to grow in the last period of the Macmillan government, and was extended in the subsequent Labour government.

It is well that a case can be made for both the British and

American forms of government, for it is very difficult to alter whole systems of government. Even revolutionaries find, once they seize power, that they must retain much of the *ancien régime*, as that is the form of government to which their subjects are accustomed. The durable persistence of differing forms of government within Britain and America makes them virtually proof against wholesale change.

The value of comparing systems of government is intellectual: it makes one conscious that one's own system of government is *a* model of democracy, and not necessarily *the* model. The fact that common problems of government can be treated differently has practical significance for the thoughtful public man. It means that one's own form of government cannot be taken for granted as the inevitable outcome of history; therefore it could be made different in many significant respects. Any Englishman who studies the American form of government must admit that it is possible to confer judicial protection upon individual rights, to give voters a choice of their party's candidate through a primary election, and to decentralize powers to major cities (not to mention historic kingdoms like Scotland). Reciprocally, any American who gains passing familiarity with British government must admit that popular attitudes may in many circumstances be as strong a safeguard for individual rights as judicially enforced laws. He will learn how an electoral and party system that reduces the individual's range of choice may simultaneously confer greater power on the government chosen by the majority. The integration of local and central authority illustrates how landuse planning is made more effective without a federal division of powers. The steady flow of legislation through Parliament provides a reminder that disciplined parties and legislatures co-ordinated with executives may do more together than they can as separated powers.

The encouragement of self-doubt is particularly important at a time when both the great English-speaking nations find that their achievements are lagging in relation to their own professed aspirations and goals. The casual traveller may find comparison a means of bolstering his ego. An Englishman may consider his own method of protecting individuals superior, if a Bill of Rights is not proof against assaults upon individuals by White House security agents as well as brutal county sheriffs. Reciprocally, Americans may see little point in surrendering their international role as a powerful, sometimes raging Prometheus to emulate the foreign policy of a country which, if its own jeremiads are to be believed, may replace the Ottoman Empire as 'the Sick Man of Europe'. The thoughtful traveller can gain a critical, even stoic awareness of the problems and limits of government everywhere.

6 Exporting the Pursuit of Happiness

Tom Hooson

Director of European Operations, Benton & Bowles

Far more than any other country, America has shaped the consumer society in which virtually all the peoples of the Western world now live. American ideas are so fundamental to consumer society that it is arguable that the national genius of the Americans was necessary for originating the modern consumer society. It is the product of the same principles on which the American nation itself is founded.

We shall never know whether something akin to modern consumer society would have developed in other countries without American pioneering. But we do know that the majority of people elsewhere have taken to this American import with enthusiasm. There may be aspects of Americana which do not travel well to other countries, but American consumption patterns have been highly exportable. The world follows American leadership in this respect more than in many others.

The fruits of prosperity are highly acceptable, but it is not always clear whether America's imitators wish to accept the price to be paid for them. England exhibits more schizophrenia than most contemporary states. Englishmen are now whole-hearted consumers, but they have a half-hearted appetite for working hard enough to expand the system that provides their livelihood. There is a respectable case to be made for choosing the American-style consumer society or for choosing a more leisurely, almost anti-materialist way of life. There is nothing to be said for those who wish to lead a leisurely traditional existence – with all the modern consumer conveniences.

I. THE AMERICAN IDEA

The modern consumer society was pioneered in the United States. If that country did not exist, the world might still have become familiar with many of the following phenomena, but possibly not with all, and probably not with their present level of development:

Advertising	Leased goods and services
Branding	Mail order
Convenience packaging	Market research
Discount retailing	Mass production
Disposable products	National distribution
Easy-payment credit	Out-of-town shopping centres
Economies of scale	Sponsorship
Fashion waves	Supermarkets
Incentive economy	Trade-ins
Keeping up with the Joneses	

The list could be lengthened almost indefinitely. It could include some unattractive things too: dishonest selling, disgruntled buyers, slipshod workmanship and over-indulgence. But while these imperfections are a reality, many defects of trading existed in more primitive trading societies. The Roman law of sale records most of the unpleasant possibilities which can arise in buying and selling. And the seven deadly sins are as old as human nature.

The prominence of American brand-names, companies and techniques around the world attests the source of origin of the ideas on which a consumer society is based. The language of this society is American, as appropriately as the language of music is Italian, or that of cuisine is French. Not every feature of the system originated in America: with ingenuity, one can show that something akin to, say, brand-names or advertising predated the discovery of America. London's oldest advertising agency goes back to 1801, four decades before an American agency was founded. But wherever features of consumer society first arose, America has developed them more completely than any other country.

The beginnings of America's modern consumer economy

go back to the 1870s. From that period date such phenomena as mass production (Singer sewing machines probably
have the best title as the pioneer), mail order (which Mont-
gomery Ward began in 1872) and manufacturers' branding,
advertising and national distribution of their products. Today's advanced model is largely the product of the decades
since the Second World War, when such mainsprings of the
consumer society as supermarkets and television advertising
became significant. The majority of today's leading products
have been launched in this period.

Through the century in which America has led the world
in consumer innovations, it has enjoyed virtually unrivalled
material prosperity. But the emergence of the consumer society in the United States cannot be explained by industrial
wealth alone. In 1870 three countries accounted for two-
thirds of the world manufacturing capacity: Britain, 32 per
cent; the United States, 23 per cent; and Germany, 13 per
cent. By the turn of the century America had taken over the
lead from Britain in all essential respects. Germany was also
emerging as an industrial power. One can trace journalistic
comment then which anticipated comparisons which have become familiar reading in the era of the enlarged European
Common Market.

Several factors explain why America was a natural leader
in shaping what was to become the dominant pattern of the
twentieth-century economy for much of the world. First,
Americans had at that time a much larger income *per capita*
than Britons – and even more than Germans. Secondly, the
United States had the largest and fastest-growing population
of any industrialized country. Thirdly, it was a new country
in which ideas were less set and in which any innovation
could be tried. Fourthly, there is the go-getting and inventive
spirit of the people, a characteristic already noted by Tocqueville, Dickens and other travellers. Fifthly, the American
aptitude for neat engineering solutions has extended far beyond man-made artefacts described elsewhere by Reyner
Banham. American producers and consumers found many
ways to 'do a deal' outside established institutions. This is
true not only of the discount warehouse finding new ways to
bring cheap goods to masses of consumers, but also of disc

jockeys and record company representatives, finding new ways to exchange advertising for payola. The verb 'to fix' has an honorific connotation among engineers and handymen, just as it is malodorous in politics and horse-racing.

America's consumer society is a highly attractive model to most people throughout the world. The diffusion of American goods and American-style aspirations is the most notable evidence of this. Even the elder statesmen of the new Europe, men nurtured in an age when affluence was for the few and subsistence the concern of the masses, have recognized this. Konrad Adenauer in Germany, Charles de Gaulle in France and Harold Macmillan in England were each ready to preside over the rapid growth of a consumer society in place of older models, and each reaped rewards from a grateful electorate.

The Communist world is vulnerable to the appeal too: a visitor to Moscow is liable to receive an offer for the suit he wears and to discover surprising things like razor blades stolen (and even worn-out blades hoarded by the hotel staff). A mark of privilege in such a society is access to Western goods. Only two nations, the Chinese and the Cubans, may arguably have rejected voluntarily all that goes with American consumer society, but in each case what their people desired is debatable.

The consumer society, not least in its American form, has its shortcomings and deplorable effects, as well as absurdities that some find amusing and others tasteless. Not all products for a mass public are equal to the quality of more traditional products. Generations ago the European ancestors of modern Americans were eating better bread than most Americans do nowadays. There are shoppers who do not think out carefully enough what they want to buy, and who are too easily swayed to make purchases beyond their means or needs. Products which have harmful effects occasionally go on sale without thorough testing; the results can, at their worst, be fatal. The drive to sell or buy can become an end in itself, rather than a means to the end of pleasurable consumption. There are people, not least in America, who reject the whole system. But the evidence in elections as in market-places is overwhelming; the great majority in almost every Western country want the fruits of this type of society, and most accept the price.

Japan provides the most striking example of the attractions of a consumer society. Little more than a century ago the Japanese were leading a traditional life, as alien as it was remote from the world of New York or Manchester. A generation ago the Japanese were governed by traditional rulers, and consumption was for the achievement of national greatness (i.e. military expansion) rather than for the masses. Today Tokyo threatens to overtake New York as the most intensely commercial city in the world. It also threatens to overtake New York in the competition for being the 'best bad' example of disadvantages of great commercial activity: crowding, noise and other types of pollution.

If America had never existed, a consumer society could still have come into being. It would probably have been very different, because of the originating stamp of England, Germany or France. Yet the American parentage of the consumer society seems more than an accident of history. If a country were designed to become a consumer society, that country would have had some important points of resemblance to the United States. Major assumptions upon which a consumer society is based can be traced back to eighteenth-century ideas that have also moulded the American nation. It was mainly through American application that they have now spread to much of the world.

The Declaration of Independence appeared in the same year as the publication of Adam Smith's *Wealth of Nations*; the coincidence reflects the liberal milieu of thoughtful men of the day. The American Declaration of Independence proclaims every person's right to 'life, liberty and the pursuit of happiness'. Early in the life of the Republic, democracy – rule by the masses of the people – also became enshrined among the nation's guiding principles. Market economics became the accepted theory and, pressure-group politics permitting, the practice of trade and industry. These principles have been applied in real life, not totally or consistently, but to an impressive degree. The American record makes a great contrast with the ringing words (without many of the corresponding deeds) of the French and Russian Revolutions.

Liberty implies the widest possible range of choice for an individual deciding how he will live. For the majority of people in society, such liberty did not exist when their life was determined by their status in society and when that status was rarely capable of being changed from that into which they were born. European society has been stratified until very recent times. Despite the weakening of traditional ideas about what is proper for each rank of society, the behaviour of millions of English consumers is still constrained by ideas of status. Social background can be as influential as income in determining tastes. In English public houses the same drinks are served in each of the different bars, and the prices are almost the same. The consumer's choice between the public and saloon bar reflects his perceived status in society and not his taste in drinks. A clergyman's tastes can be above what is a normal standard for his income, and a self-made millionaire may display 'vulgar' tastes far below the standard expected of a man of wealth and breeding. In each generation the individual American has felt less constraint on his life-style than has his European cousin. Europeans are going American in this respect, but they still lag behind.

America's economic advantages go part of the way towards explaining such contrasts. The difference in incomes between England and America has made the middle class the largest single American social class, while Britain's largest group is the working class. Numerous differences in ways of living need no explanation beyond the relative amount of money in people's pockets after adjusting for different costs in different countries. The contrast is evident not only in people's behaviour as consumers but in the relative importance of political issues. American politicians are sensitive to the home-owner and the motorist, two middle-class roles; British politicians have retained a remarkable preoccupation with full employment, primarily a working-class concern.

Money and space have been great advantages to America; a very particular sort of psychology has also contributed to the liberated man. The American has been brought up to the theory (though not necessarily the practice) of equality between people, and to the equally important idea of confidence in his chance of success. He sees great contrasts of wealth, but as often as not he can recognize that the wealth is of recent origin. He can see nearby examples of people no abler than he, many perhaps less able, who have made it big. Their often ostentatious homes, tennis courts, swimming pools and cars are beyond his pocket today, but they are not necessarily beyond his aspirations for tomorrow. He may envy them, but he does not think their privileges improper: he hopes that he too can attain them, or the particular forms of consumption that satisfy his own individual tastes. He has more basis for his hope than an Englishman has for becoming a lord. Even flagrantly successful politicians may command a kind of respect. Congressman Adam Clayton Powell's hold on his Harlem constituency was the despair of his earnest opponents. A detailed condemnation of his extravagances to a crowded audience culminated in an admiring cry from the back of the hall: 'Man, that's *living*!'

The democratic basis of the country makes it normal for the ordinary man's wants to be the preoccupation of producers. In traditional societies such as England and France, much of the finest production was concentrated on the needs of a small, affluent public; a product's reputation began from the achievement of a Royal Warrant. In a small-scale market, where only those of high status had money to spare, it was better to recommend a product as 'Supplied to His Majesty, George III ...' than to advertise a product as the country's biggest selling line. America led the way in developing good-quality products for a much larger public; there the common man was sovereign and the patron was replaced by the anonymous market. This development presupposed the existence of an affluent populace.

The extension of democracy from politics to economics allowed the citizen not only to choose between politicians but also to choose between products. Americans have usually seen economic monopoly as being just as 'authoritarian' as the one-party state. Europeans, by contrast, have tolerated economic monopoly, whether capitalist or by state socialism, far more readily. A self-service supermarket offering competing products permits the expression of personal choice just as much as a voting booth. An American businessman feels himself at the mercy of the consumer; his thoroughness in studying consumer needs, tastes and whims through all possible means is at least as great as the politician's use of opinion polls to divine the wishes of the electorate. The wealth of research into preferences for frozen vegetables or weedkiller compares favourably in depth and volume with the sum of opinion research on major questions of political policy. What is learned is heeded – in the economic realm, at least.

Market research is, as one might expect, an American invention. It is a curious fact that much commentary on American marketing is preoccupied with advertising, and little concerned with market research. Perhaps this is natural, since advertising is a public act whose objective is to gain as much favourable attention as possible from its potential market, while market research is private and usually confidential. Advertising is always good for colourful and provocative copy; market research is as unobtrusive as competent engineering. The only best-selling book about consumer research, Vance Packard's *The Hidden Persuaders*, broke out of the pattern by sensationally treating types of psychological research which are a tiny part of market research and have impressed advertising professionals (by contrast to the impression made on journalists) as verging on quackery.

The relative obscurity of market research leaves an impression that marketing consists of manufacturers haranguing the public with their advertising, while the passive customers are herded in. In reality, the marketer who intends to survive will maintain long silences while he listens, as intently as he can, to the customer's wishes. Professor Kenneth Galbraith's assertion that American corporations are able to perpetuate themselves by imposing their desires on customers does not ring true for anyone with first-hand experience of the power of the ordinary customer over large corporations. Companies which used to rank among the top hundred in the country twenty years ago have dropped to obscurity or gone out of business. Some of their replacements have been businesses which began with tiny resources but outstanding products and extreme attentiveness to, and respect for, the market. Submissiveness to the popular will can even be carried to a fault; the real leader in business as in politics has to go with his market, but he should also try to lead it to better standards. Galbraith's fear of consumer habits being virtually imposed by established corporations is less real than the opposite fault: the over-slavish interpretation of consumers' wishes without an effort to cultivate higher standards of taste.

The consumer is king, and a seller who forgets it is punished by a drop in his revenue. Money is the basis which gives the American the chance to be any man's equal – so long as he can earn it. The American preoccupation with money can strike some foreigners (and many Americans too) as crass, shallow and materialistic; often it is. Yet money is an essential solvent of a fluid society; a man can change his income more easily than his sex, skin colour, religion or parents. The attention money gets reflects an American talent for concentrating on essential factors. However crudely he does it, the American is reaching for the source of power. Whereas the six-shooter was the equalizer on the frontier, the dollar bill is the equalizer in contemporary America. Scott Fitzgerald, novelist of the life of the rich of the 1920s, once wrote: 'Let me tell you about the very rich. They are different from you and me.' Ernest Hemingway repeated this remark in *The Snows of Kilimanjaro*, adding: 'Yes, they have more money.'

The absence of a national status system in America means that what status fails to define, a person's own behaviour must articulate. While there is a narrow sense in which 'we are what we eat', there is a much more extensive sense in which modern American man is what he consumes: books, boats or bourbon. His identity is largely for him to choose.

Never has the world known as many possible life-styles as America offers today. Sociological predictions of twenty years ago about trends towards uniform suburbanites with uniform ideas, dressed in uniform grey-flannel suits, make unreal reading today. Individual expression has prevailed. The dominant ideal remains a stable married life, with children, pets and friends. But a multitude of variations and alternatives exists. The most idyllic 'all-American' communities have their rebels, their pot-smokers and their alienated children. Hippy communes, group living, free love, homosexual liaisons are openly available. Both normal standards and deviant groups luxuriate in America. This is most of all true in California, the state that symbolizes, within America, what other states may become tomorrow.

While many Americans (like their strait-laced European counterparts) find some of these life-styles hard to accept, the remarkable fact is how calmly and tolerantly American society has adjusted to and co-exists with the assertive minority of nonconformists in its midst. With understandable delay, hesitation and controversy, the big system is getting used to the idea that there are varied ways in which its citizens choose to pursue their own goals. It remains recognizably true to the Founding Fathers' aim to create a rational, open society, which tolerates and encourages the competition of ideas, of men and of products, in the belief that competition or debate about alternatives would be beneficial for all. Most Americans remain confident in Adam Smith's praise of competition in the market-place of commerce, and in John Stuart Mill's faith in competition in the market-place of ideas.

II. MARKET TRENDS

A restless subject complicates the task of a painter or photographer. Few subjects in the world are as restless as the American market-place. Its salient features today are best caught by examining a few points at which change is clearly evident.

The American consumer is asserting himself. Nowhere else and at no other time have consumers been so demanding, so selective, so individual and so sceptical as in America today. They have developed these characteristics mainly because they have grown sophisticated in their tastes and in their knowledge of the market. Quality is, more than ever, the key to any lasting success with the American consumer. With almost every type of product there are 'price buyers'. But there is usually a predominant middle group of the market which has standards for quality as it perceives them, even if this is not always the way in which an engineer or a chemist or an economist perceives them. This group expects to pay a premium over the minimum price to receive the quality it desires; moreover, the size of this group is growing.

The buyer is willing to see a portion of his growing affluence go on paying for better quality in some of the things he already buys. The husband moves up from ordinary to premium-quality (and premium-price) petrol; the wife does not buy the most economical but what she perceives as the best toilet soap for the family. More than half of American spending on toilet soaps goes on products having demonstrable qualities of superiority over the lowest-priced brands in cleaning efficacy, deodorant performance, lathering, mildness on the skin or scent. By contrast, much less English spending goes to such brands; the difference can be extended to many other examples. There is a wide range of products – even in areas close to being commodity products, like table salt – for which Americans will pay for assured quality an extra 10 or 15 per cent over the minimum they need to pay. The market tells producers in the language they understand instantly – money – that it will not grudge the premium price for quality where it perceives it. This factor is important in encouraging manufacturers to improve products or add secondary styling attributes to attract the consumer. Every buyer has his own scale of values; he wants the very best in some lines of products, but sees little reason to spend more than the minimum necessary for others.

The means of a purchaser have, of course, great bearing on the margin he can afford to pay for quality. In most product categories a clear pattern of the influence of income can usually be seen. The meat section of a supermarket in a fashionable suburb will offer little but the finest cuts; there will be a different selection in a supermarket in a decaying inner-city area. Yet black consumers, although they cluster so heavily at the bottom of the income ranges, are ready to pay a premium for some quality goods. A high proportion of the American consumption of leading Scotch whiskies is accounted for by blacks; this tenth of the population with less than average spending ability buys one-third or more of some prestige brands of whiskies. A group long denied more important forms of recognition need to assert something about themselves by their shopping tastes.

Americans will respond to a better idea by buying the product, and at a sufficient price to provide a spur for manufacturers. Sellers show endless enterprise in what they bring to market, and the public responds speedily. Americans are willing to experiment with a completely novel idea: newness is often a recommendation. Something new deserves to be tried, if it holds out the promise of being in any way an improvement upon what went before. Sales of a new product which meets with approval will quickly accelerate; if it keeps an advantage against competitors its momentum can be great.

The market can also punish swiftly if a new product is a disappointment when it is used, or if an old favourite deteriorates in quality. Consumers in the mass can be remarkably perceptive; their purchases will start favouring what they perceive as the better product. Half the brands to be found in American supermarkets did not exist ten years ago, and half the products which were available that long ago are no longer available. The chain of marketing is taut at all points. New ideas are continually coming on to the market, retailers are responsive in giving them circulation or distribution, and there are plenty of bold consumers ready to try them out. Product areas not undergoing change are the exception rather than the rule. In most fields there are products in decline as well as products on the rise.

The trend today is towards a shorter and shorter period in which a product enjoys a heyday, before one or another factor makes it obsolescent. The life-cycle of home electrical appliances illustrates this trend. Appliances which appeared early in this century, such as refrigerators, took thirty-four years on average to reach their best year of sales as a category. For post-war products the equivalent average has been eight years. In fashion fields like clothes the cycle from the first appearance of an innovation to unwillingness to be caught dead in the garments can take months rather than years.

The decline in brand loyalty to products is a sign that the public is increasingly exacting in its standards, and alert to the possibility of gain from transferring its allegiance. A Darwinian would find in the endless battle of brands plenty of evidence of a struggle for the survival of the fittest. The whole pace of American life is speeding up, and cycles, whether of products or of ideas, are becoming shorter. The trend is away from permanence, to the short-term rental of expensive goods and use-and-discard inexpensive products.

If a product is to prosper or even survive in this atmosphere, its managers must work to find points of possible improvement and remove its vulnerable attributes. If they do not (or even if they do), they can expect to hear any day the patter of big feet coming up behind them: competitors offering a product that is bigger, better and newer than their own. They should assume that a product which has been launched successfully is almost out of date as soon as it is nationally available. Their own improvement and not a competitor's should be the one that supersedes their original product. The advertising of product reintroductions and new models should bring to buyers a continuing cycle of improvements.

A manufacturer can make two different types of change in his product. He may improve its intrinsic performance characteristics, or he may improve its styling. Performance characteristics are measurable and usually unambiguously desirable. A longer-wearing make of bedsheet would be an example of a product where improvement affects intrinsic performance characteristics. A disinterested industrial chemist could explain where, how and why the new product is superior to the old. To produce a new range of sheets in pastel colours, or in polka dots, stripes and vivid flowered designs, does not provide any intrinsic performance advantages. (It may even lead housewives to discard plain white sheets before they are worn out.) Such an innovation is purely stylistic. One cannot go into a laboratory and demonstrate that plaid bedsheets are intrinsically superior to white bedsheets. But one can turn to marketing figures, and demonstrate that the sales of sheets in variegated colours are superior to the sales of plain white sheets.

Nothing is as American as the automobile, and nothing better demonstrates the difficulty of applying criteria of performance and style to specific products. The American motor-car industry and its mass-production equivalent elsewhere annually offer 'new' models. For the most part, the models retain the same properties as the car of last year. But each annual model change incorporates new features promising superior performance as well as features that stake a claim for superior styling. The basic concept of the horseless carriage has hardly changed in seventy years. But the performance and comfort of motor-cars has changed out of all recognition. While annual changes in automobile models may be small, cumulatively these provide a car with superior performance, as well as more up-to-date styling. The owner of a Rolls-Royce may feel that he has a car with classic styling that will last for twenty years. Given what it costs him, it ought to last four times longer than its American equivalent. An American resolves the problem of obsolescent styling by getting a new car every three to five years. He gains on an English equivalent with a Rolls-Royce by the fact that when he trades his automobile, he will acquire new performance characteristics, as well as a restyled automobile. The owner of an ageing but still roadworthy Rolls may see nothing particularly attractive in the newly restyled exterior of an American car, but he may wish that his automobile enjoyed the technical advantages that have spread in America – automatic transmission, power brakes, power steering and air conditioning – while his car is ageing gracefully.

The criticism of styling change most often heard in Europe is not derived from the seventeenth-century religious scruples of the Puritan, but from eighteenth-century aristocratic fastidiousness. European intellectuals criticize the American motor-car because it is a machine product, rather than handcrafted. This is true. It explains why the masses can have an American-type car, whereas only an elite can enjoy a European sports car with special coachwork. By contrast, contemporary American critics of the automobile industry do not ask for qualities capable of production only for an aristocratic few, but rather for improvements in the technical performance of mass-production products such as greater safety features and less pollution from engines.

Americans do not believe that the aristocrats of culture should be the ultimate arbiters of taste, especially where consumption goods are concerned. They prefer to make their choice by a more democratic means: consumers can vote with their pocket-book. The point is illustrated by Detroit's own history. Henry Ford senior, an autocrat if not an aristocrat, thought he could tell the American people what style of car to buy. He kept selling his successful cheap car and cheerfully justified its standardized attributes and styling by saying:

'You can have it in any colour you want as long as it's black.'
General Motors' Chevrolet division saw the chance to inno-
vate in styling terms, while producing a slightly dearer car of
equal or slightly superior technical quality. Chevrolet also
offered its product in a variety of colours. Buyers were willing
to pay extra for a choice of colours and other styling changes.
By the time Ford began to compete on these counts too,
Chevrolet had passed Ford in sales before the Second World
War, and has never since lost its lead in the American car
market. It would take a peculiarly narrow-minded Puritan to
claim that because Americans have been buying cars in every
colour from turquoise to desert bronze, they have somehow
damned themselves. There is nothing intrinsically immoral
in driving a chartreuse Chevrolet.

Specialization is another form that innovation can take.
The American economy is confusing because pressures to
specialize and diversify product appeals exist concurrently
with the economic logic of standardization for purposes of
production and nationwide advertising. The scale and intensity with which big manufacturers specialize leaves a large residue of unmet demands. If, for example, the standardized
lines ignore the priorities of 10 per cent of the market, this
creates a market potential of 20 million consumers for speciality products. This market is greater in size than the whole
of Scandinavia. For example, the freedom of choice of American automobile purchasers has been greatly widened by the
entry of European cars to the American market. The original
minority market for European cars was too low to attract Detroit manufacturers, but so great as to offer simultaneous
openings for many small-scale European manufacturers. Today Americans can choose between American or European
cars. Europeans are effectively confined to purchasing the
products of only one continent.

The trend in product development is for an increasingly
differentiated market, as life-styles and consumer tastes become more heterogeneous. Manufacturers seek to find a
special advantage for their product, and a category of consumers who will be uniquely committed to the special goods
they offer for sale. The trend is very evident in the communication media, which do much to give people ideas about life-

styles. Magazines with an appeal to a large, undifferentiated middle mass of readers, like *Life, Saturday Evening Post* and *Look*, have died. Meanwhile, magazines with specialized appeals are prospering and multiplying. The range of radio stations available to a listener in a metropolitan area is great and growing. The choice of programme content is extremely varied – news, country and Western music, hard rock, soul music, classical music, ethnic interest and religious. A country subdivided by region, state and city is also beginning to subdivide significantly into groups of people with specialized interests – golf, money, home decoration, scuba-diving, hunting or baroque music.

New York City, the capital of the communications industry, illustrates the variety and specialization of the media. Radio and television outpourings for specialist, non-network audiences are greater than its nationwide network output. Its newspapers, except for the *New York Times* and *Wall Street Journal*, do not circulate outside this one metropolitan area. Within New York, the number of general daily newspapers has declined to three, yet the real diversity of New York journalism has grown. Similar evening newspapers owned by newspaper chains have disappeared, but such publications as *New York* and the *Village Voice* have risen. The *Voice* is a refuge for every challenging opinion and attacks the 'system' ceaselessly. The 'system' uncomplainingly rewards it for its authentic hold on its audience. Its weekly issues of more than a hundred pages are obese with advertisements. In a comparative perspective, the important point to note is that New York City does not dominate the American communications industry. No single production centre determines consumer choice in the media, as London or Paris set standards in England and France. New York-based communicators must watch competition from Washington, Chicago, Los Angeles and San Francisco, as well as remember the concerns of an audience scattered across a continent between these points.

Only a foolhardy manufacturer would launch a new product without a special reason for the product's existence. Consumers are expressing increasing individuality in their choice of brands. Within a given product area, there are constantly increasing degrees of choice in colours, flavours, sizes, packaging. Products such as coffee and syrup have different formulations for different market areas' tastes. The rapid increase in the different forms that make up the range of one brand makes inventory control an exasperating task for the distributive outlets. For a foreigner who has not experienced such a luxury of choice, this freedom of choice may appear trivial or tiresome, but it is a concrete expression of individual freedom. There are plenty of people who will not accept a substitute when the precise product or flavour they want is not at hand.

Orators who remind Americans on patriotic occasions that political liberty and market choice are related have an unexpected ally for their argument. A *New York Times* reporter, Fox Butterfield, accompanied Chinese journalists on an extensive tour of the United States in the summer of 1972. The Chinese consistently refused to indicate personal preferences. At Howard Johnsons, proud of their twenty-eight flavours of ice-cream, their unwillingness or inability to choose a flavour gave their waitress a perplexing problem. 'Just give us three ice-cream cones,' said one of them. 'Any flavour will do.' Any foreign visitor who remembers ordering his first ham sandwich in an American delicatessen will understand the befuddlement of the Chinese. What kind of ham does he want – baked, boiled, smoked, Virginia? What kind of bread – white, rye, pumpernickel, whole wheat, roll? What dressing – relish, ketchup, mustard, mayonnaise, Russian, Thousand Islands? Does he want a pickle with it?

The burden of choice is the price an American must pay for enjoying a richer variety of material life than an Englishman having tea in a café. The tea will be ready-poured with milk and perhaps sugar. The possibility of individual preference – that the customer might not want any milk – is not on people's minds. The waitress might never have heard that some people like a slice of lemon in their tea instead. England is the world's main market for tea, yet most of its tea-drinkers have undifferentiated tastes. The tea-packers find that smaller markets elsewhere are fussier and more interested in alternative flavours.

Although these illustrations are trivial in themselves, the contrast that they illustrate is not trivial. It is a comparison of two cultures, one offering a relative dearth and the other a wealth of choices; the freedom they illustrate may not be as sublime as the freedom that Beethoven celebrates in *Fidelio*, but neither is it inconsequential.

An intellectual may intersperse puffs on his pipe with mockery of the competition between laundry detergents, yet he may be extremely articulate about the character of his favourite pipe tobacco. He might also talk with some feeling about other pipe tobaccos which he accepts as substitutes, and those he would never want to smoke. If an intellectual studied a handful of product categories in detail, the clarity of his distant view might yield to a more complicated reality. He might discover that what appears to an uninterested observer as much of a muchness under different names (as products such as laundry detergents, peanut butter or wine can appear to non-users) can often have quite important variations of performance and appeal. He would find regular users sensitive to the differences and some of them willing, as he is with tobacco, to try three or four shops to find a preferred product before accepting a substitute.

When products are virtually identical with their competitors in all essential qualities, this very equality owes much to the competitive discipline of the market. Manufacturers sometimes have to match their competitors on pain of suffering business losses. The pressure has usually been an influence for the good by raising minimum standards, as the new, improved, best buy drives out the cheapest – and is in turn copied by competitors. A businessman who understands the market well respects his competitors' ability to stimulate his own efforts at all forms of improvement. Pioneers in new markets sometimes yearn for the arrival of a competitor, knowing that a fight often has a way of expanding a market.

The search for a distinctive product feature compelling a specialized loyalty can be an extraordinarily difficult one. There is always a tension between the desirability that a product should fulfil a very special role and contrary forces which tend to make competitors alike. If one airline does well by pioneering in-flight films, the rest follow. Competitors are not always necessary to spoil a good thing. If the businessmen are not good enough to keep a clear strategic direction, they may even be afraid of continuing to plough their own furrow. Decisions to stick to a special product can easily be diluted. Was the American Motors Corporation right to panic at a trend towards larger luxurious cars and to diversify beyond its utility Rambler, which had given the company some very successful years? Perhaps it acted out in real life the line of the board chairman in a *New Yorker* cartoon: 'Gentlemen, we're going to bring out the biggest compact car the world has ever seen!'

The assertion of more individual consumer tastes is not limited to manufactured goods. There are some interesting swings in consumer expenditure for services and other forms of consumption – everything from hairdressing to packaged tours. The market is close to saturation point for many appliances. Some of the spending that went earlier to keep up with the Joneses' automobiles, deep-freeze and colour television set is now released for other uses. There are growing numbers whose taste leads to some non-material forms of consumption: travel to distant sights, a fishing expedition and self-improvement courses. There is more scope for individual expression in these than in many forms of ownership of goods. The hedonism of the American consumer is not declining, but a change of emphasis is on the way: it is taking the form of hankering for experience rather more than for acquisition of goods.

There is nothing discreditable in any of the trends which are emerging: in looking for the best quality, in alertness to the possibility that a new product may be an improvement, in seeking an individually satisfying product or service and in displaying a growing interest in adventurous forms of experience. They are sane and understandable preferences, suggesting an abundance of collective wisdom and maturity among the American public. Despite the quirks which all humans show in their relationship with some consumer product or another, rationality is predominant in individuals' buying patterns. The share of the consumer's dollar that is spent without a rational (if sometimes badly reasoned) basis is very small. This should cause no surprise within a frame of reference which sees modern American consumer society as a logical consequence of a state itself devoted to developing a country by free individual choice.

The practicality, efficiency and efficacy of American products has had much to do with their initial appeal to other countries a century or more ago. The surprise is only in the difference between this reality and widely held impressions that American consumers are controllable, uniform, gullible and governed as no other people by advertising. There is an extensive literature – *The Greening of America* by Charles Reich is one example – which sees the American consumer as a moronic plaything in the hands of advertisers, doing their bidding and barely able to assert an individual personality. American advertising has made whopping overstatements in its time, but its critics sometimes match it.

In truth, advertising is a limited selling weapon, and today some of the least effective of it is the type lacking a rational appeal. Advertising can rarely sell – certainly not for a second time – an unsatisfactory product. It is most useful in encouraging the growth of a product which would sell in lesser quantities without it. It usually influences individual preferences marginally and on details. Its justification as a *selling* tool depends on its usefulness as a *buying* tool for the consumer. It can inform, stimulate or suggest. But the consumer alone decides whether to take notice of its promptings. If the consumer rejects the appeal – and more new brands fail than succeed – funds for advertising dry up. The brands which survive are not to everyone's taste, but like the politicians with whom they share media time, their continuing presence indicates that they have a satisfied constituency somewhere.

Today there are currents moving American marketing towards rationality of selling appeals. The strongest of these is the consideration – it is not the first time it has appeared in business – that the more edifying, ethical course also produces the greatest effectiveness. Informative advertising is the likeliest to be rewarding for the advertiser, as well as for the reader or viewer. This is not a new phenomenon, but realization of its truth is spreading. Compared with a decade ago, the standard of advertising has improved greatly in accuracy, interest, informative content and in its craftsmanship. Yet some of the most technically proficient advertising fails, because it is trying to persuade people to buy something they decide they do not want.

Compared with the average person in almost any other society, the average American is relatively well educated and his basic intelligence has to be respected. As a consumer he receives a postgraduate education from the media. Advertising has often been described, sometimes justly, as aimed at the minds of twelve-year-olds. Advertisers are beginning to respond to this comment in the way that Groucho Marx did on being told that a three-year-old child could understand the problem with which he was grappling: 'Send for a three-year-old child.' The twelve-year-old American has a wide range of information and well-developed scepticism about the claims of salesmen, advertisers and politicians. He knows about 'hyping', that is, efforts at manipulation, and he refuses to be hyped. To a considerable degree, he can even refuse to pay attention. Television advertisements must become distinctive and fresh if they are not to fade into the wallpaper. People of all ages have the ability to 'switch off' salesmanship. They successfully ignore most of the advertising they see which lacks relevance to their lives, and soon forget most of what they did not ignore.

The consumer is not under the control of advertising. Its inherent prominence often causes its significance to be exaggerated. It is a modest part of the distributive economy; all its forms, even including classified newspaper advertising, take only 1 per cent of the national income. This share has long been static and could conceivably decline. The original justification for advertising was its efficiency in enabling products to be marketed more satisfactorily than through salesmen, wholesalers or special promotions. It is required to continue justifying itself against alternatives as the most economical mechanism for selling goods. Its survival, like that of the products it sells, depends on performing some service to the economy.

Consumers who show increasing ability to look after themselves are now receiving an unprecedented amount of protection and aid from government and other sources. The growth of the consumer protection movement is greatest in America, and politicians have taken up consumer protection as a battle-cry. To say that American business welcomed the arrival of self-appointed protectors of its customers would be an exaggeration, but it is adjusting to life with more active government agencies, public-interest law firms, and groups and individuals expressing particular concerns. Characteristically, the main concern of the American consumer movement is not to attack mass consumption but to ensure that the consumer economy delivers what it promises to deliver – a fair expectation. The purchaser of an expensive appliance is entitled to expect it to perform as advertised. The user of a pharmaceutical product should be able to rely upon tests eliminating risks from its use. The audience for salesmen, either on the doorstep or over the air, is entitled to information it can rely upon.

Honestly run businesses have a major stake in eliminating dubious practices. The bodies they have supported for decades, such as the Better Business Bureaus, have contributed much, if not enough, to such efforts. Better voluntary adherence to standards is the most important step towards improved commercial standards. The Canadian advertising industry gave an example of a constructive initiative when, hoping perhaps for guidance from a higher authority than a Minister for Consumer Affairs, it invited a group of theologians to study criteria for advertising. *Truth in Advertising*, a statement of the norms they devised, is an admirably mature and fair statement.

If trends towards a more critical, demanding, consuming public in America are a sign of future trends elsewhere, then consumer society is in good shape, and evolving into something better. People are able to guide their own buying decisions and they understand how to keep the market in a highly competitive condition. The evidence suggests that the public exercises a good collective judgement and that confidence in the consumer's good sense and in the ability of competitive businessmen to serve him is not misplaced.

III. THE WORLD JOINS IN

An American-type consumer society has arrived in large measure in every country in the Western world. There is no doubt about its acceptability to foreign consumers, and fortunes have been made from the introduction or imitation of American products and methods. Among the most striking converts have been Japan, West Germany and Italy, which were all in the grip of very different social and political ideas a generation ago. The question is no longer whether but how completely foreign countries will follow American patterns.

A total duplication of America is not imaginable, if only because ideas can undergo mutations for better or worse in new cultures. Businessmen continually wrestle with the question whether an idea should change when it crosses frontiers. Any type of answer could be right in special circumstances.

It is impressive that the most successful internationalizers of American ideas have been Americans. In the Common Market, American firms have set the pace with numerous categories of products and generally shown greater skill than European businessmen in marketing in new countries. Superior management policies are almost certainly the main explanation. A bias frequently shown by these companies is to assume that what has succeeded in America will probably succeed elsewhere too. American exporters are open to discussion, but they will usually resist more tenaciously than Europeans any argument that Belgium is different from Germany or France. They have been told often enough in their own vast country that Oklahoma is different from Ohio to assess how much weight to allow for local factors and how much for general influences upon consumer behaviour. Perhaps it takes the detachment of outsiders like Americans and Japanese to see unities in the European countries, while Europeans think first of the differences.

There are bound to be differences in how people in different countries will respond to any product or idea, and there are cases in which American confidence has been disastrous. American cake-mix manufacturers came to England in the late 1950s convinced that they could cash in on a great opportunity. The particular tastes of the English defeated them; food habits everywhere are particularly strong and unshakeable. There are cases in which a product's reason for being (say, saving of the housewife's time in food preparation) may be all that can be transferred; what is virtually a different product can emerge in response to the new market's tastes. Cultural patterns also result in market differences. An aid for female hygiene will be far harder to sell in a prudish Mediterranean country than in an uninhibited Scandinavian land.

Variations in market potential are not a surprise to an American manufacturer. He is prepared by his own country's experience for variations between markets in Europe. Great variations in consumption of such things are found within America. The great unifying forces in the country – network television, coast-to-coast retail chains, and nationally distributed brands in almost every conceivable product category – are effective only in reducing the extremities of contrast. Research can often explain up to three-quarters of variations in sales by regional factors. The explanations will mostly be rational considerations such as income, climate, living conditions and cultural background. If the product is fish, proximity to the ocean and the incidence of Roman Catholics, who have a custom of eating fish on Fridays, could emerge as significant influences.

Hypotheses about cross-national variations in contemporary consumer behaviour can be devised to explain the conditions in which American patterns of consumption will be adopted elsewhere:

*Differences in disposable discretionary income will influence the relative penetration of products, particularly expensive ones, more than any other factor.
*Americanizing influences will usually gain initial acceptance among younger people; the young are more open to new ideas.
*Cultural factors will obstruct many ideas, and often, being more emotional than rational, they can be powerful obstacles.

Of these three influences, the first two operate independently of national traditions. As European (and non European) countries grow more prosperous, American-style consumer goods will be increasingly sought and acquired. This has already happened with such things as television sets, and the trend appears irreversible with the family automobile

and washing machine. With the death of the elderly, raised in
a tradition of handcrafted goods or of austerity, there will be
a decline in the proportion of European consumers to whom
American-style goods are uncomfortable as well as alien.
Gradually, all generations will take for granted automobiles,
television, refrigerators, use-and-discard goods and other ac-
coutrements of the American-style consumer society.

We already see in common dress, grooming, music and folk-
heroes – the surface froth of our lives – as total an acceptance
of shared ideas as we are ever likely to see in our weightier
habits. This pool is not exclusively of American origin, but
its tastes are influenced more by Americans than by anyone
else. As multinational companies develop more fully, their
need to keep ahead of competitors' innovations will reduce
differences in products available in different countries. Until
recently, even a really notable innovation could be expected
to take several years to begin from its country of origin. Nowadays a marketer has to move very quickly if he is not to allow
imitators to beat him into foreign markets. For example,
Gillette's Trac II razor was introduced in major European
countries within nine months of its American launching; the
company had once been satisfied with time-lags of two or
three years for diffusing its products in Europe.

England is naturally one of the countries that appears most
susceptible to American consumer influences. No other country except Canada is so close to America in language and
heritage, or has had so much American capital invested in it.
In the last twenty years England has shown vast changes taking her towards American consumption patterns. But by
comparison with Continental Europe, the country has slip-
ped well down the ranks of consumer societies.

The English appetite for the fruits of consumer society is
enthusiastic enough. Certainly something is wrong, and it
seems to be rooted deeply in the people's ways of thinking –
consumers, managers and workers. The symptoms of trouble
are easier to specify than the nature of the distemper. Consumers have been trained to be uncomplaining: complaining
is not nice; it is something that a raw American or German
might do. The loyalty of the English consumer is intense
enough to bring tears of joy to the eyes of a product manager

– and tears of exasperation to the eyes of an economist intent on perfection of competition. An old favourite, like Persil in the laundry-soap market, can survive technical developments which reduced comparable products to also-rans elsewhere. Managers are often aware of the very latest ideas in their fields, yet the businesses they run can go wrong, because of simple inadequacies that call not for management science but for applied common sense. Workers are dissatisfied with their poor incomes, but they have a rigid conviction that their own inadequacies at work have nothing to do with the problem. The parties complain about each other, but they deserve each other.

Is there an ingrained English aversion to a competitive world? It is curious that a good proportion of the businesses which have developed most aggressively in England have been headed by Americans, Canadians, Australians, Continentals, Jews or Scotsmen and not by true-blue Englishmen. Roy (now Lord) Thomson arrived in Scotland from Canada in his mid-fifties; for twenty years he found easy opportunities which no one else had beaten him to. He made a fortune out of a commercial television licence, after failing to persuade a host of distinguished Scotsmen to risk their funds on the venture. He invigorated the *Sunday Times* and its sister papers, markedly improving them. He launched a colour magazine supplement to derision from Fleet Street, and again led the way towards good journalism and new profits. He found that extensions could be made from his newspaper business into packaged holidays, chartered flights and many profitable publishing side-lines. Some of his best ideas were not original; he simply transferred what he knew had succeeded in North America. Along the way he commented: 'There must be something wrong with a country where it's so easy for me to make money.'

The later years of Lord Thomson are equally instructive. In 1963 he became a British citizen, and the following year received a hereditary peerage. Lord Thomson then began to act like an Englishman. His most significant move to establish himself as an Englishman was to buy *The Times* newspaper, as unprofitable as it was prestigious. He then demonstrated that he could lose even more money running this newspaper than could his aristocratic predecessors, the Astor family. Generations previously, the Astors had also laid the basis of their fortune by starting as American entrepreneurs.

The evidence of Europe seems to confirm that a dynamic atmosphere on the job is a crucial factor missing in England. Consequently, Continentals are nowadays the more apt pupils of American marketing, and they sometimes surpass their model. Germany has been the most vigorous European market, but the French have shown acute receptivity to outside ideas in recent years. The innovative French marketing of yogurt with fresh fruit in neighbouring countries and the triumph of a French ballpoint pen in America shows that they have the potential to emerge as formidable consumer marketers. A French shopping centre as spectacular as Parly II on the outskirts of Paris surpasses the modernity and imagination of equivalents in Orange or San Jose counties in California. There are closed-door discount stores in Germany as efficient as any American retail discounter.

The popularity of American-style consumer goods throughout Europe does not necessarily mean that this trend should be welcomed, even if it is inevitable. Many arguments are heard against Europeans embracing mass-consumption societies.

The first objection is moral. European countries already enjoy far greater wealth than most countries in the world today. They should not enrich themselves further, but give some of their resources to the underdeveloped world. If public opinion agrees strongly enough, politicians will respond by finding funds for such aid. But European governments of all political shades have been slow to transfer their growing wealth to other continents.

Another objection is that the growth in consumer affluence will only accelerate the depletion of the world's finite resources. If these fears are justified, the American people will have been worse malefactors than any other. Half the world's consumption of many resources is accounted for by America alone. There is an intellectual vogue at present for theories of 'zero economic growth', based on forecasts of the rapid exhaustion of many of the resources on which consumer societies depend, or upon the ecological imbalances resulting from the dynamics of consumer societies. Whether these projections are valid remains to be seen. The example of Malthus and his followers shows that unexpected factors can upset calculations; but two centuries after the time when Malthus was writing, his fears may actually be realized.

Ideological opposition to profit-seeking activities constitutes a third objection. Teachers, nurses and other members of service professions have undertaken careers in which pecuniary reward is not the chief motivation. In America this spirit is weak. The attraction of a medical career is the income that a doctor enjoys and not the service he performs. In European societies today the service ethic is waning, not waxing. From Italy to England, public servants, teachers and other respectable professional groups threaten or take strike action for higher wages. Gentle European socialists may object to the new consumer society because it is based upon competition, not co-operation. Proponents of the American system can argue that the economy works well only when producers, consumers and workers are all co-operating in a 'benign' circle of activities. Producers improve products to increase sales, earnings and wages; this in turn benefits their own employees and shareholders, who in turn become more prosperous consumers for other producers of the goods and services.

The consumer society cannot be dismissed simply as a product of capitalism, though this it indubitably is – if the capitalism of America can be equated with nineteenth-century European models. In Western Europe ideological opponents of all forms of democratic capitalism have but to use its own procedural forms to persuade the majority of voters to reject it. In Eastern Europe this alternative is no more available than are the full fruits of the consumer economy; the record of divided Germany provides the most succinct comment on individual preferences for democratic capitalism as against state socialism. During the fifteen years when Germans could vote with their feet by migration, one German moved east for every hundred moving west.

The most profound comment by critics of the consumer society is that material goods do not necessarily bring happiness. In the abstract, the comment is no more plausible than its opposite: poverty does not necessarily bring happiness. While America is, according to its Constitution, dedicated to the pursuit of happiness, American society in the mid-1970s is conspicuously not a happy place. Yet material well-being is not the cause of unhappiness; it is independent of it. The most visible of protest groups take for granted standards of mass affluence unknown anywhere else in the world today, and even unknown in America a generation ago. Blacks demand a bigger share in the material benefits of society, and student radicals are the expressive consumers of the most expensive mass education provided anywhere in the world. Even drop-outs find that it pays to 'drop in' to straight society for a time, to earn the money to support them in their urban or rural communes. They accept the very American dictum: 'Happiness doesn't buy money.'

Americans would accept that the accumulation of goods has its limits for a life that makes sense, and – as the trends in their own behaviour show – they are exploring many more individual possibilities of self-expression. Goods in themselves do not bring happiness, but their easy availability in varied and competing ways can help in creating the conditions for a pleasant existence. The extensive freedom of choice that is integral to a consumer society also gives individuals many opportunities to express their own personality. This is true especially in America today, where competition between consumer goods is evolving into a competition between competing life-styles. You can choose to be anything from a 'straight', dressed in a business suit with attitudes to match, or a dropout in Indian gear or overalls perched on an expensive motorbike.

While new and better consumer products cannot resolve the problems that trouble America today, they cannot be blamed for them either. The breakfast-food manufacturers did not take America into the Vietnam war, nor did the television industry create America's racial problems today. Just as European societies cannot hope to match American living standards in the immediate future, so they may take comfort that they also cannot match its problems. In importing the patterns of mass consumption, Europeans are in the fortunate position of members of any market society: they can pick and choose what to accept and what to reject. The evidence, judged by the massive rise in affluence in post-war Europe, is that most Europeans want more of the advantages of a consumer society.

7 Public Broadcasting Policy

JOHN WHALE

Journalist, 'Sunday Times'

Broadcasting, and in particular television, is a clear case where British practice has been significantly changed by American example. In the 1920s the broadcasting systems in the two countries set off on different paths. In the 1950s the two paths converged; and it was not the Americans who had changed their line. The direction of British broadcasting since then is in large measure the result of a lesson from America. Whether that particular lesson was a useful one is a matter for doubt.

Although broadcasting arguments are now mostly about television, the pattern of broadcasting was set in both countries by the way in which radio was established. The spirit of the British Broadcasting Corporation's early radio operations can still be detected in the 1932 dedication to be seen in the front hall of Broadcasting House – a rescripted version of Philippians iv. 8 ('Whatsoever things are true...') done into Latin and cut into stone. The spirit of early radio in the United States was not the same. It is better caught in the flat dictum of Calvin Coolidge, the President who signed the 1927 Radio Act: 'The chief business of the American people is business'.

That Act was largely concerned to keep the ether tidy. It said nothing about advertisements except that they must be identified as such, and nothing about the programmes which went between them except that they must not be obscene, indecent or profane. The five-man federal licensing authority which the Act established was specifically denied any power of censorship or of interference with free speech. The first station-owner who was refused a renewal of his licence because of bad programmes was a Kansas country druggist, John Romulus Brinkley, on the comparatively narrow grounds that he prescribed his own medicines over the air to patients whom he had never seen; but only after he had been doing it for seven years, and made a fortune in the process.

Dr Brinkley's speciality was goat-glands to boost progenitive power; he certainly fathered the dominant strain in American broadcasting, since his private planes and his 16-cylinder Cadillac were an early demonstration to other broadcasters of what they too could pluck out of the air if they used it rightly. Clearly, the right use was to sell. No other system of financing radio except by advertisements, and thus no other use for radio, seems ever to have been seriously considered in the United States in those pre-war years. To make advertisements pay, the audience had to be as large as possible. So it was necessary to recognize the unregenerate level of public taste: to give people what they wanted, rather than follow the early BBC maxim of giving them something a little better than they thought they wanted. In the United States the National Association of Broadcasters' first code of ethics, drawn up in 1929, contented itself with forswearing 'the broadcasting of any matter which would commonly be regarded as offensive'. Yet Sir John (later Lord) Reith, first head of the BBC, had already published the view that the 'pursuit of entertainment alone' on radio, without a consciously elevating social purpose, was in a deep sense offensive: it was 'an insult to the character and intelligence of the people'.

A commercial element was not wholly absent from the beginnings of the BBC. While the initials stood for British Broadcasting Company, between 1922 and 1926, revenue came from a royalty on the sale of wireless sets as well as from licence fees. But the company was already a monopoly; once it became a state-chartered corporation the royalties were dropped. Shielded from even that limited contact with the market-place, broadcasters did not need to make the size of their audience a dominant consideration; it was anyway assured by the absence of competition, and they could set out in search of public rather than private gratification. In the United States, on the other hand, the commercial principle was central from the start. As long as broadcasters stayed away from one another's frequencies and from the grosser forms of social nuisance, they were at liberty to get on with what interested them, which was in most cases the making of money.

There were a number of reasons for this difference. One was that the governing classes in America did not have, and would not have thought it right to have, that sense of mission to the less privileged which still survived in the British governing classes from the specialized system of education to which the British Empire had given rise. Another was a simple scruple for free speech: the First Amendment to the Constitution demanded it, and the 1934 Communications Act – based on the 1927 Radio Act, and to this day the main authority to which American broadcasters look – reaffirmed it: no censorship. Freedom in America, then and for years to come, was a less qualified concept than in Britain: if free speech meant freedom to broadcast not just the third-rate but the actively misleading, that was part of its price. Growth, too, in the economy of the citizen and the nation, was still held an unmixed and transcendent good, to be fostered by government at almost any cost. The Federal Communications Commission which the 1934 Act set up was able to make a civic virtue of its inertia. It was the American ethic itself which made virtually inevitable a broadcasting system regulated by the need for advertisements and by little else.

The crucial decision about broadcasting, in a tolerably free society, is how you finance it. The broadcast word needs more help from government than the printed word, because frequencies have to be allotted and no one but government can do it. Since no government service can be provided unconditionally, this loads the government with a number of decisions about what kind of broadcasting it should countenance. But most of those decisions are pre-empted the moment a government chooses to finance broadcasting commercially. Choose any other method of finance, as Britain did, and you are still left with all the questions about whether you should try to use broadcasting as an instrument of social or cultural change, who should decide what change is desirable, and so on. Choose advertising, as the United States did, and those questions hardly arise. The only kind of broadcasting which will survive will be the kind which attracts the most listeners and viewers. How that should be done is an empirical rather than a political or moral judgement.

In the United States, as in Britain, television grew out of radio without any structural change: in the late 1930s the same organizations simply added the pictures to the sound. The prevailing attitudes of American radio were carried over whole into television when the National Broadcasting Company began transmitting regular television programmes from the New York World's Fair in April 1939, with the Columbia Broadcasting System not far behind. (BBC television had been established a little earlier: it went off the air for the duration of the war.) Except for developing their news services to report the fighting, the American networks continued much as before. The FCC made a brief effort to assert itself in 1946, when it suggested in a 'Blue Book' that broadcasters could afford to carry more unsponsored or local material and fewer advertisments than they did, and that subsequent performance on these heads might become a criterion for granting or renewal of licences. The squeals from the industry, the use made of terms like 'censorship' and 'communism', the comparisons of the FCC with Goebbels or Goering, were so loud that the Commissioners retired abashed.

The Blue Book set out at length the record of one Baltimore radio station in particular which had been broadcasting as many advertisements and as few programmes worth hearing as it could. It belonged to the Hearst group. Hearst newspapers were especially virulent in attacking the Blue Book: one editorial invoked the Bill of Rights and the Minute Men of Concord. A few months later the station applied for a Baltimore television channel. The FCC granted the request unheard. Life was to go on as before. The same men and the same rules as had governed radio were to be in force as television entered on its heritage. In television the pressure to make money would be stronger still, because the costs were higher.

The American viewer sees the results of this every day. Since few stations have the means to put out their own programmes, the choice of what is broadcast is largely in the hands of three networks headquartered in New York. The fierceness of their competition further reduces the viewer's freedom, since no network can allow a rival's success to go unchallenged: they must run horse opera against horse opera, documentary against documentary, and the viewer who values either may see only one of each. Their chief aim is to persuade the viewer into a habit of loyalty. To that end, surprise must be avoided; novelty must be avoided; single items, plays or reports which stand by themselves must be avoided. A finite sequence of programmes is scarcely better. The ideal is a series which need never end, in which a young man of proven amiability talks late at night to notables in New York, or in which a fictional doctor or detective wraps up a problem a week.

Nor are the networks much in favour of the real world, of actuality, a thing which television is commonly held to be good at representing. The main network news shows are put out in the early evening, long before the news of the day can be properly assembled; and although huge human and mechanical expertise can be deployed on some public happening, the event chosen is usually richer in form than content, like a convention or an inauguration. Programmes offering a regular review of current events lead brief and irregular lives, and are sometimes not to be found at all in the network schedules.

This is partly because news from the real world is expensive, and partly because viewers do not in fact rush to watch it, despite what they tell pollsters about their dependence on the small screen for information. In consequence, advertisers are not fond of news and current affairs shows. The real world disquiets them, anyway, because it tends to have a messy complexity which is at odds with the simple optimism of their advertisements. They take this sensitivity further, into the wider world of fictional television. Car manufacturers see no reason to put their money into programmes in which cars, and particularly cars of their make, are seen to crash. (They also dislike reminders of their rivals: Chevrolet once had a reference to '*ford*ing a stream' rewritten.) Cigarette advertisers banned scenes where smokers coughed – until their own advertisements were banned. A mention of what the Nazis did with gas chambers was unacceptable to the American Gas Company. Those are examples taken from the 1950s; but the same attitudes persisted long after formal sponsorship of programmes by advertisers had become the exception rather than the rule. In 1970 Coca-Cola shifted all its network advertising to CBS and ABC (the American Broadcasting Company) after NBC had put out a documentary programme about migrant fruit-pickers in Florida. A company which profited from their services was Coca-Cola.

None of this ought to have occasioned any surprise. Many of these battles had been lost long before, in the 1950s. It was in 1954 that Elmer Rice, suggesting a series of programmes based on his play *Street Scene*, was told by an agency that no advertiser would knowingly allow his products to become associated 'with the squalor and general "down" character of *Street Scene*. On the contrary, it is the general policy of advertisers to glamorize their products, the people who buy them, and the whole American social and economic scene.' In 1955 the metals firm Alcoa ended its four-year sponsorship of CBS's *See It Now*, a current affairs programme in which Ed Murrow and Fred Friendly had taken editorial lines which Alcoa's customers disliked. In such an atmosphere, neither journalistic nor even fictional presentation of the world as it is could long survive. Television of any consistent intellectual rigour was discouraged almost into extinction.

For a time, after the war, the BBC had been able to look on this picture with gentle contempt. The same conditions did not apply in Britain. Indeed, they were exactly reversed. Under the terms of the BBC's Charter, and its Licence and Agreement, it was obliged to put on the air or keep off it whatever the government asked it to. Yet even in wartime this power was put to significant use very sparingly, and in peacetime not at all. The effective editorial force in BBC television remained the social conscience of men trained in the Reith tradition; and they were free to follow it because the BBC's income was not from advertisements. It still came in great part from licence fees paid by individual viewers and listeners and collected through the Post Office. There had been a suggestion from a government committee before the war that a measure of sponsorship might be necessary to pay for the costs of the new television service, but the argument had been interrupted by the war and was not resumed after it. The need not to give offence to advertisers, and to win them the largest audience possible, was something from which the BBC was delivered.

It could disregard audience figures for another reason too: it had no competitors. The sole television channel in Britain was the BBC. Monopoly may have generated, by the early 1950s, a certain flaccidity. Both music and plays of certain established kinds were well presented, but the handling of current affairs was unadventurous: admirers of the BBC's main middlebrow radio channel, then called the Home Service, did not find the same steady level of attainment on television. But this shortcoming was at least as much dictated by the nature of television itself, and its appetite for pictures rather than ideas, as by the fact of monopoly; and in so far as it proceeded from a lack of other channels which might offer other choices, the lack could have been supplied within the state-sponsored, licence-financed system – as was shown by the ultimate establishment of the BBC's second television channel in 1964. If the monopoly needed breaching, there was no logical reason why it should be breached by the system operating in America.

Yet it was at exactly this point that the American example began to be important. In Reithian terms, it was into this Eden that the serpent of American influence was introduced. (Lord Reith himself, in the Lords, roundly likened the introduction of commercial television into Britain to the introduction of smallpox, bubonic plague and the Black Death.) In 1949 a committee under Lord Beveridge was asked to advise the Postmaster-General on the future of broadcasting in Britain – a routine move before the BBC's existing Charter was renewed. The committee's recommendation, when it reported in 1951, was for more of the same. Although television should be produced from other places besides London, control should remain with the BBC, and the money should still come from licence fees. A number of committee members crossed the Atlantic to examine American broadcasting, and they viewed the fruits of a commercial system of financing with appropriate distaste. All except one member: Selwyn Lloyd. Mr Lloyd had not then entered on the astonishing string of public offices which took him from the Foreign Office through the Treasury to the Speakership of the House of Commons; but he was already supremely representative of Conservative opinion, and for the BBC the jig was up from the moment he laid eye on American advertisements and observed that 'There were some in television programmes which were amusing and entertaining'. It was Mr Lloyd's dissenting report which became the blueprint for advance. *Independent* competition, he said, would be healthy for broadcasting.

The very word, as a euphemism for commercial, was gleefully seized on by advocates of a new system. They were mostly, it so happened, Conservative politicians; and they had their chance because the second post-war Labour government was put out of office before it had fulfilled its intention of renewing the BBC's Charter on the terms recommended by the Beveridge majority. By 1954 a new Act had established an Independent Television Authority. By 1955 ITV, advertisement-financed, was on the air with a national network to rival the BBC's.

On the face of it, it was an odd reversal. There was no mention of commercial television in the Conservative manifesto for the 1951 general election, and members of the new Conservative Cabinet disliked the idea; yet within three years they had adopted it and passed it into law. The principal argument used to persuade them by a determined group of their back-benchers was the argument from the evils of monopoly: any monopoly could become lazy and dictorial; a monopoly of a means of communication was particularly undesirable. The BBC had shown that its monopoly could be used in wartime on the government's behalf, but a less scrupulous government would be able to use it in peacetime for less laudable ends. Conservatives were after all pledged to dismantle the state monopolies which Labour had been busily constructing since 1945. If steel and road transport were proving unexpectedly difficult to denationalize, all the more reason to reassure Conservative supporters by denationalizing a more pregnable fortress, the BBC. The BBC was not particularly popular with Conservatives anyway. They believed that it was sympathetic to their political opponents, and the belief was not shaken by the fact that their opponents held exactly the same belief in reverse. In the mind of Winston Churchill, once again Prime Minister, the recollection of tussles with the BBC still smouldered. Further, the country as a whole, and the Conservative Party with it, was becoming more interested in the kind of high-consumption society which advertisements on television would suit and foster. There was also a significant group of people who expected to make a lot of money out of commercial television; their interests were sympathetically represented by the Conservative back-benchers who made the running in Parliament.

The arguments used against commercial television were the arguments from social responsibility, from the usefulness of what the BBC had been trying to do. It was not primarily an anti-American case – though it was helped along by the news that, while the Coronation of Elizabeth II was being shown on American television, the Communion service was interrupted by an advertisement for Pepperell's bedsheets. This anti-commercial view was shared by most Labour politicians, and by a few senior Conservatives like Lord Halifax and Lord Hailsham. But they were not in the Cabinet, and Cabinet ministers yielded to the persuasions coming from the parliamentary party because they had no firm views of their own.

Certainly it would have been difficult to resist commercial television for ever. Very few European countries have managed it: the difficulty of financing a television service entirely by licence fees is daunting. Only Belgium, three Scandinavian countries (Denmark, Norway and Sweden) and three Communist countries (Albania, Bulgaria and Poland) carried their television services into the 1970s unspotted. Even in Eastern Europe, more countries have allowed advertisements than have forbidden them.

The example of commercial television in East Germany or Hungary was not available in the early 1950s. Canada was there to be studied: Canadian television had commercial as well as public backing from 1952 onwards. But the commercial element followed directly from the proximity of the United States; it was inevitably the American model which was most zealously examined both by the opponents of commercial television in Britain and by its ultimately successful advocates. Much stress was laid by the Conservatives on the fact that their scheme did not incorporate what they conceived to be the one serious failing of the American system – sponsorship. Advertisers in Britain would only provide advertisements, not the programmes which went between them as well. It was a distinction without a difference. When sponsorship later largely disappeared from American television practice, the distribution of power was unaffected. Advertisers had already found other ways of guiding the content of programmes. The American magazine *Broadcasting*, unfailing upholder of the commercial ethic, was right when it wrote of the Conservative scheme: 'One can't be just a "little bit" commercial. Either it is or it isn't.'

From the moment when commercial television in Britain became a real prospect, and when the BBC took its first faltering steps towards a prophylactic and yet unavailing self-vulgarization, the gap between American and British broadcasting began to narrow. The BBC fought, and continues to fight, a rearguard action of fluctuating intensity on behalf of the public-service principle in broadcasting against the commercial principle; but it now began to feel for the first time the pressures which the American networks had known for thirty years.

Commercial influences on the Corporation were not direct. Its revenues were still derived from licence fees. But those fees were mediated to it by the Treasury, after the Chancellor of the Exchequer had first withheld whatever proportion he thought fit: until 1950, that proportion had varied between 15 and 46.5 per cent. The fees themselves could be increased only with government consent, however rapid the increase in costs. So ministers could turn the BBC's money on and off like a tap. If they wanted to turn it off, as the eternal search for ways to keep taxes and living costs down impelled them to, the task was easy in proportion as the BBC was unpopular. It therefore became a prime object of BBC policy to gain as many viewers as it could before ITV began, and after that date to see that it had at least as many viewers as ITV had. Any other policy would have been suicidal. If the BBC had gone after excellence (as it was often urged to) while ITV went after the viewers, the consequent slump in the BBC's audience would have enabled ministers to cut its money to the point where excellence was for ever unattainable. The Corporation was thus firmly bound on a commercial wheel.

Competition may well make for high quality with some products. Mousetraps and motor-cars are doubtless the better for consumer democracy. But newspapers and broadcasting organizations react to it less well. In face of the fact that the paper with the largest sale in Britain is the *News of the World*, and the paper with the fastest-growing sale is its companion and imitator the *Sun*, it is difficult to argue that newspapers are improved by a successful struggle for sales.

The natural coin in competition for big audiences is low quality. And this depressing influence is even stronger on broadcasters than on newspapermen, because broadcasting organizations can transmit only one thing at a time, whereas newspapers can offer several. A bored newspaper reader skips to another item in the same paper. A bored viewer skips to another place on the dial.

It is in this hard school that BBC men have learned to respect a new set of names on the honours board: 'audience research' (over two thousand interviews a day, in order to have figures to beat the ITV figures with); 'channel loyalty' (the wished-for state of mind and body in the viewer, where his switching arm atrophies); the 'inheritance factor' (which delivers to each programme at least part of the audience for the programme before it); 'pre-echo' (whereby a programme is lit upon and taken up by people switching on for the more popular programme which follows it); and so on. One or two American devices for securing channel loyalty, like the late-night talk show, are less successful in Britain than the United States; some of them, like staying on the air for most of the twenty-four hours, are proving in the end irresistible.

ITV, naturally, has learned these lessons even better. Its ingestion of American material has been more enthusiastic, its assimilation of its own product to American standards more industrious. Both the 1954 and the 1964 Television Acts put a limit on foreign material, at the instigation of the production unions: they were anxious to keep down the import of programmes from America. A quota of 14 per cent was set by the ITA, but the effect is not exactly what the law intended. The programme companies are not obliged to spread the quota over the whole day's viewing: in fact they concentrate it during the evening; and they also increase the American tone, if not the American content, of their output by making sure that as many as possible of their programmes can be subsequently sold in the United States.

There are other points of likeness. ITV's main news show, *News at Ten*, was modelled when it began on the *Huntley–Brinkley Show* then on NBC. The system of time-buying on ITV does indeed preclude overt sponsorship; but nothing is easier than for an advertiser to get his advertisements close to a programme he likes or away from a programme he dislikes, on something very like the continuing American pattern. The ratings, the audimeter readings, are as deeply respected in both systems. ITV's networking arrangements give London at least as much national dominance as New York has. Although control of advertisements is tighter in Britain, it is no more rational: the ITA can allow advertisements for the *News of the World*, but not (because of rules about religion) for a new translation of the Bible. Advertisements, in the end, are the great common influence on the two systems. Because of them, ITV exhibits essentially the same chief characteristic as American commercial television: its source of revenue is gauged to the public taste as it is, not as it might be.

In so far as the BBC travels the same path, it is not entirely out of rivalry. Even without ITV, even without the sounds and sweet airs borne on the breeze from the New World, the BBC would have changed. The old, Reithian certainties have been changing and dying all the time. The 1960s introduced into the English mind a whole new range of doubts about what constituted acceptable standards: in the arts, in behaviour, in habits of dress and speech. The BBC could not have escaped the prevailing uncertainty. For all that, it never quite lost sight of the belief that there were other standards besides commercial success; and where British broadcasting has neglected the American example, the BBC remains both the origin and the chief sign of that neglect. The flow of influence between ITV and BBC was not all one-way. What would ITV have been like, after all, if there had been no BBC?

Both the commercial and the public-service approach to television were founded on a single belief: broadcasting is uniquely persuasive. In the body of the report to which Mr Lloyd entered his momentous dissent, the belief was stated at its most uncompromising:

> Broadcasting is the most pervasive, and therefore one of the most powerful of agents for influencing men's thought and actions, for giving them a picture, true or false, of their fellows and of the world in whch they live, for appealing to their intellect, their emotions and their appetites, for filling their minds with beauty or ugliness, ideas or idleness, laughter or terror, love or hate.

The words were written by Lord Beveridge himself, and none of his colleagues seem to have suggested to him that 'the most pervasive, and *therefore* one of the most powerful' was a crashing *non sequitur*. The potency of broadcasting, then and for several years afterwards, was widely taken to be on a par with the wetness of water. The effects of the belief, especially about television, were in any case more important than its truth.

To Reithians, this vision of power suggested uplift. To men of commerce, it suggested sales. But those were not the only interested groups. To politicians, it suggested votes. From the beginning of television, the people who controlled its legislative and financial shape were also watchful of its political effects, and anxious to ensure that those effects were as beneficial or as little harmful to themselves as possible. From the moment in 1947 when both the Republican and Democratic parties decided to hold their 1948 nominating conventions in Philadelphia for no other reason than that it was on the coaxial cable which could reach the largest viewing audience, this watchful anxiety was part of the air which television breathed.

It is a peculiarity of commercial systems of broadcasting that their free-for-all attitudes do not as a rule extend beyond commerce. Liberty of commercial statement is not as a rule accompanied by liberty of political statement. The reasons are plain enough. There is a marked community of interest between successful men in commerce and successful men in politics. Businessmen, whether advertisers or station operators, want a world in which investments and currencies keep their value. They want to see the present state of affairs stable and persistent. So do politicians, if they are either in power or near it. Businessmen, particularly advertisers, want no enemies for their product, since an enemy made is a customer lost. They do not want contentious political views aired. Nor do politicians in power. Businessmen as station operators are also direct vassals of the government of the day because they depend on it for their franchise to broadcast, and they know that this could easily be bestowed elsewhere: there are other candidates waiting to take it up; whereas a non-commercial service with its specialized sources of finance, and still more an entrenched state service, can be replaced only with great difficulty. Hence the reluctance of commercial broadcasters to broadcast anything which might involve them in political argument, represent them as over-critical of the established order, or make them seem indulgent to those who wish to change it.

One manifestation of this spirit was the uneasy deference paid to the views of men like Senator Joseph McCarthy and Vice-President Spiro Agnew. Another was that the networks were far outdone by the newspapers in their readiness to embarrass the administration, particularly over the Vietnam war. But the most striking sign of thraldom to commercial principles was that candidates for political office were not given any opportunity to address the voters over the air as they thought fit. They had no allocation of free broadcast time of the kind that was enjoined by law in Britain. If they wanted to make a broadcast whose form they controlled themselves, they had to buy the time at commercial rates, without discount, cash on the nail. True, they could buy as much as they wanted (even after an attempt in 1971 to limit the staggering sums laid out). But the effect was to make it the most important quality in a candidate that he should either possess wealth or command it, and therefore to intensify the identification of government with commercially safe views.

If politicians had been allowed such influence as they paid

for and no more, it would at least have been a logical interpretation of the commercial principle. But the real difficulties in the relation between politics and broadcasting were left unregulated. The system of political time-buying worsened candidates' financial problems – by the 1960s the television cost of a senatorial campaign was reckoned at 10 cents a citizen, which was a lot of money in states with populations of over 10 million – without serving as any guide to the day-to-day handling of the multitudinous issues in which candidates were interested. That still required a ponderous and at the same time unspecific body of rules from the FCC in elucidation of its 'fairness' doctrine, of which the net effect was to paralyse the will of broadcasters and strengthen their resolve to stay away from anything which savoured of controversy.

The BBC had mapped this minefield from end to end before television began. Although it submitted to a good deal of government control during the war, in the end the Corporation taught the government the lesson that unfavourable truth – or at least the appearance of it – was better propaganda than favourable untruth. It emerged from the war with its title to decide the contents of its own broadcasts clearly made out. Throughout the most difficult years of the cold war, therefore, it had a standing which the American networks lacked, as well as the practical immunity to flank attack which came from lacking rivals. ITV, when it began, taught the BBC something about alertness in the coverage of news and current affairs, but it also profited from the long tradition of BBC resistance to politicians' more pushful claims.

It was the touch of obstinacy about that resistance, as compared with ITV's readiness to live by its commercial logic and yield where it could, which in the end forced the BBC to change its ways. Starting from the Suez adventure of 1956, the Conservative Party's picture of the national interest diverged steadily from the Corporation's. 'Why bother to knock out Cairo Radio', an irate British ambassador cabled to the Foreign Office at that time from a Middle Eastern capital, 'when the BBC is doing its work for it?' And Sir Anthony Eden seriously considered some formal bending of the BBC to what he conceived to be the national will. But matters did not then come to an open breach. Harold Wilson, becoming Prime Minister in 1964 at the head of a party which until a year before had seemed destined for permanent opposition, was vigilant for any sign of insufficient respect from broadcasters, and prepared to make an issue of it. He rapidly found it, or thought he did, at the BBC. At ITV, without a word being said by the people in charge, producers and reporters on the staff understood the essential dictates of a commercial system. Needless offence was never given. At the BBC very few people thought like that. Early in his rule Mr Wilson undertook a great number of visits to other European capitals, to spy out the prospects for British entry into the Common Market. It was the practice for him to give television interviews at London Airport as he came and went. Almost invariably, the ITV man there would be a political correspondent known to the Prime Minister, while the BBC man would be the rawest product of their school for reporters. It represented on the BBC's part an accurate foreknowledge of what Mr Wilson's Europeanism would be worth in the end, but a low level of worldly wisdom.

Part of the formal power of the government over the BBC was the fact that the BBC chairman was a government appointment. The sign that the BBC was at last operating in a different and harsher climate was Mr Wilson's appointment of Lord Hill to the chairmanship in 1967. Lord Hill had begun his public life nearly thirty years before as the BBC's radio doctor; but his attitudes to broadcasting had been learned – after a spell as a Conservative Cabinet minister and co-ordinator of government information under Harold Macmillan – in the post of chairman of the ITA, the high command of the BBC's commercial rival. His training showed. He was still at the BBC when Mr Wilson went out of office in 1970, and he prepared the Corporation in the way he understood best for the time when its fifth successive Charter would need renewal in 1976. Finding strong criticism of the BBC, on moral as well as political grounds, among back-benchers of the new Conservative government, Lord Hill sought to comfort them during 1971 by setting up a private complaints service – nominally within the BBC, but staffed by eminent men from outside. The effect was only to redouble the cry that the BBC had lost its own ability to tell right from wrong. In the same year Lord Hill sanctioned a virtual ban on conversations with members of the Irish Republican Army, who had become the British government's chief scourge in Northern Ireland. The government changed its policy before the BBC did. Lord Hill knew by what kind of methods ITV had kept its nose clean, and he could see that the BBC must henceforth stay alive in exactly the same world.

The BBC's difficulty derived from the fact that many people had forgotten in the commercial era what state-sponsored broadcasting was for. They supposed that just as commercial broadcasting upheld commercial values, so state broadcasting was to uphold state interests and values – which they further took to mean the interests of the governing party and the values of the property-owning class. In fact the BBC was vowed in origin to a far more elusive aim, the pursuit of the good. Philippians iv. 8 looked a little solemn over doorways through which passed Tommy Handley or Vera Lynn, but it was a not inaccurate statement of the things which the BBC's founders did indeed want its listeners to think on. Yet the idea of the good was too impalpable and even shifting a mark for Conservative back-benchers to hold in their minds with any degree of comfort. So the BBC, set up by men who believed in the moral and cultural power of broadcasting, was gradually reduced in stature by people who were chiefly interested in its political power.

Publicly financed broadcasting in the United States was never allowed much stature in the first place – out of the same fear of the political consequences. In July 1972, twenty years after its first introduction, President Nixon vetoed the Bill which would at last have given non-commercial broadcasting a measure of financial security. His telecommunications adviser had already spoken scathingly of public broadcasting's habit of 'taking the taxpayers' money and using it to express controversial points of view'. In pursuit of official approval, it had in fact expressed far fewer controversial points of view than it might have done. Set up to copy the BBC in its Reith phase, American public broadcasting ended by copying it in its Hill phase. Watched chiefly by people who could have secured its cultural benefits from other sources, it made only a marginal difference to the character of American television. Once commercial broadcasting exists, non-commercial broadcasting cannot help being assimilated to its standard.

Given this osmotic effect, it is surprising that commercial television in Britain should have had to wait so long before being joined by commercial radio. Legislation establishing it was only passed in 1972, and transmissions from a few centres began late in 1973, eighteen years after the start of ITV programmes. Advocates of commercial radio had chosen to base themselves on the plea that what Britain needed was local radio – a station in every large town. The BBC duly discovered in itself a zeal for local radio which had been dormant for nearly fifty years, and its attempt to head off the new invader duly failed. In both camps this emphasis on geographical dispersal was a pity. It increased the likelihood that the new diversification in radio would not mean a diversification of choice. Every large town could look forward to a pair of stations, one BBC and one commercial, identical with each other and with all the rest.

It is of the nature of competition to foster similarities, not differences. Rivals compete by producing the same article, not different ones. The only way to get genuine variety in broadcasting would be to have a number of different channels within a monopoly. Competition homogenizes programmes; and since competition must be for numbers of listeners or viewers, and since the wider the audience the lower must be the average level of intellectual or cultural nourishment which that audience believes it wants, competition also has a tendency to debase programmes.

British broadcasting's lesson from America, then, is already learned, and not reversible. The only countries now able to profit from the lesson of that lesson are such few free societies as have not yet admitted commercial broadcasting: Belgium, the three Scandinavian countries, Israel. The best that can be done in Britain is to see that the ideals of the BBC's foundation are not completely wiped away. Even that will require a degree of moral self-confidence in the Corporation's servants which they have understandably lost the habit of showing.

Bibliographical Note

There are several useful volumes of reminiscence about American broadcasting: one of the more illuminating is Fred W. Friendly's *Due to Circumstances Beyond Our Control...* (New York: Random House, 1967), and one of the more recent Les Brown's *Television: The Business Behind the Box* (New York: Harcourt Brace Jovanovich, 1971). The indispensable study is Erik Barnouw's three-volume *History of Broadcasting in the United States* (New York: Oxford U.P., 1966, 1968, 1970); on a much wider canvas he has done almost as exhaustive a job as Asa Briggs has in his *History of Broadcasting in the United Kingdom* (London: Oxford U.P., 1961, 1965, 1970).

Much of the relevant official material is in Frank J. Kahn (ed.), *Documents of American Broadcasting* (New York: Appleton-Century-Crofts, 1968). The Beveridge Report which opened the door to British commercial television when it meant to shut it is the *Report of the Broadcasting Committee,* 1949, Cmd 8116 (London: HMSO, Jan 1951); and the story of how commercial television was then foisted on a mildly reluctant government is told in H. H. Wilson's *Pressure Group* (London: Secker & Warburg, 1961).

8 Compensatory Education and Race Relations: What Lessons for Europe?*

ALAN N. LITTLE

Head of Reference Division, Community Relations Commission

Most societies are seeking to expand educational opportunities as a means of overcoming social and economic inequalities. The underlying social theory is that if children can be given equal access to education, then they may compete on more equal terms for privileged positions in society. Unfortunately, all children cannot benefit equally from exposure to education because of genetic and environmental differences. It is further quite clear that, as education becomes an important influence on status in society, parents seek the best possible education for their children. There is, in consequence, a 'built-in' tendency for education to be used by parents as a means of maintaining existing social advantages for their children. The existing elites have an advantage in doing so over underprivileged groups, whether social, racial or ethnic. Therein lies a fundamental dilemma for education and other social policies.

In the United States this dilemma has become particularly acute – not only because of the faith of that country in education as a key to social and individual equality but also because sharp racial and ethnic differences in opportunity have brought the problem to the forefront earlier than in other countries. It is typical of American society that recognition of the problem has brought a burgeoning of programmes and projects to solve it. Phrases such as 'compensatory education'

---

* Some of the arguments presented in this paper have been taken from G. N. Smith and A. N. Little, *Strategies of Compensation: A review of Educational Projects for the Disadvantaged*, Paris: (OECD, 1971).

and 'the socially disadvantaged' can cover a wide range of educational programmes, and can be applied to groups as diverse as the isolated rural poor, or ethnic minorities in the city centre.

The United States was the first country to mount a massive national programme recognizing the importance of education for socially and economically disadvantaged children. This concern is now spreading to a number of European countries, which have begun to plan and mount programmes of 'compensatory education' for socially disadvantaged groups, as small-scale research projects and on a national basis. This has in part been influenced by similar work in the United States.

An aspect of American life that has been widely publicized in Europe is the discussions about the American city centring around the word 'ghetto'. Anthony Downs describes two distinct meanings which seem relevant to the British situation:

> In its *racial* sense, a ghetto is an area to which members of an ethnic minority, particularly Negroes, are residentially restricted by social, economic and physical pressures from the rest of society. In this meaning, a ghetto can contain wealthy and middle-income residents as well as poor ones. In its *economic* sense, a ghetto is an area in which poor people are compelled to live because they cannot afford better accommodation. In this meaning, a ghetto contains mainly poor people, regardless of race or colour.[1]

This distinction is possibly more important in the United Kingdom, with its long history of class differences (second meaning) and a relatively recent history of domestic racial differences (first meaning), than in the United States. It is perhaps not too glib to suggest that the current concerns of both countries are similar, but the path by which they have arrived at them dissimilar. Many would argue that poverty has become an issue in the United States largely because of race, whereas in the United Kingdom race has become an issue because of poverty.

[1] A. Downs, 'Alternative Future for the American Ghetto', *Daedalus*, xcvii, 4 (1968).

I. THE AMERICAN EXPERIENCE

But how far does the current American urban racial situation provide a portent for the United Kingdom and its policies, particularly educational decision-making? Initially it is important to point the differences between the two situations:

1. *Size*

There is no comparison in the relative size and concentrations of racial minority populations in the United Kingdom and the United States. Well over 20 million Americans are black; this is between one American in eight or nine, compared with an estimated $1\frac{1}{2}$ million 'coloured' in the United Kingdom, less than 3 per cent of the population. Many American cities are anticipating that well over half their population will be black by the mid-1980s; already Washington DC is over 50 per cent black. Public school populations of many major cities are already over half black; in Washington, fewer than one pupil in twenty in public schools is white. In his classic report James S. Coleman demonstrated that two out of three American blacks were in schools that were 90 per cent black.

This contrasts with the United Kingdom situation; it was impossible a decade ago to find even census enumeration districts that were exclusively black. Currently only two local education authorities have more than one-quarter of their pupils defined as 'immigrant' and a further four between one-fifth and one-quarter classified in the same way. Although two out of three West Indian children are in schools in the Greater London area and half in the inner city area, few schools have concentrations of minority groups as in America. In central London 60 per cent of so-called immigrant pupils are in schools with fewer than one-fifth immigrants, and only one immigrant pupil in six is in a school which is more than half immigrant. In the country fewer than 150 schools had more than half of their pupils defined as immigrant in 1971.

2. *Homogeneity*

Although the United States minority population is not exclusively Negro, the difficulties of Puerto Rican, Asian and European immigrants have been given little emphasis. By contrast, the United Kingdom settler population is highly differentiated: of 270,450 pupils defined as 'immigrant' in 1971, 40 per cent were of West Indian origin, 20 per cent Indian, 10 per cent Pakistani and a further 10 per cent from Africa: all these groups would be defined currently as black. The importance of this point is that the reasons the parents of these children had for coming to this country, the experiences they brought with them and their adjustment or maladjustment to the host environment are different from and independent of the dominant white culture. Certainly, the African and Asian populations have their own cultural identity even in the United Kingdom; this contrasts markedly with the disorganized situation of many American blacks, whose culture is largely that of the dominant and rejecting white majority. How far the settlers from the Caribbean have an autonomous cultural identity and how far they are in a similar situation to the American Negro is debatable.

Even in the United States it is misleading to treat the black community as a one-dimensional group of people; again to quote Anthony Downs:

In reality, each racial ghetto contains a tremendous variety of persons who exhibit widely differing attitudes towards almost every question. Many are very poor, but just as many are not. Many have radical views – especially young people; many others are quite conservative – especially the older people. Many are on welfare, but many are steadily employed. This diversity means that public policy concerning any given ghetto problem cannot be successful if it is aimed at or based upon the attitudes and desires of only one group of persons affected by that problem.

A second widely prevalent oversimplification of ghetto problems is concentration of remedial action upon a single substandard condition. For instance, improving the deplorable housing conditions in many slums would not in itself eliminate most of the dehumanizing forces which operate there. In fact, no single category of programs can possibly be adequate to cope with the tangled problems that exist in ghettos. Any effective ghetto-improvement strategy must concern itself with at least jobs and employment, education, housing, health, personal safety, crime prevention, and income maintenance for dependent persons.

This quotation indicates the extent to which the American black population is differentiated both by its resources and by problems requiring a variety of social policy responses. Similarly, recent settlers in the United Kingdom must be internally differentiated. Initially (and sensibly) it is possible to distinguish them by country of origin, but even these national origins are cut across by rural and urban differences, by class or even colour distinctions even in their country of origin. The extent to which the host white population reacts in a uniform manner will determine how far historical, ethnic and colour differences remain significant within the United Kingdom, or are swayed by a common experience of living in a 'white man's' country.

3. History

The American black is an internal migrant, until a generation or two ago the inferior member of the Southern plantation society. Migration to the cities was always a way out of a caste society. Industrialization in the Northern cities and the economic boom of the Second World War enormously widened the opportunities for the black population and chances for migrating north. But many urban blacks are still living in the shadow of the slave plantations; settlers in the United Kingdom have never been dominated by the cultural and economic standards of the whites. Even in the West Indies, domination of blacks by whites was never as severe as that in the United States. One illustration of this is that some of the leaders of recent black militancy in the United States had their origins not in the ghettoes of the United States cities or in the American South but in the West Indies. A major reason for this was that the whites both in the West Indies and in Asia were always outnumbered by the blacks. As a result, a black bourgeoisie was always in evidence. Further, a peculiar mixture of missionary zeal and transient colonial exploitation gave the relationship between whites and blacks in the West Indies a different flavour from its counterparts in the United States.

The capacity of the Asian culture(s) to withstand the pressures of commercial, political and religious colonization is legendary: 'resilience' is a word that has frequently been used to describe the capacity of Asians to preserve a cultural integrity and identity against colonization. As a result, the settlers in the United Kingdom do not present the same kind or degree of cultural disorganization or show the same need to value themselves by white standards as do American blacks. The phrase 'American blacks' has been an apt description of the situation of the Negro in the United States in a way that 'black or brown British' is not accurate for settlers in the United Kingdom.

4. *Institutional framework*

A further difference between the countries is the institutional framework within which race relations take place and which structure the economic and social opportunities and life-styles of minority populations. The different relationship between central, regional and local authorities in the United States and the United Kingdom inevitably makes problems and opportunities differ. The fact that nearly one-third of housing in the United Kingdom is controlled by public bodies means that the public policy (in this case, local authority policy) could (if we wished it to) have a profound effect on the housing opportunities of settler and minority groups. The fact that the state is a major employer not only in the bureaucratic sense of the civil service but in industrial sectors like mines, public utilities and steel, in services like transport, post and telecommunications, means that public recruitment, training and promotion policies could directly change the employment situation of minorities and serve as an example to private employers.

Finally, parallel with immigration control in the 1960s came a legal framework for race relations. This included legislation against incitement to race hatred, discrimination in employment, housing and recreational facilities, and the creation of Community Relations Commissions. The positive effort to discourage discrimination was established within a decade of the arrival of sizeable numbers of black settlers in this country. This contrasts with the American situation where legislation and action against discrimination were imposed upon set conventions and behaviour established generations previously.

5. *Commitment to change*

So far the bulk of the argument suggests that the United States and the United Kingdom problems are different in their scale, history and ease of amelioration. There is one important respect where this is not only an over-simplification but also distorts the situation, namely the commitment to a positive effort for changing the situation and the mobilization of sufficient resources to achieve some effect. The cost of the British Urban Programme (which was explicitly stated not to be an immigrant programme, although it is the only major programme for assisting areas where immigrants have settled in large numbers) between January 1969 and November 1971 was £18 million; the extension of the programme until 1976 will bring the provision of funds up to £40 million.

Contrast this with the estimates for the first year of the anti-poverty programme in the United States of $1 billion, and the criticism that was levelled at Congress when the Office of Economic Opportunity had its budget cut from $2·1 billion to $1·8 billion. In so far as willingness to mobilize resources is a measure of commitment to change, there can be little doubt about the relative seriousness of United States and United Kingdom efforts. For example, the Community Relations Commission budget in the United Kingdom is currently around two-thirds of a million pounds. One project to assess the impact of negative income tax on minorities in the United States received twice as much.

11. THE LESSONS TO DRAW

What, then, can a European learn from American experience? First of all, the variety of practices and projects that have been initiated. Gordon and Wilkerson, in *Compensatory Education for the Disadvantaged,* included as an appendix a comprehensive 'Directory of Compensatory Practices', an annotated list of projects under state and city headings.[2] They quote a statement made in 1964 about the education of the disadvantaged in Chicago: 'There is probably not a single suggestion made anywhere in the country for the improvement of the educational program for such children that is not being tried out, *within the limits of available resources,* in some Chicago school.'

Since that remark was made, to mention only large-scale efforts, there has been the Headstart Program, set up under the Economic Opportunity Act of 1964, which provided funds for local groups to organize pre-school facilities. In the first summer of Headstart more than 500,000 four- and five-year-olds from depressed areas were enrolled in thousands of pre-school centres for an eight-week summer course; these centres were set up by local school boards, schools and community action groups. Inevitably, these different forms of organization resulted in a considerable diversity in the type of pre-school curriculum that was operated. Rather than a single programme, Headstart covered a range of approaches.

Similarly, there have been many programmes under the various headings of the Elementary and Secondary Education Act of 1965, particularly Title I, through which several thousand projects were supported in the first year of operation. Under this Title, local school districts received funds in proportion to the number of children in schools from families with an income of less than $2,000 per year. These Title I funds, which were estimated to be about $1 billion per year, were intended for projects designed to raise educational standards among the disadvantaged.

The number and diversity of projects under these various

[2] E. W. Gordon and D. A. Wilkerson, *Contemporary Education for the Disadvantaged: Programs and Practices – Pre-school through College* (New York, 1966).

programmes means that a European is bound to be sceptical about the chances of such varied and expensive projects taking root in his own country. Neither the wealth nor the political will is there for them.

It is tempting, therefore, to adopt a more prescriptive approach, providing specific findings and lessons that could direct European efforts in developing programmes for the disadvantaged. Yet this approach is immediately undermined by the present position regarding compensatory projects in the United States. The early confident optimism about the success of such projects, reported for example by Maya Pines,[3] has given way to considerable pessimism about the long-term effects of past programmes and the likely results of future work. This impression is supported by a study of the literature, which has changed from predominantly reporting successful programmes to articles questioning the criteria by which such successes were measured and, more widely, an investigation into some of the assumptions upon which such projects were based.

The apparent failure of many compensatory projects has been used by Jensen as additional evidence for reopening the debate on the relative effects of environmental and genetic factors in determining intelligence.[4] Though such fundamental discussions about the basic assumptions of compensatory education may be timely and beneficial in the long term, they cut the ground from beneath any attempt to derive a specific set of proposals for action. What emerge instead of detailed proposals are general guidelines for developing programmes for the disadvantaged, and a set of ideas that could be translated into action but which as yet are largely untried.

1. *Objectives*

The most significant question about objectives is what the policy is seeking to achieve for both majority and minority populations. Two types of long-term objectives for race relations have been suggested by the American situation: the

---

[3] Maya Pines, *Revolution in Learning* (London, 1969).

[4] A. R. Jensen, 'How Can We Boost IQ and Scholastic Achievement?', and 'Reducing the Hereditary–Environment Uncertainty', *Harvard Educational Review* (1969).

'melting-pot' and the 'mosaic'. The 'melting-pot' is an attempt to achieve a social structure in which distinctions between majority and minority, indigenous and new arrivals, cannot be made in social, economic, political, educational and cultural terms. The 'mosaic' is the attempt to preserve the cultural identity of minority groups and provide a diversified social structure, within a framework of equality of treatment and consideration. As far as racial minorities are concerned, the most obvious practical reason for arguing for the mosaic is the impossibility in the short run of loss of identity by skin colour. Clearly, other reasons can be given for advocating the mosaic objective, but the one characteristic that marks the current situation off from other minority groups is identification by their skin colour.

Given this, the problem remains of identifying those aspects of minority cultures that are preservable as part of a pluralistic society and what action is needed to preserve them. Many would agree that the West Indian tragedy (like that of the American Negro) is the absence of a cultural inheritance that has not been destroyed or dominated or damaged by the white culture. Hindus and Moslems from Asia are in a different situation. Questions are more concerned with tensions that might be generated by preservation of cultural identity (for example, inter-generational conflicts or problems of direct conflict with majority culture over issues like relationship between the sexes).

Related to these points are the discussions that have taken place in the United States about the theory of the 'poverty cycle'. These initially emphasized the closely interrelated aspects of poverty: 'Inadequate education, low or non-existent income, limited job opportunities, dilapidated and overcrowded housing, poor physical and mental health, an inclination towards delinquency and crime – these and many other characteristics of poverty both cause and are caused by each other, interacting in a maner which renders it virtually impossible for the disadvantaged child, adult or family to break out of the "cycle of poverty".' Later the theory was interpreted to mean that the cycle could be broken by intervention at one point, and succeeding stages avoided. Education seemed to offer a suitable period of continuity early in the sequence where the chain could be broken. Changes in educational theory have provided support for this emphasis on educational programmes to solve the problems of poverty, and recent research had produced fresh evidence on the potential effects that educational programmes might have on basic human skills previously thought to be largely prede-termined by genetic processes.

Educational programmes for the poor and the black had two distinct sets of objectives, the first being strictly educa-tional, e.g. the raising of educational performance levels, and the second vaguer social objectives, 'breaking the poverty cycle' and so on. Both types of objective imply some theory or assumption about the ways in which such objectives could be reached. To set meaningful objectives entails some under-standing of the changes necessary to attain these goals. At the more general level, the educational objectives themselves be-come the means to achieve wider social goals. This implies a relationship between improved educational standards and subsequent occupational position. The importance attached to such aims as equalizing educational opportunity derived in part from the belief that greater equality of educational opportunity will contribute to the achievement of wider social and economic opportunity.

Yet the relationship between educational attainment and subsequent occupation is far from clear, particularly where there is discrimination in employment. As there is no simple relationship between educational change and change in other social institutions, it becomes uncertain what are appropriate educational objectives for compensatory programmes. Rather than raise intellectual standards, it may be more appropriate to develop self-confidence and social purpose, if job discrimi-nation is the main obstacle to advancement.

These two sets of objectives have added to the uncertainty surrounding the goals of many educational projects. Marris and Rein report a similar finding for community action pro-grammes: 'What are you really trying to achieve?' asks the naïve critic, and finds he has thrown down a provocative chal-lenge.[5] The stated aims of compensatory educational pro-

[5] Peter Marris and Martin Rein, *Dilemmas of Social Reform* (London, 1967).

grammes range from the very broad objective of breaking the poverty cycle to the very specific goal of producing measurable improvements in a particular skill area. The dilemma for the large-scale programme is that the setting of a non-educational objective such as breaking the poverty cycle gives very little guidance for selecting a particular educational approach. The result is that the programme may well include almost any educational change that can be justified as a way of helping to break the poverty cycle.

At the other end of the scale, the small-scale research project, by concentrating on the specific outcomes of a particular approach, does not avoid the dilemma. Though the project may have made significant improvements in a particular skill area, it still has to be shown how far this improvement has relevance for wider objectives. The pre-school programme, which has achieved its immediate objective of skill improvement, is committed to a series of follow-up studies to see whether this improvement is maintained.

Neither approach has, as yet, an adequate framework within which it can fit its activities: at one end there is lack of knowledge about how far changes in educational standards can affect other areas of inequality; and at the other there is uncertainty about how far gains achieved at one level of education can be maintained later.

2. *Strategy*

American experience suggests two broad possible strategies for change: 'dispersal' and 'enrichment'. The former refers to the attempts to break up the housing, educational and occupational isolation of minority groups; the latter attempts to work within existing enclaves to achieve the objectives of equality of opportunity and condition without explicit attempts to disperse. In education it is the contrast between bussing and a compensatory education programme; in housing it is the attempt to shift the ghetto population contrasted with attempts to improve the housing stock within the ghetto.

As far as Britain is concerned, two points are worth making. First, in most areas of the country 'dispersal' in the American sense is unnecessary simply because the scale of the problem is much less. A second point is that no single solution is likely to be satisfactory. Although most settlers do not live in ghettos in the American sense, concentrations undoubtedly do exist: over 1,000 schools are more than one-third immigrant and four schools have more than 80 per cent of their pupils defined as immigrant. Therefore a limited and localized dispersal policy is arguably necessary and in certain areas practical. But the extent to which a far more effective and more popular way of dealing with these problems might be a programme of positive discrimination (i.e. enrichment) deserves more consideration than it has been given.

Several studies have attempted to assess the effects of changing some of the pressures on the inner-city schoolchild by moving him to suburban schools. Wilson's study shows the normalization of divergent standards between schools drawing from different socio-economic status areas. He also showed that pupils from low socio-economic status backgrounds who attended predominantly middle-class schools had a higher level of performance than similar children who attended predominantly working-class schools, though he pointed out that such differences may be the result of 'self-selection' by brighter families from poor areas who have moved to better districts.[6] The Coleman study demonstrated the effect of pupil characteristics on achievement level, and found that it explained more variation in achievement than any other school-based characteristic. Students from minority racial groups who attended schools with a high proportion of white students tended to show higher patterns of achievement. The effect appeared to increase at higher grades, suggesting that it was more a result of attending an integrated school than any prior difference in background. The study's findings 'that the apparent beneficial effect of a student body with a high proportion of white students comes not from racial composition *per se*, but from better educational background and higher educational aspirations that are on the average found among white students', indicate that there may be academic grounds for integration on a social class as well as racial basis.

As far as educational 'enrichment' is concerned, classroom

[6] A. B. Wilson, article in A. H. Passow, *Education in Depressed Areas* (New York, 1963).

and curriculum innovations for the disadvantaged can be grouped into several categories, depending upon their relationship with innovations in the wider educational system. There are innovations aimed specifically at eradicating the intellectual deficits of disadvantaged children; such changes are not necessarily applicable to education as a whole. Some indeed might be received with hostility by middle-class groups. Then there are innovations which try to build on the strengths and interest of disadvantaged children; these again would not necessarily have wider application without extensive modification. Many so-called innovations are merely the creation of facilities that already exist in other areas; only in depressed areas are they innovations. Finally, there are genuine innovations that have relevance for education in general, but on a basis of 'positive discrimination' they are initially set up in depressed areas. Many projects included innovations of several different kinds.

Programmes designed to change the learning situation raise a number of separate points: (*a*) the most suitable age group to form the target population, i.e. how young should the intervention be; (*b*) the details of programme content and method at different levels of education, and (*c*) the problems of increasing the quality and quantity of the teaching force in depressed areas.

3. *Impact*

One generally accepted lesson from American experience is the difficulty of making any significant impact on the problems presented by the underprivileged in general and the ghetto-dweller in particular. This is the most depressing result of United States experience, especially because it comes from a society that believes in immediate technocratic solutions to practical problems and is wealthy and concerned enough to mobilize resources that would lead an observer to expect a positive impact.

The catalogue of disappointing and apparently ineffective programmes and projects is long; the reasons given for ineffectiveness are a mixture of the intrinsic difficulty of the task (overcoming generations of discrimination and disadvantage is impossible by any instant programme) and the extent to which any effective strategy is likely to be threatening to the short-run interests of the majority and the privileged (for example, the way desegregation in housing and school bussing is resisted by many members of the majority population). Certainly, the early optimistic expectations have not been realized. And where rigorous evaluation has been conducted, results have often been disappointing or, where significant, have not been maintained for any length of time.

The American writers Light and Smith lament: 'Our ability to detect failure has outrun our power to instill success.'[7] They attribute part of the problem to the 'make or break' method of the traditional evaluation approach, and suggest the need for 'improved development and evaluation strategies'. Others would lay most of the blame on the design of the action programmes; research evidence has been poorly used and programmes have worked within a limited frame of reference that neglects the child's wider experience outside school. Others would criticize the overall level of resources and the short time-span within which measurable return was expected.

The disappointing results of compensatory programmes have raised basic doubts about the influence of education in tackling the problems of poverty. Several critics have argued that the educational system alone has little independent effect as an agent of social change, and that improvements in educational facilities, however radical, could never achieve the kind of objectives that were set. Even if these objectives were apparently 'educational' themselves, for example an increase in pupil performance, the influence of other social factors far outweighed the influence of school characteristics. More fundamentally still, it has been questioned whether the observed intellectual differences between social and ethnic groups are principally determined by social factors rather than genetic differences. In the face of such basic criticisms, it may well be asked whether the whole compensatory education movement has not been a series of 'paper programmes', founded on inadequate assumptions and poorly articulated theory.

[7] R. J. Light and P. U. Smith, 'Choosing a Future: Strategies for Designing and Evaluating New Programs', *Harvard Educational Review* (1970).

Some programmes have set unrealistic objectives; this problem is particularly marked where vague non-educational goals are put forward. In general, the more extensive and varied the programme, the more likely it is to have vague objectives. 'Umbrella' programmes such as Headstart or Title I of the Elementary and Secondary Education Act of 1965 almost inevitably become associated with broad objectives. The relationship between these objectives and the educational changes promoted by the programmes were never clearly thought through and, as in the case of the 'poverty cycle', the theories on which such relationships were based are often very inadequate. Yet it would be wrong to dismiss compensatory education as a series of 'paper programmes' because of weaknesses at this level of theory. Clear knowledge about such relationships is inadequate on any analysis; perhaps it is only by experimenting this way that better theory will be developed.

While American experience does not provide a portent for the future of British cities, race relations within them or educational action, we can learn something about styles of intervention and possible outcomes. In particular, the following would seem to emerge from the United States experience:

1. There is no single or instant solution to the many-sided problems of race relations in the urban context; the chronic nature of the problems (especially when recent settlers have visibly provided an extra dimension to existing class differences and inequalities), its presentation as a crisis and the resistance of the majority population to support necessary action must all be taken into account when outlining expectations from action.

2. Given agreement on the need for action, the question of objectives has to be examined and the desirability and practicability of attempting to achieve a 'melting-pot' seriously debated. Certainly, the assumed objective of many American projects has been to make the 'black man white'; the cultural implication of phrases like 'compensatory education' illustrates this tendency. Equally, the implications of the alternative, a 'mosaic', have never been systematically worked out or its viability tested. What, for example,

are the aspects of differentiated cultures that are preservable, what types of cultural tensions are generated by
cultural diversity and what action is required to achieve
cultural pluralism with minimum tensions?

3. Once agreement about objectives has been reached,
the question of strategy should be considered and the extent to which objectives are best met by policies of dispersal or by programmes of enrichment thought through.
This is partly a choice between strategies in a particular
context, and partly a question of attempting to develop an
appropriate mix of dispersal and enrichment policies; for
example, educational enrichment could co-exist with a
policy of occupational dispersal.

One thing that is underdeveloped in race relations policy
in the United States and Britain is any clarification of policy
objectives and strategies for change on local, regional or
national levels. A conscious effort is needed to create a climate of opinion favourable to the achievement of any strategy.
Many of our cities now contain a substantial black minority
population. The implications for living in a multi-racial
urban society for education, housing, employment and social
relations generally need thinking through. Taking thought
will not of itself solve our problems, but it is a precondition
of understanding how this might be done.

9 On Some Perils of Imitation

NICHOLAS DEAKIN*

Department of Planning and Transportation, Greater London Council

This paper is about two government-sponsored programmes designed to deal with the endlessly rediscovered problem of poverty in two of the most prosperous societies in the world – the Poverty Program in the United States and the Urban Programme in Great Britain. Superficially, the parallels between the two are very close. Each begins with a human situation anatomized in a book: Michael Harrington's *The Other America* (1962) and Peter Townsend and Brian Abel-Smith's *The Poor and the Poorest* (1965). Each was launched with a speech: Lyndon B. Johnson's at Howard University, Harold Wilson's at Birmingham Town Hall. Both leaders chose to dramatize one particular aspect of the problem by underlining the particular problem of race; and part of the difficulties that arose subsequently stemmed from the association with such a contentious topic. As the struggle to break away from this association led to a broadening of focus, each turned to the particular difficulties experienced by deprived children. This was a situation analysed in the United States in the Coleman Report on equality of educational opportunity (1966) and in Britain in the Plowden Report on primary education (1967).

It is hardly surprising that the specific programmes adopted in each case have a strong family resemblance; in many important respects the British programme was quite consciously modelled on its American predecessor. Only the trajectory of the two is strikingly different. The Poverty Program rose to greater heights in the strictly practical sense of the injection of resources on a far greater scale, and in the metaphorical sense of investment of confidence and hope.

---

* The opinions expressed in this paper are solely the author's own and in no way reflect those of the GLC.

Failure, when it came, was correspondingly more complete. The brief period when the solutions to the problem of poverty seemed within reach, and to consist essentially of vastly increased expenditure scattered broadside over hundreds of different cities and programmes, had never had a direct parallel in Britain; indeed, that stage had already passed when the British policy-makers set up their programmes. But the basic assumptions of that period, when, in the immediate aftermath of the trauma of John F. Kennedy's death, the social engineers of the New Frontier turned their attention to the drastic problems of their own country, had left their mark, and in turn influenced the approach adopted to the problem of poverty in the British programme. At the same time, the architects of the British programme adopted from the outset a more cautious approach: the financial resources which were provided for the task were far more limited, almost farcically so by comparison. The politicians who were called upon to justify this modest expenditure were also studiously cautious in their claims for the programme. But their caution and the restricted scope of the operation have not saved Britain's Urban Programme from passing into an equivalent phase of disillusionment.

In both cases the accepted verdict is one of failure; yet what is striking to anyone examining the present situation is the sense of vigorous, apparently spontaneous growth from the remnants of the original plans. The American situation is once again the more dramatic: the efflorescence of new activity under new leadership in the deprived areas of American cities stems, in part at least, from the initiatives undertaken as part of the Poverty Program, especially in community action programmes and in some of the Model Cities areas. While the equivalent activity in Britain is on a far smaller scale, hardly to be graced with the name of ferment, the indications are that out of the original restricted design of the Community Development Projects introduced in 1969 as part of the process of broadening the scope of the Urban Programme, something new and welcome in the community action field may well emerge. Even if these developments do not always reflect the original intentions of the two programmes, they suggest that to talk of failure may be premature and misleading.

Yet it is not too early to draw one conclusion: many of the mistakes that were indisputably made on both sides of the Atlantic in the course of devising and executing the programmes were unnecessary. This is perhaps particularly true in the case of the Urban Programme in Britain, because so many of the possible pitfalls had been charted in the course of the American programe – often in the most direct possible way, by falling headlong into them. It is this theme that I shall be exploring in the course of this paper.

I. THE ORIGINS OF THE URBAN PROGRAMME IN BRITAIN

When Harold Wilson rose in Birmingham Town Hall on 5 May 1968 to make the speech that launched the Urban Programme, he did so in circumstances that were distinctly unfavourable politically. Unfavourable, that is, both because of the general situation in which the government that he headed found itself – they were about to suffer one of the most drastic of all their local election defeats during their period in office – and specifically, because of the state of disarray into which their race relations policy had fallen. The structure that had been elaborately put together over the preceding three years – known facetiously, after one of its architects, as Foley's tripod – rested on three legs: the control of immigration, the creation of special agencies designed to promote integration, and the provision of financial aid to areas affected by immigration. This third limb was perhaps the most rickety of all; it had been created in 1966, in redemption of an election undertaking. By section 11 of the Local Government Act of 1966, provision was made for grant aid to local authorities 'required to make special provision in the exercise of any of their functions in consequence of the presence within their areas of substantial numbers of immigrants from the Commonwealth whose language or customs differ from those of the community'. In all, £1·5 million was being spent annually under this provision. Expenditure on such a meagre scale provided no ready defence for ministers when, early in 1968, Enoch Powell (Conservative Member for

Wolverhampton South West and a former Cabinet Minister
seized the opportunity presented by the collapse of the first
leg of the government's policy to launch his campaign. In essence, Powell took advantage of the Labour government's
failure to achieve a humane solution to the problems of
United Kingdom citizens of Asian origin displaced by Afri-
canization in East Africa. In doing so, he projected himself as
the champion of the neglected rights of the indigenous white
working class.

In some ways Powell's ability to create such a political
tempest seems surprising, given the relatively small size of the
black and brown population in Britain, and their comparative quiescence. Although immigrants had encountered substantial discrimination in the labour market and especially in
housing, no indigenous civil rights movement of any substance had developed; by comparison with the United States,
the temperature of British race relations remained cool.
Powell's success lay in his capacity to dramatize social problems, and in order to do so he drew (in Wilson's phrase) on
'abundant transatlantic analogies'. The resultant threat to
Labour's political base in the white working class (though it
proved in practice to have been greatly exaggerated) was
sufficient to make some form of reply an urgent necessity.

In the voluminous memoirs to whose production he (like
Lyndon Johnson) devoted himself on losing office, Harold
Wilson puts a bold face on the situation that confronted him,
seeking reassurance about the course of action he adopted by
repetition. 'It was right,' he says, 'that I should meet this
problem head on in one of the areas where the controversy was
most heated. It was Birmingham's annual May Day celebration and I devoted the whole of my 55-minute speech to
immigration and to Mr Powell ... whether it was politically
wise or expedient, others can argue; but it was right.' In the
speech itself, Wilson adds, 'taking as my May Day theme the
brotherhood of man, I decided to challenge racialism directly.'

In fact the speech reads rather differently. After comment-
ing that 'at this time of change the problem of immigration
has aggravated many of our inherited difficulties; and all the
adjustments necessary to cope with the problem of immigra-

tion, to assimilate and to integrate, are painfully limited by our economic resources', Wilson went on to offer an elaborate defence of the government's immigration control policy. He advanced the proposition that 'there cannot be any doubt that in many areas we have reached absorptive capacity in respect of new immigrants. This is totally irrespective of race, colour or national origin.' He described the urgent review that the government had undertaken of the extent of this problem, which had isolated sixty towns where 'the problems of immigrants and their families have made a great social impact', in part because 'those who have come among us have their own religion, customs and conventions, to which they will want to cling'. Only then did he come to the government's new initiative. 'We are ready to embark on a new urban programme, over and above the massive increase in expenditure since 1963–4.' The sting was in the tail: 'Every penny spent will have to be met by corresponding economies and this at the end of the day means some contribution by more favoured areas.'

The speech attracted considerable publicity, as Wilson correctly records; but it was not so much the Conservative press's reluctance to see the Prime Minister 'take a national line' (as he contends), as uncertainty about the government's precise intentions that was reflected in the immediate reaction. A point widely fastened on was the question of the source of financial aid: the prospect of additional grants set off, as might perhaps have been expected, an immediate scramble to qualify for 'unfortunate' status.

Birmingham was one authority particularly quick to stake a claim: a conference between the chairmen of the Children's, Education, Finance, General Purposes, Health, Housing, Priorities (Expenditure) and Welfare Committees was held on 14 May. It reported to the City Council that

> immigrants tend to settle in specific localities forming their own communities which reacts against integration with the general population. It would seem that immigrant communities are formed because of circumstances (e.g. relatives, suitable surroundings) and the advantages to be gained by collective settlement in a manner not dis-

similar to the selection by individuals of the established population of neighbourhoods in which to live. Some services tend to be overburdened by this concentration of immigrants in specific localities because of the above normal demands which they make.

In this context, the implication was that any new subsidy should take the form not of meeting extra, abnormal, burdens, as the provision in the 1966 Act was intended to do, but of a straightforward subsidy to those local authorities with an immigrant population. The report complained that 'the limitation to immigrants whose language or customs differ from those of the community presents problems both in defining an immigrant for grant purposes and in determining eligible expenditure'. Additional funds should be made available, the report concluded, and the proportion of expenditure for which central government should take responsibility increased from 50 per cent to 100 per cent.

But the government, although they had now reached a point where they had almost nothing to lose in local political terms, had already recognized that opposition on the part of 'more fortunate authorities' was a likely obstacle to acceptance of their proposals in the form that Wilson had announced them. A process of back-pedalling began almost immediately. On 8 May one of the Conservative Members for Liverpool asked for clarification of the form of the proposals, and whether assistance meant 'a reduction in the help to other local authorities without an immigration problem but where there was overcrowding'. The Parliamentary Secretary at the Ministry of Housing, James MacColl, answered simply 'no'. In a subsequent exchange about the proposals, on 22 July, the Home Secretary, James Callaghan, was pressed by Edward Heath, then the Leader of the Conservative Opposition. Callaghan had assumed responsibility for the initial planning operation after the Prime Minister's speech and was presenting the preliminary conclusions that the Home Office had reached about the structure and scope of the programme. Heath argued: 'The help that he will give to deprived areas will not be most effective unless these fears [of continuing immigration] are removed by better control and regulation, and the reduction of the numbers coming in.' But Callaghan replied:

'The immigration factor is only one factor, though an important factor, in the assessment of social need. I am certain that this is the right approach.' In anouncing the government's intention to find £20–24 million in grants for the programme, he added: 'There are areas of severe social deprivation in a number of our cities and towns – often scattered in relatively small pockets.'

Moreover, when proposals to deal with the problems of these 'small pockets' of deprivation emerged, they were pitched in distinctly cautious terms. The initial Circular sent out from central government to local authorities talked of areas 'which bear the marks of multiple deprivation, which may show itself for example by way of notable deficiencies in the physical environment, particularly in housing, overcrowding of houses, family sizes above the average, persistent unemployment, high proportion of children in trouble or in need of care, or a combination of these. A substantial degree of immigrant settlement would also be an important factor.' As a result of this Circular, thirty-four local authorities were identified as qualifying for grant aid, the criteria for participation being overcrowding in housing and the presence of immigrants in the local school system. The programmes for which these authorities qualified for assistance consisted of new provision for nursery education and child-care facilities. They were chiefly building programmes, which would be likely to show a tangible pay-off. This first, non-statutory, phase of the programme was necessarily experimental, but in the most cautious vein: only £3·5 million was spent on the projects approved.

The emphasis within this first phase on aid to the under-fives presents an interesting parallel with the emphasis in the Poverty Program, and in particular the Headstart Program. In addition, the hurried de-emphasizing of the race issue had also had its parallel in the American situation. Not merely had the trumpet blast against racialism that Wilson had sounded proved to be more than a trifle uncertain; his troops had set off in a direction radically different from the one to which he had summoned them. Instead, broader issues of the relief of poverty had led to the consideration of issues that had been raised in the Plowden Report on primary education and, in particular, problems of positive discrimination in favour of areas of underprivilege, defined generally without reference to race.

II. THE EVOLUTION OF THE URBAN PROGRAMME

During the earlier stages of the Urban Programme, three linked issues assumed particular importance: the selection of areas for grant aid, methods of delivery, and the type of programme selected. In all these instances the experience of the Poverty Program was of the utmost importance. While the Home Office was in the course of launching Circular 225/68, their approximate equivalents on the other side of the Atlantic were sitting out the last stages of the Johnson administration, before the apparently inevitable victory of Richard Nixon at the 1968 Presidential election.

Robert Levine, in *The Poor Ye Need Not Have with You,* has charted the various stages through which the Poverty Program passes; he characterizes this period as one of 'suspense and routine'. But suspense and routine should not be equated with inactivity. In fact this stage was marked by a positive fever of activity, as battle-scarred poverty-warriors jostled each other in their rush to get into print about their experiences in Washington. The Poverty Program has spawned a substantial literature; by contrast, the documentation on the Urban Programme is miserably inadequate. But it was of particular importance to the planners of the British programme, hesitating on the brink of a new initiative, that accounts were available in 1968 for them to draw upon. The most cogent of these was Peter Marris and Martin Rein's *Dilemmas of Social Reform,* which analysed the development of the Poverty Program from the Ford Foundation's initial experiments in the grey areas, through to the first Presidential task-forces, to the hectic rush to produce legislation after the assassination of John Kennedy and the creation of the Office of Economic Opportunity.

The lessons that the civil servants responsible for designing the British programme drew from Marris and Rein and other

American studies were those to which they were by instinct favourably disposed. Unrealistic goals should be avoided, no excessive claims made for the efficacy of a particular programme and, above all, disorderly and wasteful procedures for distributing funds must be avoided. This implied a decision not to create *ad hoc* agencies in Britain, either a central body at the top by analogy with OEO or the kind of informal coalitions and local organizations that had been put together in American city neighbourhoods. The Urban Programme would remain strictly within the existing framework of government, and the procedures for dispensing grant aid would be in accordance with customary administrative rituals.

It was in this specific sense that the marks of American influence were present when, in December, 1968, James Callaghan came to launch the legislation which formally inaugurated the Urban Programme, the Local Government Grants (Social Need) Bill. The Bill authorized grants to local authorities covering up to 75 per cent of expenditure incurred 'by reason of the existence in urban areas of special social need'. The criteria for establishing need were not written into legislation. It was made clear in the obligatory financial memorandum that expenditure would be unlikely to exceed the £20–25 million originally envisaged for the period up to 1972. The scope of the programme therefore remained limited, to an almost ludicrous extent, by comparison with the Poverty Program.

The style of proceedings remained another area in which the contrast between different sides of the Atlantic was total. The British legislation itself is of great brevity – two brief clauses[1] – and its introduction was accompanied by no rhetorical fanfares. The contrast is complete with the Economic Opportunity Act, with its grandiose definition of aims – to 'eliminate the paradox of poverty in the midst of plenty by opening to everyone the opportunity to live in decency and dignity' – and the resounding Presidential proclamations that accompanied it. But a close association was explicit in the

---

[1] The second of which states simply 'This Act does not extend to Northern Ireland' (s. 2 (2)). The exemption was thoughtless – in the strict sense that it was done mechanically, for constitutional reasons; but the time was to come when it would be regretted.

exchange that Callaghan had with Sir Edward Boyle, leading for the Opposition; both men agreed that the American parallel was instructive and Callaghan revealed that a Home Office official was actually in the United States attempting to profit from it. Connections were also implied in the emphasis on the problems of unmet need. In his opening statement Callaghan had referred to needs which 'are felt by citizens who are incapable of matching the requirements of the situation, [which] create apathy, and the apathy then gives rise to further needs'. The problem, Callaghan implied, was one of delivery. The Home Secretary's attempts to put the final quietus on the question of the significance of immigration was less successful. 'It would be wrong,' he said, 'to assume that all areas in which immigrants are concentrated represent areas of acute social need. We have not hit upon this programme as a means of dealing with any aspect in particular but the problem caused by the inflow of immigrants. It is a programme designed to meet the needs of the poorest, whatever their colour.'

Conservative Members present were patently not convinced and pressed the issue of immigration control strongly during the ensuing debate. Nor did Callaghan set at rest the anxieties of those who were anxious to expand the scope of the programme and give it a different emphasis, critics who argued, as Robert Holman of Birmingham University had done in *New Society*, that there was a need for 'non-institutionalized organizations, dependent not on local authority funds, but on local involvement, an acceptance of conflict strategy and an insistence upon "rights"'. This line of criticism assumed greater importance as the lines on which the government were proceeding gradually became clearer. Meanwhile the legislation passed through Parliament without difficulty.

Selection of areas for aid was the theme uppermost in the Circular issued once the Act had become law; it launched the second phase of the programme. The Circular offered expanded scope of the initial programme to teacher centres, language classes, educational material and family advice centres. Housing, it was suggested, might be tackled in the course of a later stage of the programme. Meanwhile the re-

sources made available were once again extremely limited –
on this occasion £4·5 million. Altogether, the implication of
this second Circular was that the development of a programme had not proceeded very far. But the difficulty which
was assuming greater significance, as the switch in emphasis
away from a programme designed to deal specifically with the
problems of immigrants took effect, was the question of finding alternative criteria for selection. The Circular was therefore devoted, in part, to following what proved to be a blind
alley – the attempt to devise a rigorously scientific basis of
selecting the areas for grant aid.

When, in October 1969, the draughtsmen of the British
initiatives came to a formal interchange of views with their
American colleagues, they were able to present a coherent
picture of a programme in the course of evolution. The occasion for the interchange was a gathering at Ditchley Park,
Oxfordshire, the Anglo-American conference centre frequently employed for quasi-official interchange of views, experiences and prejudices. The Home Office paper for the
meeting painted a consistent picture which deftly concealed
the internal debate that had been taking place. The Urban
Programme, its author stated, 'is not an immigrants' programme but a programme mainly concerned with urban
need wherever it exists'. Immigrants might well be a component in such a programme, 'but they could never form
more than a limited part of the programme as a whole'. The
account given of the programme laid stress on what the
Home Office considered to be the specific distinguishing
characteristics of the programme: the capacity to deliver assistance rapidly, to reach the roots of social need, and to be
experimental. In such an approach the determining role of
central government, with its power to approve of grant aid,
was stressed.

At the same time, problems of identifying areas for receipt
of aid still preoccupied the Home Office. The Ditchley paper
reflects this: the question of devising indicators of need was
discussed at length. In the course of this discussion an em-
barrassing discovery had been made. Although indices had
been developed, with the aid of data derived from the 1966
census, it had proved impossible to devise a method which

would allocate sufficient aid on this basis to areas outside London. When attempts were made to assess the problems of Wolverhampton and other West Midland boroughs through the use of these indices, rather than on the basis of the presence of blacks, 'the differences between these areas and London were sufficient for their maps to look unacceptably clear of deprivation'. Thereafter this particular problem was resolved by reverting to a system whereby local authorities identified areas for assistance on a rule-of-thumb basis and central government rubber-stamped their decisions. This change sets the seal on the move away from an immigrants' programme to an urban poverty programme, in which the basic aim would be to spread benefits evenly over as many areas as possible, on political as well as social grounds.

III. EMPHASIZING COMMUNITY ACTION

From this point onwards in the life of the Urban Programme another theme began to assume increasing significance – community development, This took the tangible form of the Community Development Projects (CDP), established in 1969. CDP was initially intended to deal with problems of deprivation, defined on a geographical basis, on the assumption that more of the same, in terms of simply providing additional resources, would not itself solve those problems. The areas selected were intended to release the potential for self-help in the community affected, in part by closing the gap between need and demand caused by inadequate communications.

Marris and Rein, in their introduction to the revised edition of *Dilemmas of Social Reform*, lay particular emphasis on the American influence on this new departure. 'The CDP projects promoted by the Home Office', they argue, 'set out explicitly – on a much smaller scale – to imitate the American experiment, with all its evident virtues and hidden contradictions.' But they also detect the influence of a number of strands of thought about social policy in Britain: concern about the disparity between needs and resources, the pressure for greater efficiency in delivery of services, and the desire for increased participation. This new approach also reflected the influence of a civil servant, Derek Morell, on the evolution of official thinking on this subject, and represented, in departmental terms, the incorporation of earlier thinking within the Department of Education and Science into the general thinking on the Urban Programme. More particularly, the line of thought initially developed in the Plowden Report, with its emphasis on the need for positive discrimination in favour of areas affected by multiple deprivation, was carried over into the planning of CDP. In part this was the result of the involvement of an Oxford sociologist, A. H. Halsey, who had been responsible for developing the educational priority areas demonstration programme which stemmed from the Plowden Report.

After the launching of CDP, the Urban Programme proper began to sink back into providing (in the Home Secretary's words) a 'useful supplement' to the government's existing programmes for schools, housing, health and welfare (see Table 1). Launching the third phase of the programme in

TABLE 1

PHASES OF THE URBAN PROGRAMME IN ENGLAND
AND WALES

	Phase 1	Phase 2	Phase 3	Phase 4	Phase 5
Date approvals announced	Jan 1969	June 1969	Jan 1971	Aug 1971	Nov 1971
Amount	£3·5m	£4·5m	£5m	£450,000	£5m
Type	Capital schemes	Capital/ non-capital	Capital/ non-capital	Non-capital	Capital only
Number of successful authorities	33	89	107	93	26
Number of separate projects	199	515	530	263	102

Source: T. and G. South, 'Urban First Aid', *New Society*, 30 Dec 1971.

May 1970, James Callaghan could reasonably claim that the programme had been 'generally welcomed by local authorities and social workers alike'. Callaghan was also able to announce that the programme had been extended to 1976 and the funds made available increased to £40 million. Participa-

tion of voluntary associations in the programme was also
provided for, although the main emphasis remained on nursery schools, day nurseries and play-groups. More important,
the participation of voluntary organizations in the schemes
was subject to vetting and approval by the local authority in
whose area the proposed scheme would be undertaken.

IV. AMERICAN PARALLELS REVISITED

As CDP got under way, the validity of the American experience as a model became increasingly questionable. Certainly,
the lessons to be drawn were mixed, to say the least. If the
initially naïve hopes of the architects of the Poverty Program
that underprivilege could be drowned in a flood of government expenditure had not survived the revelations of waste
and inefficiency that dogged the programme from the mid-
1960s onwards and the debilitating effect of the Vietnam war,
confidence in the capacity of the poor to organize their own
salvation remained alive far longer. What Sar Levitan calls,
in *The Great Society's Poor Law*, the 'great society's numbers
game' – the fervent claims to have reached solutions to the
problems of poverty by manipulating statistics about incomes
– fell into disrepute fairly early on. Even the most favoured
of all programmes, the Headstart program, lost a degree of
credibility when the first evaluation by the Westinghouse
Corporation showed that children who had passed through
Headstart programs were not appreciably better off as a result than equally disadvantaged children who had not. But
the second line of defence, the assertion that the Poverty Program had provided the opportunity for the poor to participate in decisions that affected their lives, proved hardier. It
was a reassertion of the basic American virtues of self-help on
the new frontier of the city.

There was nothing fundamentally new about this approach to poverty. Saul Alinsky had pioneered it during the
1930s, though in very different circumstances. In his *Reveille
for Radicals* (1946) he refers to the 'dirty, monotonous, heart-
breaking job of building people's organizations', which can
only be achieved by 'possessing the infinite patience and faith
to hang on as part of the organization disintegrates; to re-

build, add on, and continue to build'. Programmes like his had a heavy emphasis on the practical obstacles, on the lack of resources and on the capacity of organizers to survive intimidation and other setbacks. The emphasis in the community action programmes of the 1960s was rather different. The responsibility for providing funds and devising programmes rested not with the poor or with the dedicated community organizers to which Alinsky referred, but with federal agencies under whose benign wing community organizations could now operate. Hence the curious paradox by which the Black Panthers came to birth in a Poverty Program local office in Oakland, California – and the incredulity of the older city bosses who found themselves in a situation where one level of government was financing attacks upon another.

Sometimes the situation that resulted was little short of ludicrous. Tom Wolfe's account of one particular episode is a caricature, but a caricature with a painful kernel of truth. 'Everyone but the most hopeless lames knew that the only job you wanted out of the Poverty Program was a job *in* the Program itself,' he writes in *Maumauing the Flak-Catchers*.

Some of the main heroes in the ghetto, on a par with the Panthers even, were the Blackstone Rangers in Chicago. The Rangers were so bad, the Rangers so terrified the whole youth welfare poverty establishment that in one year, 1968, they got a $937,000 grant from the Office of Economic Opportunity in Washington. The Ranger leaders became job counsellors in the manpower training project even though most of them never had a job before and weren't about to be looking for one. This wasn't a case of the Blackstone Rangers putting some huge prank over on the poverty bureaucrats, however. It was in keeping with the Poverty Program's principle of trying to work through the real leaders of the black community. And if they had to give it the protective coloration of manpower training then that was the way it would have to be done. Certainly there was no-one who could doubt that the Blackstone Rangers were the most powerful group in the Woodlawn area of Chicago. They had the whole place terrified. The Rangers were too much. They were champions.

There is a legitimate question about whether these pro-grammes none the less helped to speed the evolution of black leadership in the ghettos. Saul Alinsky thought not: he char-acterized the community action programmes as 'political pornography', promising what they could not deliver, and de-rided the black leaders who emerged as a result as 'Uncle Talk-Toughs'. Robert Levine is less sure. He refers lyrically to 'Social, economic and political institutions [that] prolifer-ate and flower in a tangled undergrowth so thick it is impos-sible to find a way through without a seeing guide'. More soberly, he argues that there are 'clear indications of institu-tional change' resulting from the activities of community ac-tion projects; perhaps a moderate type of confrontation does pay off. In perhaps the subtlest analysis of the Poverty Pro-gram as a whole that has yet been published, *Regulating the Poor*, Frances Fox Piven and Richard A. Cloward argue a different case. In their view Great Society programmes were 'managerial politics', designed to 'prod the local Democratic Party machinery to cultivate the allegiance of urban black voters by extending a greater share of municipal services to them, and to do this without alienating urban white voters'. The chief function of community action projects was to 'facilitate the chanelling of blacks into the electoral system'; in this they were generally speaking successful.

Limitations on resources and different demographic pat-terns would in any case rule out such an attempt in Britain. The restricted scope of the Urban Programme also carried another, rather different implication. It ensured that the pro-gramme did not become an election issue in mid-1970, when Britain, too, passed through a change of government. From the point of view of the survival of the programme, this was fortunate: the advocacy of even a very moderate degree of conflict through local community action would have been un-likely to command approval from a Conservative government that had chosen to campaign on behalf of law and order. But after the Conservative victory in the general election, the main lines laid down for the Urban Programme by the Lab-our government were followed with virtually no adjustment. Initial confusion about the extent to which the government could trade off the Urban Programme against increased

severity of immigration control was succeeded by the implementation of the third phase of the programme without
modification, and the growth of community development
projects continued unchecked.

Criticism of the initial definition of priorities for the
Community Development Project began to grow. In *Socially
Deprived Families in Britain* (1970), Robert Holman argued that 'The CDP is the part of the British poverty programme with room to promote different forms of community
work to meet social deprivation. This it has failed to do.' To
the extent that the subsequent phases of the Urban Programme itself, launched by the Conservative government,
offered little that was new to supplement the first appearance
of voluntary organizations in the third phase, Holman's criticisms were fully justified. But CDP was passing through a
very rapid evolution. The programme had initially stressed
co-ordination and co-operation, with a particular emphasis on
different local authority services. Four teams began operating
in 1970, in Coventry, Southwark, Liverpool and Glyncorrwg
(Glamorgan), with the eventual expectation of extending the
operation to twelve areas. Each team was to contain both an
action and a research component: as the Home Office's
official description puts it, 'the lessons learnt can then be fed
back into social policy, planning and administration, both at
central and at local government level'. After the reforms introduced into local government structure as a result of the
Seebohm Report on personal social services, there was less
emphasis on vertical division within local authorities and a
correspondingly greater emphasis on trying to involve the
public in decision-making on such issues as the provision of
services for local communities. However, the basic difficulty
of operating within a local authority framework remained. As
one sympathetic critic put it: 'Having to operate by sweet
reason sometimes means that the CDP teams are scarcely able
to operate at all.'

Perhaps more important, after 1970 the CDP teams were
operating in a new climate of opinion. This was compounded
of general disillusionment with orthodox forms of political
action, which affected a large number of those who were involved in the community action field, and a more specific

scepticism about the capacity of central government to solve the problems of the inner city. The initiatives that had been taken in the course of the 1960s were wide-ranging, yet the results were disappointing: the problems of urban poverty demonstrably persisted. Concern with the persistence of these problems and their causes, which had lain at the root of the definition of the programme's goals, remained and even intensified. A sharp controversy raged around the question of the extent to which the Labour government's programmes had been effective in this area; the Child Poverty Action Group, which had been set up specifically to deal with this question, was able to show, through the melancholy device of striking a poverty balance-sheet, that the proportion of those in poverty had continued stubbornly static or might even have shown a slight increase.

In the circumstances, several of the local CDP teams began to evolve new approaches. They set up information centres, conducted local surveys and acted as a channel for local authority grants to community groups and community newspapers. They came to consider their areas of activity as laboratories for working out new programmes which would have wider implications, and even to think in terms of redistribution of political power, in the first instance through the promotion of increased participation in decision-making. The Coventry CDP team have described the assumption behind their revised approach as follows:

> Local government as the major single operator for and on behalf of the community at large must develop an efficient and effective policy-making and planning capability. It can only do this by linking itself into existing communities to discover the needs, to make sure that they are represented and to resolve the inherent conflicts. This can only be achieved by increased communication and participation between local government and the community.

In adopting this approach, the Coventry team were following a course that had become familiar in the United States, though in a less dramatic style.

V. ENVOI

In his influential *Maximum Feasible Misunderstanding* (1969), D. P. Moynihan, who had been heavily involved in the planning stage of the Poverty Program under the Johnson administration (and was shortly to return to Washington as Special Assistant to a Republican President), pours derision on the social scientists, from Cloward and Ohlin onwards, for their part in providing the intellectual underpinning for the programme. As a result of their quite illegitimate claims to provide authoritative advice in areas where social scientists have no particular competence, Moynihan argues, the indigenous white working class found themselves in danger of being offered up as a guilt sacrifice to assuage the misery that these social scientists feel about the sufferings of the black proletariat. 'Social scientists love poor people,' Moynihan reports. 'They also get along fine with rich people (not a few are wealthy themselves, or married to heiresses. In any event, in the 1960s, persons of great wealth have been a major source of support not only for social science research but for radical political activity). But alas, they do not have much time for the people in between.' On their chief allies outside government, the young radicals, the old radical, Saul Alinsky, was tougher still – but then perhaps he had earned the right to be. 'If Lenin were writing about our present far out left,' he comments in his afterthoughts to *Reveille for Radicals*, 'his work would be titled "Left Wing Communism, A Womblike Disorder". They will divide and redivide into multiple cults of fragments in futility.' Neither Moynihan or Alinsky, from their very different perspectives, has any time for attempts to redress the balance of power in city neighbourhoods by channelling resources direct to community organizations and bypassing state and city governments.

All these strands in the American debate have some relevance for Britain. Civil servants paid close attention to the machinery devised for implementing the Poverty Program, and applied the lessons, as they conceived them, in the structure they devised for the Urban Programme, centrally controlled through existing departments, but with a key role played by local authorities and a tight rein kept on the activities of voluntary bodies. Politicians have been sensitive to the possible political lessons of the American experience – Ben Whitaker's Fabian essay, *Participation and Poverty* (1968), is an early example. Within the Urban Programme itself the role of the social scientists had been held in check – though they were present at the creation of the Community Development Project and had much to do with the modifications that have been introduced into it subsequently. Limitations on funding and the constricting devices for allocating those funds that were available has meant that the process that has taken place in the United States, by which black radicals had been equipped with the resources for rebellion by the federal government, has had no parallel in Britain. Even if funds had become available, it is doubtful whether full advantage could have been taken of them by black or brown organizations. As Gordon Lewis argues, the Black Power movement in Britain is still at a confused and uncertain stage in its evolution. Moreover, the constraints imposed by the relatively small size and lack of concentration of the black community in Britain have set additional limits to the prospects of the same processes occurring in this country.

In these circumstances, the kind of dangers against which Moynihan felt it necessary to preach are less relevant, if at all relevant, to Britain. At the same time it is possible to identify certain specific points at which the embryonic movement for community participation in Britain is especially vulnerable to criticism, and there are dangers of money and efforts running into the sand.

For example, there is the belief that often characterizes community action movements that local demands are necessarily to be supported by virtue of their point of origin alone. The recent history of certain local residents' associations in Britain and their resistance to the arrival of black newcomers is strangely neglected by the advocates of community power. What does it profit if there is a responsiveness to local demands, if those demands are selfish or even racist ones? The argument about the balance of the relationship and distribution of power between local and central government is also a real one, with important implications for community action. A Fabian study group (admittedly likely to be *parti pris*) has commented acidly on this problem in *People, Participation and Government*. 'Past experience,' they argue, 'tells us that whereas the central government is inclined to protect the weaker members of the community, the lower down one gets in the hierarchy of authorities, the more parochial and selfish the majority becomes.' In addition, the emphasis on participation tends to obscure the importance of broader factors which may have a decisive influence on the future of local communities – such questions as changing patterns of employment in the inner city. If changes are to be made on this level, they will not be achieved through what David Donnison calls 'micro-politics', but through the existing structures of decision-making.

Yet however deficient some of the arguments deployed may be, there can be no doubt that new channels have been opened as a result of the debates of the past two years, which have infused new life into the argument about the goals of social policy. The range of activities, from the spontaneous action of squatting groups through the half-formed revolt against urban renewal to the formal election of fully fledged neighbourhood councils that have engaged in elaborate community planning exercises: all these developments illustrate the existence of a new climate of opinion. So far has the pendulum swung that a well-known firm of property developers (in as one-sided a sellers' market as this century has seen) feels it necessary to emphasize to potential purchasers that 'In every project, we participate with our customers, from arranging meet-your-neighbour parties to the encouragement of residents' associations'. All this goes far wider than the activity that has taken place under the specific heading of the Community Development Project: but the various processes are complementary and flow into one another.

In another critique of the Urban Programme, Robert Holman argued that the only ultimate justification for the programme would be to return a measure of power to the inhabitants of underprivileged areas. Power is an infinitely elusive concept. Peter Marris has suggested that one crucial ingredient in influencing decision-making is knowledge:

If we extend the right to be heard, to submit evidence and

present argument, to all manner of decisions which affect the communities of the city; if this right is backed by the power to challenge proposals which ignore the evidence; and if the professional skills needed to prepare and present evidence are available to rich and poor alike – then the balance of power will change, because information is itself a form of power. New information alters the context in which a decision is taken – the perception of the problem, the arguments to be answered, the claims to be met. I am not thinking so much of formal hearings, as the informal meetings and circulation of papers through which a decision evolves. The more actors to whom this process is open, the wider the network of consultation, the more democratic the discussion becomes: and if officials know that their decisions may be challenged, and they will have to defend them, they prepare them more carefully.

These are also the objectives of some, at least, of those who are now involved in the community development programmes.

The kind of approach epitomized in the creation and evolution of programmes like CDP is often caricatured as 'disjointed incrementalism', a process of carrying all parties and shades of opinion in a crabwise progression. Infuriating though it often seems, it is a technique that can often secure effective gains. As Michael Cassidy argues: 'It appears to be a good deal easier politically to launch a new small special programme, relating to some newly defined need, and to add to its fundings incrementally over a period, than to replace a programme by a new big comprehensive one.'

Yet a doubt remains: was an opportunity missed in Britain in 1968? Could policy-makers have profited more fully from American mistakes? It can be argued that the experience of the years since demonstrate only that the British situation is fundamentally dissimilar from the American; that the role of central government and the attitudes of citizens alike are too widely different for the parallel to have any real significance, in terms of the practical tasks of devising policies. Clearly there is something in this; but the better view seems to me to be that there were fundamental similarities about the problems facing the two societies, and that the British government found themselves attempting to deal with them in very much the same kind of context, albeit in a style that was 'more tentative, unassuming and diffuse', to employ the government's own phrase.

If the parallel is accepted, why did the measures that were adopted fail to meet the case? Four main reasons suggest themselves. First, the identification of the main focus for action. The original emphasis on race relations can be criticized from a variety of different perspectives, but it had the merit of simplicity, and of focusing attention on a social problem area where the expenditure of funds of the order available might have made a perceptible difference to the situation. As it is, funds have been spread thinly across a wide range of projects, and expenditure has not always been well co-ordinated. Meanwhile, the government spends more on the immigration-control system than it does on agencies designed to promote integration.

Second, there is the decision not to establish a separate agency to administer the programme. The objections to the establishment of *ad hoc* bodies are well known: they tend to be the object of suspicion within Whitehall, and to lack the status and facilities of an established department, which can be vital when conducting negotiations about resources. But it remains surprising that a Labour administration, which was prepared to consider the establishment of separate agencies in other fields, closed their mind so firmly in this case, despite the American precedent. Linked with this was the decision to allocate a central role to local authorities, and to allow voluntary organizations to participate only with local government consent.

Third, and perhaps most important of all, is the question of resources. The amount of funds made available to the programme was quite simply inadequate, by any standards, to make any direct impact on the root causes of poverty. In these circumstances the Urban Programme was rapidly reduced to the role of an occasional source of supplementary funding: useful in certain contexts, but too often of little more than symbolic value. An alternative purpose might have been served if the programme had been undertaken as a demonstration project; but here the fourth failing becomes relevant – the absence of systematic means of monitoring and feeding back results. The programme was neither the subject of rigorous evaluation by social scientists, nor was it made accountable, in a more basic sense, to the population whose needs it was intended to meet. A programme that had been subjected to this kind of scrutiny might have become a more flexible one, and more responsive to local community needs. It is significant that in the exceptional case of CDP, where both these factors were present, the programme passed through a rapid series of evolutions and became in several individual cases genuinely innovatory. As Hilary Rose suggests in her pamphlet *Rights, Participation and Conflict,* it might have served as a focus for the whole series of activities grouped together under the broad title of the 'welfare rights movement'.

It would be wrong to end on a wholly critical note. Despite the missed opportunities, and the lessons not properly assimilated, or wrongly applied, the series of activities that makes up Britain's miniature poverty programme has, in the first years of its existence, produced measurable progress towards goals that are of fundamental significance for this society. As Marris and Rein conclude in their own review: 'Through all the disappointments, the false starts and turning back, there appears at the end the uncertain outline of a subtler and more sensitive pattern of government, where people will be at once more in control of their own affairs, and better able to legislate for a common good.'

A NOTE ON READING AND ACKNOWLEDGEMENTS

There is a copious literature on the Poverty Program, of which I have found the following particularly useful: Sar A. Levitan, *The Great Society's Poor Law* (Baltimore: Johns Hopkins Press, 1969); T. R. Marmor, *Poverty Policy* (Chicago: Aldine, 1971); R. A. Levine, *The Poor Ye Need Not Have with You* (Cambridge, Mass.: MIT Press, 1970); and F. Reissman, *Strategies against Poverty* (New York: Random House, 1969). Daniel Moynihan's views are in his *Maximum Feasible Misunderstanding* (New York: Free Press, 1969); a very different interpretation is Frances Fox Piven and Richard A. Cloward's *Regulating the Poor* (New York: Vintage Books, 1971). Indispensable background reading in this context is Peter Marris and Martin Rein, *Dilemmas of Social Reform*, 2nd ed. (London: Routledge & Kegan Paul, 1972), which makes explicit connections between the British and American situations.

By contrast, the literature on Britain is sparse. Robert Holman's important criticisms can be found in his article 'The Wrong Poverty Programme', *New Society*, 20 Mar 1969, and in *Socially Deprived Families in Britain* (London: Bedford Square Press, 1970). There is a useful factual description in T. and G. Smith's essay 'Urban First Aid', *New Society*, 30 Dec 1971, and a polemical review in *Community Action*, 1, 3 (July–Aug 1972). The publications of the Coventry CDP are of very considerable interest; the Home Office issues a brief information sheet ('Notes on the Urban Programme'). The Child Poverty Action Group have issued a great deal of relevant material (obtainable from 1 Macklin Street, Drury Lane, London WC2). There are also a number of Fabian tracts that are of relevance, notably Anne Lapping (ed.), *Community Action* (Tract 400). The report of the Educational Promotion Area project, A. H. Halsey (ed.), *Education Priority* (London: HMSO, 1972) is also helpful.

Apart from these published sources, Michael Cassidy and Peter Marris have allowed me to draw on unpublished material. Peter Marris also commented very helpfully on an earlier draft of the paper. I am most grateful to him. Maree Ley typed the successive versions of an increasingly lengthy paper: my thanks to her too.

This paper began at a seminar given at the Adlai Stevenson Institute of International Affairs, Chicago, in April 1972. I am grateful to Professor William R. Polk and the Fellows of the Institute for stimulating me into further thought and activity.

10 The Welfare State: The Costs of American Self-Sufficiency

HUGH HECLO

Research Associate, The Brookings Institution

When non-Americans complain about Americanization overtaking many areas of their lives, they rarely refer to social policy. United States welfare programmes are not an object of envy or imitation elsewhere in the world. Quite the opposite. Complaints are far more likely to be heard from Americans that their national policies are being 'socialized' (i.e. Europeanized) in ways inconsistent with native virtues. In caricature, these virtues teach that hard work by individuals supplies acquisitive rewards and personal independence; education opens opportunity for better work rewards; limited, divided government guarantees the competitive underpinning for individual opportunity and work; and that all this ought to be enough for anybody. Welfare is equated with antipoverty measures and treated as an affair requiring a neat, technical solution for those special residual groups that cannot succeed in the work–education competition. Americans, as the phrases go, stand on their own two feet; they pay their own way. In essence, the challenge confronting the American welfare state is to extract social equity from a credo of homogenized individualism and pulverized government.

Since the first colonial protests against British taxation, Americans have derived satisfaction from the uniqueness of their social experiment and, although occasionally lapsing into charitable hopes, usually have not expected other nations to re-create their example. Economic and social planning have been requirements deemed suitable for applicants seeking foreign aid, not for the benefactor. Having lacked the American constitutional and frontier experience, foreigners tend to be forgiven if they cannot see the presumed identity between freedom, individual independence and personal self-sufficiency. Since the domestic disturbances of the mid-1960s, self-satisfaction has had to compete with self-flagellation. But both beaters and strokers of the national social conscience retain a faith in its virtues: the land of the common man is and must be more than a common nation. America's social failings are often seen as arising from more widespread phenomena: the nature of modern life, technological maturity, post-industrial society and so on. Complaints but not virtues are exportable to other nations. If there is a lesson for others in all this, it is that pride in uniqueness and self-sufficiency yields its own social retribution; no one elsewhere need feel obliged or destined to share the resulting penalties.

I. THE MARKET FOR WELFARE

The United States, like Britain, completed initial industrialization prior to any major government involvement with workers' welfare. In both nations, liberal conceptions of a capitalist market prevailed over the more paternalistic state welfarism found in industrializing Continental nations. Unlike Britain the United States has only tardily and partially adopted forms of collective state protection, maintaining a strong sense of inherent contradiction between individual self-fulfilment and overt public action on social policy. Today it is still easy to overestimate the role of the federal government in what are regarded elsewhere as standard welfare programmes. Old-age pensions and unemployment insurance, initiated in 1908 and 1911 in Britain, were not enacted by Washington until 1935; the British sickness benefit scheme of 1911 finds no American counterpart until Medicare in 1966; the family allowances instituted in Britain in 1945 have not been accepted; lagging over a generation behind Britain, American benefits for the non-aged disabled began only in 1956. Even then, disability benefits require permanent and total incapacitation for work and a six-month waiting period for benefit.

When federal programmes finally have been instituted, their contents often demonstrate a willingness to trade full coverage of risk for self-help and state or local control. Of all the programmes in the 1935 Social Security Act (the first and last major landmark in national income maintenance), contributory old-age pensions alone established uniform national standards. Federal support for public relief covers only particular categories of clients – aged, blind or disabled adults, as well as single mothers with dependent children – and has applied very few nationwide standards. Only in January 1974 did Washington undertake a potentially important innovation when it acquired full responsibility for administering and financing cash relief payments to blind, disabled and aged adults in need. Financed from general taxation and run by the only national administrative organ available, the Social Security [national insurance] Administration, the new programme establishes the first uniform relief scales, but only for three categories of persons. Benefits for these individuals and couples are still pegged well below the official 1974 poverty line, and no additional grants are provided for dependants in the family.

Health insurance (Medicare) in the United States applies almost exclusively to the elderly; while making hospital insurance compulsory, it leaves insurance for physicians' services voluntary and gives preferential regard to administration through private insurance companies. State-run, federally financed Medicaid pays medical professionals for some health costs of the 'medically indigent'. But in almost all states it excludes the working poor, and by requiring the recipient to be not only needy but also in a category eligible for public relief, Medicaid effectively limits coverage to the impoverished aged, disabled, blind, and lone mothers with children; in half the states unemployed men and their families are excluded.

While most countries maintain the contributory principle in social insurance (i.e. financing some portion of benefit costs through separate, earmarked taxes), American social security since 1935 has been particularly zealous in upholding a supposed relationship between individual contributions and benefits. The explicit and overriding aim in doing so has been to demonstrate that protection, while collectively organized, is provided to an American by his own efforts. As one result, the first social insurance benefits were not paid until 1940. A longer-term result has been complacency towards

minimum social insurance benefits, which go disproportion-
ately to women, racial minorities and one-person households.
American social security, like most nations' social insurance
schemes, is intended to provide both minimum anti-poverty
benefits and replacement income related to previous earnings. But American policy has usually emphasized the latter
at the expense of the former. Improvements in basic insurance benefits have been deemed to require comparable increases in the higher, earnings-related benefits for the better
off. A threefold difference (depending on previous earnings
and length of insurance) persists between minimum and
maximum social security pensions; minimum benefits, going
to a minority of recipients, are also meagre compared to
counterparts in many other developed nations. Minimum old-
age pensions in the early 1960s, for example, were 19 per cent
of *per capita* consumer spending of the aged in the United
States, compared to a comparable 49 per cent for Swedish and
62 per cent for British minimum pensions (before need-tested
supplements); such basic pension benefit was 9 per cent of
average manufacturing earnings in the United States, compared to 18 per cent in France and Britain (before need-
tested supplements) and 32 per cent in Belgium.

Moreover, America's complete reliance on financing social
insurance benefits via a uniform percentage payroll tax
(euphemistically termed insurance premiums) has hit the
lowest paid hardest, since the same effective tax rate applies
to all earners at or below the poverty line but ceases at
higher income ranges. Probably well over one-half of American taxpayers in 1973 paid more in social security contributions than in personal income tax; the combined bite of
both taxes (disregarding property income and tax loopholes,
both of which benefit the better off) for a family of two rose
from a uniform 11 per cent of wages and salaries at the lowest
earning levels to 24 per cent at $10,800 income, then declined
slightly and did not return to 24 per cent until the $23,000
income level was reached. But by excluding any government
contribution from general tax revenue, American social security has demonstrated, as Franklin Roosevelt approvingly
observed, that it does not tax wealth to support workers' incomes. By rigorously maintaining benefit differentials and

myths of individualized insurance, American social security reconfirms notions of personal self-sufficiency. It also helps conceal the fact that current contributions are financing cash payments to almost 20 million persons who are not working and whose own past contributions were only a fraction (much less than one-quarter in most cases) of the value of the pension they have 'earned' upon retirement.

Most central governments probably seem remote from their citizens, but a foreigner finds it difficult to imagine how almost invisible is American national government outside Washington. An American having face-to-face dealings with his federal government is far more likely to encounter an FBI man or tax inspector than an agent of the welfare state. As far as most clients might know, the Social Security Administration exists only in the postbox. In subsidizing social programmes – from health care to cash relief for unmarried mothers – the national government has traditionally worked through state and local government agencies, where it is specifically constrained to exercise even less control over personnel than over benefit standards. The two dozen largest federally funded income-support programmes are under the jurisdiction of eleven federal agencies, ten House and nine Senate congressional committees, and usually involve as well innumerable state and local authorities in administration and control. Independence among public authorities as well as among individuals is a prized feature of America's welfare-state patchwork. Threads of financial inducement between public authorities comprise the fabric of national social policy. Occasionally state administration is induced by financial threat; unemployment insurance, for example, was spread nationwide after 1935 by creating a national tax which could be offset only if states introduced their own programmes. But in such cases substantial local autonomy in benefit rates typically has led states to compete in offering lower payroll taxes and less adequate programmes. More aggressive threats to cut federal funds are usually unproductive, inasmuch as they jeopardize clients more than state officials.

Bribery, the pull of new money, rather than the threatened loss of old funds, is the more typical inducement to action. Often the commitment behind changes in state and local policy is little more than an urge to shape social programmes so as to maximize federal financial contributions. Thus, the major factor behind the more than doubled federal expenditure on social services from 1971 to 1972 was a rearrangement of state programmes (probation, family planning, services to the aged and children) to take advantage of Washington's open-ended commitment to pay 75 per cent of costs. In the market-place where federal, state and local governments meet, other welfare programmes (such as work training, day-care centres, aid for dependent children of the unemployed) have led to meagre state and local action unless and until Washington has assumed an ever-increasing share of the cost. A few programmes (commodity distribution, food stamps for the poor, housing relief) have had full federal financing except for administrative costs. Until 1974 the only cash relief programme for which the federal government has assumed full responsibility for standards, funding and personal administration of benefits to clients was veterans' assistance. Means-tested relief for veterans and their survivors generally offers the highest benefits and easiest, least stigmatizing eligibility conditions of any form of American cash relief; almost $2\frac{1}{2}$ billion a year is paid to almost 3 million persons, of whom about two-thirds are veterans, widows or children. At the other extreme, but perhaps more representative of American policy, is workmen's compensation. Although the first such national laws were passed in Europe by the beginning of the twentieth century, workmen's compensation in America remains a state government responsibility; coverage commenced in Wisconsin in 1911 and reached Mississippi by 1949. With virtually no federal standards of funding, workmen's compensation in 1972 left uncovered 15 per cent of the labour force, usually those in the greatest need; at least one-fifth of the states lacked full coverage for occupational diseases and in most states the maximum payment for a family of four fell well below what is defined as the absolute poverty line.

Does all this mean that the United States is somehow less of a welfare state than, say, Britain? The answer depends on how we choose to use words. In its most general definition, there is little to distinguish the welfare state from Aristotle's conception of good government, that is, a policy whose governors rule in the interests of the governed rather than their own interest. Americans, like everyone else, favour well-being over ill-being. A more useful tack is to treat the welfare state as a collective noun identifying the legacy of largely improvised reactions by practical men to everyday social problems as they have arisen. Its philosophy and ethic consists, not in a kernel of meaning embedded in an abstract concept, but in that bundle of rough-and-ready interventions actually being carried out by each government. Britain and the United States are welfare states because they are interventionist democracies seeking to affect the social conditions of their peoples. Nations differ in how they act, not whether they act. In this interventionist era the relevant question is not 'Is it a welfare issue?' but 'Whose welfare is at stake?'

British and American welfare states are in practice extensive, often implicit, and occasionally accidental creations. Each nation is subject to the myth of deliberation, the notion that social interventions by government comprise a self-consciously willed whole. Nothing could be farther from the truth. Government programmes appear confused and tangled to the man in the street because they *are* confused and tangled, not because devious middlemen have subverted clear and over-arching purpose. The most deliberate interventions are likely to centre on programmes aimed at the poor, but even these usually entail unforeseen second- and third-order consequences. Other public choices affect social conditions without anyone directly deciding or choosing. Welfare considerations arise not only from questions of who *gets* what, when and how, but also from who *gives* what, when, and how. Benefits consist not only of positive grants received but also of costs avoided by shifting them on to other shoulders.

Four common elements, arranged in somewhat differing patterns, can be identified in the British and American welfare states: *entrepreneurial, contractual, fiscal* and *social* interventions. The most direct role is entrepreneurial, the state as employer of private citizens. In each nation public employment provides a direct or indirect livelihood for between one-quarter and one-fifth of the entire labour force. A large chunk of the labour market is indirectly supported through contractual arrangements for government business, with nationalized industries in Britain and defence and aerospace suppliers in America being responsible for much of this activity. The state's position looms even larger in terms of the more skilled portion of the labour force, supporting over half of all Britons with full-time higher education. The 1970 United States Census found government employing almost two-fifths of all 'professional, technical and kindred' workers, while many others were indirectly occupied through contracts and grants. The dependence of academics was amply demonstrated by the anguish which occurred at the end of the 1960s when the 22 per cent per annum post-war growth rate in federal support for academic science began to be trimmed.

A second element of the welfare state consists of public regulation and indirect support for social provision through the mini-welfare states of private enterprise. From private retirement pensions through workers' club-rooms to job safety and building standards, the state can be found helping arrange a host of supposedly private contractual conditions affecting workers' well-being. The forms of intervention can range from legislating minimum wage requirements to enforcing fringe-benefit agreements through the common law. This contractual intervention shades into the third element of state welfare activity: fiscal succour. Tax revenues are forgone to support some groups and activities but not others; artifically low interest rates, credit resources biased towards the better off, cheap insurance and loan guarantees accomplish much the same purpose. Only slowly has awareness grown that revenue forgone by special exceptions is as much a part of state support as is direct expenditure for social services. Many writers have assumed, for example, that the United States is somehow less of a welfare state than Britain because it cannot match the British effort at building and subsidizing low-cost public housing. Recent studies have shown that, on the contrary, United States public aid to housing is immense but that its major form is the $10 billion (in 1970) in tax relief to home-owners, with low-cost public housing lagging far behind. The Aid for Dependent Children and Food Stamp programmes were budgeted to cost Washington approximately $4 billion in direct expenditures in 1974, but revenue forgone through favourable tax treatment of private pension plans, life insurance savings and charitable contributions cost over $8 billion to the federal budget. Special opportunities to avoid income reduction through taxation not only benefit some rather than others, but also implicitly shift and increase the burden on to those who do pay. It is estimated that without the erosion of federal income tax through exclusions, exemptions and so on, the same tax revenue yield could be collected with tax rates at least one-third lower than those now in effect. All such cases of fiscal succour can be interpreted as welfare measures; the hidden question is 'Whose welfare?'

The fourth and final element of the welfare state in Britain and America is that familiar array of social programmes providing direct and overt services or cash transfers in health, housing, education, public assistance and so on. While many of these activities are traditionally identified with the welfare state, in terms of manpower and cost they are probably easily surpassed by the entrepreneurial, contractual and fiscal aspects of state intervention. Other subsidies, such as farm supports or industrial aid, are advanced for political or economic rather than social equity reasons. In 1969, for example, the largest fifth of American farmers (in terms of their sales), with an average income of $21,000, received about two-thirds of government farm subsidies; the smallest half got 9 per cent of total benefits.

All nations confuse the relations among entrepreneurial, contractual, fiscal and social welfare. But pervasive assumptions of self-help in the United States make it particularly easy to overlook the undeliberate mixture of welfare forms. The myth of deliberation readily co-exists with the myth of dependency: the idea that the population may be neatly divided into those who are independent and those who are dependent on the state. Supposedly, the dependants are those who participate in overt, self-declared assistance programmes, especially public cash relief. In fact an immense proportion of the population lives in a protective cocoon of indulgences, subsidies, privileges and accommodations often supplied at others' expense – benefits protective not only against privation but often against no more than marginal discomfort.

The difference in degree of dependence is hardly self-evident
between the single mother receiving public assistance, free
medical care and welfare milk, versus the rugged individualist dependent only on the Revenue Code for subsidizing his
otherwise too costly home, state-enforced credit regulations
to multiply his purchasing power, tax indulgences for his
lucrative retirement plan and expense account, and government planning agencies to make others bear social costs at-
tendant on his right to drive a large car into the city centre
with a minimum of inconvenience. Nor do notions of social
exchange and contributions in return for benefits offer any
firm basis for distinguishing dependent groups. While
many of the overt welfare dependants may not contribute
through income taxation, many also pay a larger proportion
of their income through regressive indirect and payroll taxes
than do higher income earners. Less able to acquire credit or
regular cost-of-living adjustments for their incomes, the
poorer are also likely to bear the front-line costs of fighting
inflation, of relocating for urban renewal or of making up the
revenue gaps created by tax loopholes for others. If empiri-
cally applicable at all, the idea of 'more' versus 'less' social dependence applies to the fact that some citizens rely on state
support for physical subsistence while others live in dependent abundance. It is not necessarily a matter for self-congratulation among the better off.

II. POLICY ASSUMPTIONS

The most distinctive features of the American welfare state
arise in terms of what is and is not taken for granted about
state intervention. In America, social policy tends to be
equated with anti-poverty programmes, i.e. aid to those below
a given income line. 'Welfare' is even more narrowly conceived as cash relief payments, and a smattering of services,
for distinctive administrative categories of the needy. In Britain, government provision tends more often to be seen as a
policy aimed at a shifting and inclusive body of citizens, almost any of whom might be at risk at one time or another.
The British National Health Service is probably the best-
known example. Of course, neither Britain's nor any other

nation's policies can be administered without subdividing clients, and empathy among social groups is everywhere at a premium. But precisely for such reasons it is important that a public philosophy be broad enough to accommodate competing views, including views that interpret social policy as a collective facility expressing common membership in the community. Little room for such an outlook exists within an ethic of self-sufficiency.

The American organization of social policy both reflects and promotes the sectionalization of people and rigid attitudes towards social dependency. The bulk of welfare-state interventions are interpreted as separate, semi-economic exchanges bargained out in the political market-place. Not only are fiscal, contractual and entrepreneurial activities seen as economic rather than also social interventions; overt social programmes themselves compartmentalize groups in terms of dependence and non-dependence. Some, such as social security recipients, veterans and their dependants, are taken to be getting what they paid for or earned. Others in separate poverty and relief programmes are the dependants of social policy, the 'them' who are helped by 'us'. In fact, despite the late beginnings and fragmentary nature of American welfare activity, an immense body of direct social provision has grown up; in 1973 probably over one-quarter of the American population was participating in some federally aided income-support programme. This patchwork of activities is by now the largest component of national public spending, an estimated two-fifths (or $102 billion) of the total 1973 federal budget compared to 30 per cent (or $77 billion) going for defence. This national spending for direct income support to citizens is divided into a variety of direct programmes (Table 1).

If the numbers spoke for themselves, one might imagine that at least as much concern would be aroused by retirement and related expenditure as by the $16 billion in public assistance. In the early 1970s benefit outlays for non-means-tested programmes were approximately three times those for means-tested programmes, although the number of Americans benefiting was about the same (25 to 30 million) within both types of programme. While undertaking a major foreign war, the nation has increased its yearly spending on social security benefits and health insurance for the elderly from $16 billion in 1964 to $60 billion by the time 1972 increases come into full effect. Yet despite these immense outlays, it would be difficult to imagine a system yielding a smaller social return – a lesser sense of shared community values, social solidarity and achievement – from the spending of so much public

TABLE 1

FEDERAL GOVERNMENT DIRECT SPENDING FOR
INCOME SUPPORT: 1973 BUDGET ESTIMATES
($ billion)

Retirement and related:		$72·6
Veterans' compensation and pensions	$6·4	
Military retirement and medical benefits	5·1	
Civil service retirement	3·9	
Railroad retirement	2·1	
Old-age, survivors, and disability insurance	44·7	
Medicare	10·4	
Unemployment compensation		5·9
Public assistance and related:		16·1
Aged, disabled and blind	2·8	
Families with dependent children	4·7	
Medicaid	3·8	
Food stamps	2·3	
Other nutrition	0·7	
Housing subsidies	1·8	
Other:		7·1
Student aid	3·4	
Farm price supports	3·7	
Total benefits		101·7

Source: Charles Schultze, *Setting National Priorities* (1972) Table 6-1.

money. The American poor law emphasizes the division of people into programmes rather than programmes into human needs. Since the different programmes imply that recipients have either failed or succeeded in living up to ideals of personal independence, the division also implies categories of personal worth. It is the small sub-group of dependants, the 'them' receiving cash public assistance payments, who have engendered the feeling in America that there is a welfare crisis. To appreciate the full costs of self-sufficiency, we should look more closely at American conceptions of welfare and poverty.

American professors who periodically descend on London

to find out 'what is going on in British welfare' are not abnormally energetic, only culture-bound. Similarly, an outsider who has heard about vehement American debates since the mid-1960s on the 'welfare crisis' and 'welfare reform' is likely to be perplexed by the absence of even significant pretensions towards general social policy. Welfare debates have concerned cash relief to the poor and little more. To most Americans the substance of their 'welfare crisis' is the fact that the numbers receiving maintenance payments, and thus the costs of relief, continued to grow rapidly during the 1960s. The datum invariably cited is the fact that welfare rolls and costs tripled during the decade. Most worrisome of all is the relief programme for female-headed families with children (Aid for Dependent Children), where each yearly increase has been taken to indicate a growing host of unmarried, abandoned, black mothers permanently dependent on the public purse. By 1972 the number of AFDC recipients had risen fivefold since the mid-1950s.

Arguments have raged about whether the roots of this welfare crisis should be traced to more liberal administrators, family disintegration, militant recipients' organizations, an inrush of poor Southern blacks to Northern cities, political fears of urban unrest, or what. It has provided a splendid opportunity for overstatement. American welfare policy becomes either part of a cosmic indictment of modern society at large or a particular piece of social engineering unrelated to anything else. Circumstances vary among regions, but the important point is that everywhere the key issues for social policy are framed as a question of controlling the relief rolls.

What has happened in public relief is in fact not unique to the United States; moreover it is invariably exaggerated by the American poor law's emphasis on isolated programmes for distinct groups of social dependants. Analysing the burden shows that in fact relief costs have grown little, if any, as a proportion of public spending at local, state or national levels. The federal government assumes the largest share of these costs; between the mid-1950s and 1973 Washington's expenditure for cash public assistance has remained generally stable, at 2 to 3 per cent of the federal budget. In relation to other income support dispersed from Washington, relief costs have actually declined from about 25 per cent in 1955 to 16 per cent in 1960, 14 per cent in 1965 and 10 per cent in 1972. Similarly, welfare expenditures from state governments' own revenues were at about the same level in 1968 as during the previous decade. In New York City, the home of all crises, the proportion of local revenues absorbed by cash assistance did increase during the 1960s, from 2·8 per cent of local revenue in 1963–4 to 7·4 per cent in 1968–9, but by 1972–3 the proportion had fallen to an estimated 6·1 per cent. Notions of an oppressive welfare burden seem a roundabout way of expressing the low priority that many Americans attach to relief spending.

Nor has the growth in American welfare recipients been unique. From 1950 to 1971 the proportion of Americans receiving cash relief rose from 4 per cent to 7 per cent. In Britain the proportion of the population receiving public assistance payments has gradually risen from 3·9 per cent in 1950 to 8 per cent in 1971. In Sweden a progressive rise in the welfare rate has occurred since the mid-1960s so that by 1971 6·3 per cent of Swedes were on welfare, the highest proportion in a generation. None of these welfare rates is necessarily an equivalent indicator (British relief, for example, includes housing assistance while Swedish housing allowances to the needy are under separate programmes), but they do show that America's experience with growing relief rolls is not unique.

What does lack a foreign counterpart is the fact that a portion of the relief rolls is composed of black abandoned mothers. Concentrated in urban centres, they are highly visible and socially stigmatized. But here too the welfare crisis and the actual role of such clients are grossly exaggerated. In 1971, 43 per cent of all families on AFDC were black, compared to 40 per cent in 1961; they have hardly been the dominant force in expanding relief rolls. If it is family break-up rather than blackness in welfare that particularly plagues Americans, then it is worth noting that the incidence of public assistance among one-parent families is not notably greater in the United States than in Britain. Moreover, studies have shown that for American whites and non-whites, the major force behind the last thirty years' increase in numbers of female-headed households was not growing marital instability but the higher propensity of mothers in disrupted marriages to go it alone and head separate households rather than to reside with relatives. Relief benefits have had apparently little effect on the increased tendency in all population groups to form separate households. Neither do the facts support popular views of an open-handed public assistance programme generating hosts of black unmarried mothers. Studies for the President's 1972 Population Commission showed that illegitimacy rates were not linked to the levels or changes in AFDC benefits. If it is worrisome that the American illegitimacy rate more than doubled between 1940 and 1968, then it is worth noticing that increases in whites' rates have had a greater effect on changes in the total American illegitimacy rate than have increases in non-whites' rates; moreover, it is estimated that three-quarters of the increase in non-white illegitimacy in these years is accounted for by improved health conditions affecting conception and gestation.

Looked at outside the confines of cash relief payments, mothers and children make remarkably small claims on the total American system of income support. The aged (insurance 'annuitants' and other assisted elderly) absorbed 60 per cent of total income security benefits in the 1974 federal budget; another 16 per cent went to the disabled and 4 per cent to the temporarily unemployed. Roughly 8 per cent ($8.9 billion out of total income security benefits of $115.7 billion) went to mothers and children. Such is the content of America's supposed welfare crisis.

It would also be a mistake to imagine that the difficult challenges raised by social policy are unique to America. Similar dilemmas are posed by any overt income transfer scheme in any nation. Concern for adequate benefits invariably conflicts with concerns for work incentive; economy in government conflicts with client dignity. A programme generous enough to ensure adequate benefits without stigmatizing the recipients is always likely to be regarded in some circles as too costly and prejudicial to work effort. An inexpensive and highly discriminating programme is likely to offend others as offering too little and creating a group of second-class citizens. What distinguishes American social policy is not the dilemma of competing goals or the costs, rates and composition of its public assistance programme. The distinctiveness of America is in its response to these problems. When public cash relief is viewed as a special dispensation to some dependent groups rather than an entitlement potentially available to all, it makes sense to concentrate on how many people are on relief rolls rather than on how many are failing to take up their entitlement or are receiving other benefits. The American welfare debate revolves around dependency, not needs; case 'loads', not coverage; abuse, not the use of eligibility.

The contrast with Britain is striking. Little in recent American history can match the British concern for the take-up of social benefits, first among the elderly, then among all relief recipients, and eventually encompassing the replacement of National Assistance with what was designed to be a less stigmatizing Supplementary Benefits programme. It would be almost inconceivable to arouse a controversy in the United States similar to that which followed the introduction by a Conservative government of Family Income Supplements (FIS) in Britain during 1971. FIS was designed to provide a modest but guaranteed level of cash assistance for families with children when the head was in full-time work but had an income below a certain level. From the time of its introduction, when the government projected reaching 85 per cent of the eligible population, FIS was subject to continual criticism for failing to approach this degree of coverage. Parliamentry, press and television discussion decried the government's inability to draw more of the potentially eligible population; during the first two years of operating FIS, the government was pressed into a series of publicity campaigns costing £210,000 to advertise entitlements to benefits. By 1973 FIS was being widely condemned as ill-fated and a failure for reaching no more than half of those believed to be eligible.

It is not only the stigmatized recipients of American cash relief payments who bear the costs imposed by norms of ostensible independence. Affluent America probably has as large an economically vulnerable population as any other nation. Looking behind the administrative categories of public assistance dependants and the stereotypes of poverty as a black urban phenomenon, one finds immense human insecurity. The failure for these needs to be consciously recognized and collectively met has been another consequence of formal self-sufficiency.

The American poor are neither typically black nor central city-dwellers. Of the 5 million families below the official poverty line in 1968, approximately 76 per cent were white and only 15 per cent female-headed black families. A more detailed 1966 study showed that 9.5 million poor Americans lived in central cities, 5.7 million in suburbs and 14.6 million in non-metropolitan areas. Even in New York, almost two-thirds of the city's residents live below what is defined as a 'modest but adequate' living standard, including 83 per cent of black and Puerto Rican families but also 47 per cent of all white families. Had the aged population been included, the proportions would undoubtedly have been swollen even larger. Much of New York's supposed crisis in relief has been largely a function of higher benefit levels and the resulting entitlement of a larger proportion of the population; one estimate is that those taking up benefit as a proportion of eligibles actually declined in New York City, from 59 per cent in 1960 to 56 per cent by the end of 1968. A balanced social policy perspective would address both the use of benefits and the needs of those eligible for or just outside the range of benefits. In America the one preoccupation in welfare reform is the number who have actually fallen on to the relief rolls.

One important reason for American concern with relief rolls is structural. Americans may be no more hostile to poor people than any other nation, but the poor and their overt dependence tend to appear more prominent because of the categorical American programmes distinguishing dependants from non-dependants. In a way, American attention to cash relief is comparable to claims about class voting in Britain: the prominence commanded by each is a function less of their intrinsic salience and more of the absence of other factors. Lacking British-style cash family allowances, comprehensive social insurance, a freely available health service and housing allowances, public relief stands out conspicuously. Since relief is by nature a residual recourse for those whose needs are not met by other programmes, its visibility increases as less is done by other overt forms of public provision.

But there is more to American distinctiveness than structure. Relief dependants are not only special because they are categorized; they are also categorized because they are regarded as special. The recipient of public relief fails to exhibit nearly every one of the native American virtues. He does not work and he is likely to be poorly educated; he has failed in the competitive struggle implied by equal opportunity and he is obviously dependent on the government. Americans on the relief rolls are not simply a separate group, but their very existence is an indictment of their failure to live up to the conception of national character. In Britain an increase in public assistance payments is likely to be taken as an indication that something is wrong with other policies of the welfare state. A rise in the welfare rolls in America denotes that something is wrong with the recipients.

Recent studies have documented many sharp distinctions which middle-class suburbanites draw between themselves and those dependent on cash relief. American middle-class people do not regard government as an acceptable source of income supplement; they think that relief clients see work as less important to self-fulfilment than they do and are more willing to engage in activities of dubious legality. The teenage offspring of the middle class are equally or more likely to hold a harsh view of an alien group of relief recipients. Even more interesting are the findings on actual attitudes among American relief clients. These Americans – black and white, long- and short-term recipients – have virtually the same work ethic as members of the middle class. They too regard regular work as central to their self-respect; this holds true also among teenagers raised in fatherless homes by 'welfare mothers', who have been on relief for long periods.

While questions of eligibility and take-up have come into increasing prominence in the United States since the mid-1960s, they have done so in a distinctively American way. Local protests have attacked the administrative routines, rules and legal underpinnings of American public assistance. Humanitarians, social guerrillas and emboldened relief recipients have often found a common cause in advocating welfare rights and full use of the existing cash relief system. But paradoxically, the emphasis on legal rules and rights for recipients has only re-emphasized the typically American refusal to contemplate a broader approach to social provision outside the bounds of market reciprocity. Welfare agitation has remained preoccupied with cash relief payments. Welfare rights organizers have only helped to underline the American view of segmented welfare-state groups – some of whom make claims, assert rights, demand compensation and create confrontations, and others of whom react with dispensations. That one segment calls itself poor people and another group calls itself responsible opinion does not matter. The summation of claims from the self-styled oppressed and compensations from the supposedly non-dependent no more adds up to a social policy for all citizens than did the sum of feudal estates. Militants from each modern faction can be expected to oppose and increasingly to frustrate general public provision as a threat to their own factional security. At the end of this line of development lies, not a social community, but a semi-private confederation of groups united only by contingent ties of temporary advantage.

III. A NEAT ENGINEERING SOLUTION?

Solving the welfare/poverty problem remains the preoccupying fantasy of the American welfare state. If welfare reform turns on that discrete subset of the population who are on the relief rolls, anti-poverty is the sun around which all larger social policy issues revolve. Being poor in a nation that regards itself as *the* land of opportunity is to have failed, or even to be slightly un-American. The poor must somehow be 'fixed'. American strategies for improving welfare tell us more about Americans than they offer lessons in social policy to the rest of the world. Social engineering, work and education are the three shining hopes.

The first and perhaps the greatest of these fixers is the 'neat engineering solution' for social policy. To think of society technologically is to think in terms of problems and solutions, not conditions and judgements. Conditions and judgements are untidy and indeterminant; problems are manipulable, clean and capable of being resolved. Minority-group quotas, one suspects, have become a prominent mechanism of egalitarian policy because, regardless of what selection by race and ethnicity does to those involved, a quota is a neat and easily applied standard obviating social judgement.

Given existing presumptions, nothing could be simpler than to define the criteria for solutions in American social policy: the answer to increasing numbers on the welfare rolls is to reduce the rolls; the solution for poverty is to lift everyone above a particular poverty line. Concentration on relief-roll numbers, besides reinforcing myths about state dependence and independence, facilitates a technologically satisfying interpretation of the connections among welfare, government and society. So too does the identification of social policy with the elimination of numbers below an income level. Nothing in Britain or Europe can match the thousands of man-years that have gone into United States efforts to define what exactly is a 'poverty line' income. This is not because the British are less concerned about human distress, but because British policy-makers tend to take the activity a good deal less seriously. Its meaning for general social policy is not self-evident. Setting the poverty line in the United States, however, is an intrinsic step towards solving the poverty problem. Ambiguity at this stage means that not only will the social engineer not know when he has solved the problem, but also that he may not even know what the problem is.

It is a significant fact that the intellectual impetus behind American welfare reform has come from economists rather than the softer social sciences, where scientific *ceteris paribus* assumptions and procedures are less ruthlessly applicable. The result is a debate on social policy which has centred on negative income taxes and guaranteed incomes – technically elegant mechanisms for bringing most if not all of the poor above a particular poverty income line. The computational routines are delicious. What guaranteed income level, with what 'incentive effect' (proportion of benefit lost because of earnings), related to what 'notch effect' (drop in net income from all sources as earnings rise), will yield what 'break-even income' (the point where extra earnings extinguish the last bit of state income supplement) to lift what proportion of the poor across the poverty line at what budgetary cost? American welfare reformers have revelled in debating these niceties. Similar problems are necessarily raised during any British discussion of cash relief, but they seldom form the substantive core of all debate on welfare reform.

The contrasting national conceptions of social policy are well illustrated in the British adaptation of American ideas of a negative income tax. In 1972 the Conservative government brought forward plans for a system of tax credits; a common means would be used to assess both liability to taxation and entitlement to cash income supplements from the state. Both personal tax allowances and cash family allowances would be abolished, as well as the recent FIS programme for low-income workers with children. There has been no lack of British debate about the technicalities involved, particularly important questions of where the tax threshold begins and income supplementation ends, who in the family receives the cash, and so on. But the most noteworthy point for present purposes is the fact that a plan which would usually occur to Americans as a solution to the welfare/poverty problem is regarded in Britain as scarcely more than a partial amelioration. While the tax credit idea is seen to have an important effect on relieving some social distress, it is not presented in Britain as a cure-all for reducing public assistance rolls, guaranteeing a minimum income or bringing everyone above some notional poverty line. The Conservative government remains emphatic in disclaiming any intention of offering tax credits as a comprehensive social policy solution, emphasizing instead that the plan is a tax reform adding one more item to the arsenal of general social provision.

In America, on the other hand, Democratic Presidential candidate George McGovern proposed a similar plan in January 1972, with vastly exaggerated intentions for replacing the entire cash relief (public assistance) system and certain social security benefits. Emerging from the candidate's academic/economist task-force and billed as a phase of his comprehensive economic programme, the plan left the impression that a federal payment of $1,000 to every man, woman and child (which 'would not vary in accordance with the wealth of the recipient') would lift a family of four up to the poverty line. Predictably, this abstract economic solution and half-baked presentation was used by opponents to stamp radicalism on McGovern. In the end, the Democratic candidate retreated to the heart of American faith in economic solutions to social problems: work.

Problems of work incentive bedevil any state income transfer. British supplementary benefits, for example, use a variety of administrative rules to try to ensure that those able-bodied who receive benefit are actually seeking work and not work-shy. Almost any such programme in any nation demonstrates, in practice if not on paper, similar safeguards against abuse. What is distinctively American is the tendency to see work as the positive cure to welfare issues. Probably no people in the world works so hard and worries so much about not working enough as do Americans. If the poor are poor it must be because they do not have the proper attitude towards gainful employment. By the end of the 1972 Presidential campaign both parties were competing to express their zealousness for work solutions. According to President Nixon, the voters would be choosing between 'the work ethic that built this nation's character – and the new welfare ethic that could cause that American character to weaken'. McGovern's campaign was advancing the notion that people resented the ever-growing relief rolls and that 'the reason the poor do not go get jobs ... is that no jobs exist and the Nixon policies are the prime reasons for that'. McGovern's final welfare proposal was to 'guarantee jobs for those out of work and not support those who won't work'. In making these claims, both candidates drew on the American belief in economic faith-healing.

Significantly, the major expression of the Kennedy–Johnson administration's 'War on Poverty' was the Economic Opportunity Act of 1964, which aimed to provide 'new opportunities for those who want to help themselves or their communities'. Increased earning capacity (at work) has tended to be seen as a complete and sufficient definition of American social policy. For recipients of Aid for Dependent Children in particular, a Work Incentive Program (WIN) began in 1968. Job training was intended to move people off the welfare rolls and on to the tax rolls, although readily available data showed that almost 90 per cent of all relief recipients were aged, blind, severely handicapped, dependent children or incapacitated fathers. Not surprisingly, after two full years of operation WIN had enrolled only 10 per cent and trained and placed in jobs only 1 per cent of the assessed AFDC recipients.

A later manifestation of the same approach followed in the Nixon administration's 1969 proposal for welfare reform (the Family Assistance Plan), which was characteristically described by its advocates as 'workfare, not welfare'. Whatever certain Presidential advisers may have privately believed about the possibilities of putting relief recipients to work, political considerations were deemed to require underpinning the plan with the work ethic. Cash relief would have been financed and administered nationally for the residue of unemployable, but for the rest, benefits were to be contingent on a willingness to accept work or job training. Although mothers with pre-school children – later changed to children under three – would not have been required to register for work or training, expanded day-care facilities would ease the inflow of single mothers into the labour market. Later versions of the plan completely segregated the supposed welfare population into two groups, with one programme for those strictly unable to work and a separate Opportunities for Families Program administered by the Department of Labour (rather than Health, Education and Welfare) to find jobs or training for those able to work. A 1972 Congressional version went so far as to propose a clean sweep of welfare dependency by replacing most public assistance with federally guaranteed jobs at minimum wages to all relief recipients. Welfare rolls would fall by virtue of make-work if nothing else. In the end the legislative result was no welfare reform and a three- to five-year period for local pilot projects to test experimentally the work-incentive effects of each proposal. Few foreigners are likely to see a model for their future in this way of thinking about social policy.

If the cure for lengthening welfare rolls and poverty is perceived to lie in work and improved earning capacity, the cure for any more general social inequality is the province of education. For much of the post-war period more schooling has served as the major surrogate for broader thought about social policies to deal with American inequities. Higher education expansion, scholarships, loans, early remedial education, quotas for minority admission and staffing – all these and many more approaches have been invoked as devices for assuring a more equitable society. Education has seemed the supreme expression of equal opportunity. Once that opportunity is granted, hard work can again be left to settle and justify troublesome questions of social inequality. In Britain similar motivations provided an important spur to expansions in elementary, technical and university education, and comprehensive schools, but in few quarters in Britain were the hopes for fundamental social change through education so absolute.

Because hopes were less high in Britain, the resulting disillusionment has been less as it becomes clear that education is scarcely the great solvent of social inequalities, and often their major fixing agent. Research in Britain has demonstrated that many of the most significant social advantages are settled before school age. But this finding has failed to cause the same soul-searching as results showing the ephemeral effects of remedial pre-school education in the United States. By 1973 studies had created a major intellectual stir by demonstrating that differences in the quality of education or attendance at racially integrated schools have very little measurable effect on subsequent career success and income levels. The data are startling only if it has been assumed that education must be the key to better jobs and social uplift.

Society appears much more intractable than most of the American anti-poverty warriors of the 1960s supposed. A growing stream of findings suggests that the panoply of government interventions, headed by education, have only the most marginal, if any, effect on important social inequalities and values. The causes of social division appear to extend ever more widely and to double back on themselves; equal starting chances at one point are meaningless without equal opportunities at other points in time. Unequal results acquired through earlier opportunities shape access to and use of other supposedly equal opportunities. The search for a neatly engineered economic solution, with the rest of life held constant, turns increasingly sour.

The American welfare state in the early 1970s demonstrates, if not a loss of confidence, at least malaise and immobilism. Social critics believe they must act to improve their society, yet action does no good; they must rethink their collective situation and yet thought seems to do no good. Society refuses to respond as if a morally neutral problem like traffic engineering. From the beginning to the end of the 1960s the proportion of all Americans below the line of absolute poverty fell from 22·4 per cent to 12·2 per cent. But far from being halved, America's social problems seem only to have become more intense. In short, society does not look like it is being fixed.

What difference does it make? An American citizen in need can be less sure than his British counterpart of the timeliness, amount or conditions of publicly organized aid; he probably can feel more sure of access to entrepreneurial competition in the education market-place. But there is much more at stake. The question of how to treat poor people and dependency is about social values generally as well as about poverty. Welfare policy concerns human relationships as well as disposable income. It is no accident that preoccupation with a self-help work ethic discourages a sense of collective responsibility and encourages the massed privatism of helping oneself. A generation of youthful protesters dissenting from American-style prosperity have usually disregarded the tendency for 'doing your own thing' to become selfishness and feckless self-indulgence at others' expense. If the sense of secure social position in Britain is not always inspiring, it is at least much more immune from anxieties associated with living up to a British (*sic*) Dream, or to some mythical frontier goal of individual self-sufficiency. The traditions of the Old World are not necessarily threatened by the inherent mixture of social and individualist perspectives in social policy. The American Dream, however, cannot be so tolerant of the claims of social interdependence and public authority.

IV. THE DREAM IMMOBILIZED

What is unique in the 1970s is not simply renewed domestic criticism of American materialism, but the idea that it is the responsibility of the welfare state to institute a more meaningful way of life. Far from dampening expectations, the failures of engineered, competitive opportunities and money exchanges have only escalated messianic demands to get rid of rather than cope with social problems. Somehow, America is supposed to make people happy with themselves.

Hence the immobilism of the American welfare state: home-grown critics of social policy adjure it to provide a general sense of community without really bothering anybody. Dizzyingly high expectations are counterposed with a minimal sense of collective responsibility and commitment to public authority. Few people expect so much from a government which they have equipped to do so little. Government, like the welfare programmes it operates, is seen neither to express nor to shape social values; it is supposed to fix but be external to society.

Suspicious of the statism implied by coherent political authority and professional civil service, Americans tend to be reassured by ineffectiveness in their arrangements for social provision. Few national anti-poverty programmes can claim to be administered well, and many are implemented poorly if at all. Local Work Incentive officials, for example, found 90 per cent of welfare clients in some states to be suitable for job training and less than 10 per cent in other states. Britain, of course, makes extensive use of local authorities in the delivery of its welfare-state services, but also demonstrates an administrative coherence unlike anything found in the United States. The American division between federal, state and local authority has itself become another expression of how to create mutual exchanges of money without creating joint commitment to social purposes; state and local officials can react through a calculus of following the best matching-grant formula. There is little need politically to mobilize, or reconstitute, or evaluate the substance of social policies. The premises of the 'power to the people' advocates similarly express and mould themselves to a minimalist view of political sovereignty. Idealistic calls for a heightened sense of general community are accompanied in practice by increasingly sectionalized appeals for group justice. While each newly organized intercessor group stakes out its particular claim on American society, the government is simultaneously upbraided for failing to provide a social policy which is more than the sum of group demands. At best social policy tends to become a conglomerate of compensations and at worst a form of blackmail, with the most money going to the most troublesome. In so far as government is regarded as a cash register on which each sale is a specialized programme for a claimant group, the important question will be what each is owed by others rather than what all owe to each other.

The malaise of the interventionists has led to even more impossible demands for qualitative improvement. Defining themselves (or a strip ten miles wide down each coast) as the nation, American social critics like to imagine that their dissatisfactions are shared throughout the country. In fact probably few of the *de facto* beneficiaries of the bounties of entrepreneurial, contractual, fiscal and social intervention feel that the American welfare state is failing them, certainly not in any way that requires fundamental recasting of the existing structure. Seeing themselves as the future, such coastal critics are likely to displace their frustrations with the American version of the welfare state on to the rest of the world. They risk becoming Elijahs of gratuitous doom-mongering about the failures of 'post-industrial society'. Some turn to admonishing a boycott of consumer luxuries as the true salvation, while others proclaim the advantages of zero economic growth. British listeners, who are only too familiar with the blessings of almost nil growth, cannot be expected to take very much of this seriously.

The American public philosophy has remained remarkably faithful to its eighteenth-century intellectual origins. Individual, society and state are still regarded as three distinct spheres. While all three spheres are considered to be mutually threatening (the government's rule by law, for example, may be endangered by individual or social class power), it is the danger posed to the individual by the state that most worries Americans. Yet in practice this doctrine of individual, social and state separatism has been outdistanced by *ad hoc* expansions of government activity. Placed at the strategic juncture of the three supposedly separate spheres, American social policy is well situated to expose all the strains of a social credo lagging behind the pace of events. Americans shun social dependency, but direct and indirect outlays for income support continue to mushroom; the result is a collage of programmes that divides rather than unites people and neglects many of those at risk. Americans are suspicious of government power, but they expect public authority to engineer ready-made answers to social problems; the result is a pitiful disregard of implementation, incoherent administration and unrealistic expectations of welfare solutions. Americans strive to become more individually self-sufficient, but also aspire to reduce society's self-estrangement; the result varies between frustration and hypocrisy.

Models can serve as warnings as well as inspire emulation. The American experience with the welfare state seems to serve best as a cautionary tale. Rather than facilitating a balanced competition between collectivist and individualist conceptions of human freedom, the American ethic automatically prejudges the issue. The modern American Dream is not a social vision; it is not an expression of what people are to each other, but what they are to have for themselves.

BIBLIOGRAPHY

Much of the voluminous work on American social policy is summarized in publications of the Brookings Institution in Washington, DC. On social insurance, see Joseph Pechman *et al., Social Security: Perspective for Reform* (1968), and John Brittain, *The Payroll Tax for Social Security* (1972); on the issues and attitudes surrounding means-tested public assistance, see Gilbert Steiner, *The State of Welfare* (1971), *Social Insecurity: The Politics of Welfare* (1966), and Leonard Goodwin, *Do the Poor Really Want to Work* (1972); in-depth analyses of the federal government's allocation of public resources are presented in the annual volumes by Charles Schultze *et al., Setting National Priorities* (1971 to present). A most useful one-volume collection on poverty and other issues of American social policy is David Gordon's *Problems of Political Economy* (New York: D. C. Heath, 1971). The myths of America's welfare crisis are dealt with at length in my article with Martin Rein, 'What Welfare Crisis?', *The Public Interest* (Autumn 1973).

11 America: The End of the Dream?

ESMOND WRIGHT

Director, Institute of United States Studies, University of London

America, the undiscovered and virgin continent, fired the imagination of Europe in a peculiar and unique fashion. The rumour of it stirred Shakespeare. Franklin, as epitome of its Natural Man, became part of the European Enlightenment; Rousseau, and for a while Thomas Jefferson, saw it as the *novus ordo saeculorum*. For Europeans like Coleridge and Priestley, for Du Pont de Nemours and Robert Owen, it was a place uncorrupted by power, congenial to experiments in human perfectibility, inhabited by a chosen people.

And yet the possibility of translating this uniqueness into permanent political form, making American society different from the rest of anguished mankind, died early, indeed died almost at conception. The ideal of a heavenly city on the plains, with a Nature that was more beneficent and generous than in the Old World, was imperilled at the start. Jefferson recognized it early enough. In his first comments on the Constitution, writing to Madison from Paris in 1787, he said that America would remain 'virtuous' only while there remained vacant land. 'When we get piled upon one another in large cities as in Europe we shall become corrupt as in Europe, and go to eating one another as they do there.'

But the dream of a perfectible land dies hard. It is striking that so many discussions of the state of America today start with the question: 'What has gone wrong?' Even in a secular age, a sense of manifest destiny is not deduced from sociological laws but treated as part of a providential plan. With boasts of great achievement goes the assumption that America could and should be judged by a special measuring-rod.

I. THE DREAM AND THE REALITY

In the state of American society today, many can be heard proclaiming the end of the American Dream. The country's worst critics – often its natives, rather than visiting Europeans – go further still: America is denounced as a nightmare society. Yet even here, the pride in country shows through, and shows in contradictory ways. Some Americans denounce their country as uniquely nightmarish – as if Hitler's Germany and Stalin's Russia were of no account in the history of this century. Other critics look ahead: America today is claimed to be the prototype of the nightmare existence facing European societies in the next century. The truth may be something different. Perhaps the idyllic America of an earlier era, to which the present is so unfavourably compared, is not a fact but a myth.

America was not only exceptional in origin but also exceptionally favoured. In the late eighteenth century it had an extraordinary number of statesmen who were gifted in many senses. Its constitution-makers were men of ingenuity and good sense; they were, for their time, remarkably well educated. Its Presidents were either the Virginian dynasty – Washington, Jefferson, Madison and Monroe – or their Yankee equivalents, the Adams family. These men brought to politics a high sense of personal responsibility and a sense of dignity and decorum worthy of the Senate of the Roman Republic. The majority of the Founding Fathers were graduates; four of them, Jefferson, Madison and the two Adamses, were essentially scholars turned politicians. In Philadelphia a collection of scientists, architects and politicians made that city for a while as significant as Paris as a centre of ideas and political programmes. David Rittenhouse the astronomer, Benjamin Rush in medicine, and painters like Benjamin West, John Copley and the Peales were as significant as Madison and Jefferson.

There was more than a sense of optimism and of high adventure; there was also a sense that in the New World there was opportunity to discover new social and aesthetic values, to formulate new laws, and virgin soil in which to plant new institutions. Jefferson was architect of much more than the

Declaration of Independence and the University of Virginia. If, when he came to write his own epitaph, he gave pride of place to these and to the statute of Virginia for religious freedom, there were also his drafts for the Virginia Constitution, for the Federal Bill of Rights, for the French Charter of Rights, the Kentucky Resolutions, the Ordinances for the West, the Notes on the State of Virginia, the notes of a coinage for the United States, standards of measurement for weights and coins – to name only a few. He was also architect of a charming eighteenth-century country villa which, while smaller than its counterparts outside London and Vicenza, none the less offered those who called there the prospect of greater intellectual stimulus in the course of an evening's conversation.

With a polymath's concern for matching form and substance, Jefferson wished the architecture of the nation's capital buildings to express in stone and marble the ideals that he and his friends had tried to express in the words of the Declaration. After two wings of the Capitol building were finished, needing only the central dome to crown its classical grandeur, Jefferson wrote Benjamin Latrobe, the architect: 'I shall live in the hope that the day will come when an opportunity will be given you of finishing the middle building in a style worthy of the two wings, and worthy of the first temple dedicated to the sovereignty of the people, embellishing with Athenian taste the course of a nation looking far beyond the range of Athenian destinies.'

The world in which the Founding Fathers moved had a certain unity. It was the ordered world of the New England towns or the Virginia plantations. It was a world in which movement was slow and communication difficult. It was a world of independent farmers. Some were also scholars, at home with Europeans of the Enlightenment; they were certainly no more isolated from new ideas than was Frederick the Great, condemned to life in a Prussian backwater, or Edward Gibbon, seeking education in an Oxford that was a century away from reform. Yet these men of the Tidewater also knew the problems of uncivilized lands. The trapper and the sharpshooter in his rude cabin were also part of their world. In the early years of the Republic the attraction shifted from

exploring Europe to exploring the interior of an almost unknown continent. Thomas Jefferson advised young men no
longer to go to Europe for an education. It was better to stay
on native ground. He sent his private secretary, Meriwether
Lewis, in company with William Clark, to explore the continent. The expedition not only crossed the Mississippi but
also the wide Missouri and the vast Rockies, reaching the
Pacific Ocean overland, instead of by the long sailing route.
The reports they brought back opened vast new territories to
knowledge and settlement. In the first decade of the nineteenth century the move west – away from Europe – began in
earnest. Jefferson's ideal seemed within reach. America was
to 'stand with respect to Europe precisely on the footing of
China. We should then avoid wars and all our citizens would
be husbandmen.'

Some Europeans agreed with the Jeffersonian dream. As
early as 1782, Crèvecœur saw the Americans as Western pilgrims 'who are carrying along with them that great mass of
arts, science, vigour and industry, which began long since in
the East'. They would, in his phrase, 'finish the great circle'.
The New World won the praise of Tocqueville in the 1830s,
and Gladstone, notwithstanding his pride in Britain, thought
its constitution one of the most providential acts in human
history. In 1851 Heinrich Heine proclaimed its significance
thus:

> This is America!
> This is the New World!
> Not the present European
> Wasted and withering sphere. . . .
> This is no graveyard of Romance,
> This is no pile of ruins,
> Of fossilized wigs and symbols,
> Of state and musty tradition.

Other Europeans agreed about the exceptional character of
America, only to contrast it unfavourably with the civilization of the Old. European visitors noticed many features that
would be as true of the twentieth century as of the nineteenth: the passion for speed, the worship of size, the identi-

fication of success with money, prodigious meals and preoccupation with the law – both making it and breaking it.
They noted the vestiges of a puritanical social and moral
code, and were shocked by slavery. All disliked the prevalent
tobacco-chewing and spitting habit. Charles Dickens described how he had to clean his fur coat repeatedly to remove
the dried flakes of spittle from it. Another visitor thought the
national emblem should not be the eagle but the spittoon.
But the most frequent theme, then as now, was the ease with
which weapons could be obtained, and police and politicians
bribed. Duels were sometimes deliberate murders, and every
Congressman went armed. A Southerner breakfasting at Wil-
lards Hotel in Washington, angered at an Irish waiter's service, stabbed him. The Dutch ambassador, who had just
taken up his appointment, was having his first meal at a
nearby table: 'What peoples! If they do such things at
breakfast, what won't they do at dinner!'

The wilderness, to many Americans proof of the country's
status as Eden, was interpreted by many visitors as a token of
barbarism. Mrs Trollope wrote in a distinctly un-Jeffersonian
style of the Mississippi:

> ... now we glide
> between the slimy banks; the horrent bear
> And bloated crocodile lie crouching there,
> Thy dark shores breathe miasma! on thy breast
> The uptorn forest droops its leafy crest,
> Thy storm-crushed victims; none her strength can save
> That once hath dipped beneath thy fatal wave.
> This flood contemned of nature let me free –
> Turn here again, my bark, and seek the deep blue sea.

Jefferson, the product of a settled Virginia, might also have
turned his back on less admirable characteristics of the world
of Kentucky, Tennessee and points further west. This world
was marked, in the words of James Paxton, by 'abundance,
idleness, Indians, Africans, isolation and whiskey'.

In the 1820s and 1830s the distinctive character of American politics became recognized in Europe as a potential
threat to established European ideas. Metternich, the great

exponent of European conservatism after the downfall of Napoleon, expressed great alarm at the revolutionary potential of American political ideals, and the implications of the Monroe Doctrine. Writing to Nesselrode, the Russian Chancellor, in 1824, he said:

> These United States of America which we have seen arise and grow, and which during their too short youth already meditated projects which they dared not then avow, have suddenly left a sphere too narrow for their ambition, and have astonished Europe by a new act of revolt, more unprovoked, fully as audacious, and no less dangerous than the former. They have distinctly and clearly announced their intention to set not only power against power, but, to express it more exactly, altar against altar. In their indecent declarations they have cast blame and scorn on the institutions of Europe most worthy of respect, on the principles of its greatest sovereigns, on the whole of those measures which a sacred duty no less than an evident necessity has forced our governments to adopt to frustrate plans most criminal.
>
> In permitting themselves these unprovoked attacks, in fostering revolutions, wherever they show themselves, in regretting those which have failed, in extending a helping hand to those which seem to prosper, they lend new strength to the apostles of sedition, and re-animate the courage of every conspirator.
>
> If this flood of evil doctrines and pernicious examples should extend over the whole of America, what would become of our religious and political institutions, of the moral force of our government, and of that conservative system which has saved Europe from complete dissolution?

A half-century later, Bismarck paid ironic tribute to America's ability to be different, and survive, when he remarked that there 'must have been a special providence looking after fools, drunkards and the United States'.

Even before Bismarck spoke, Americans were beginning to wonder whether providence, or some other impersonal force, was not beginning to take them away from the Jeffersonian ideal. The real divide in American history was not the firing upon Fort Sumter, or Lee's surrender at Appomattox, but Andrew Jackson's boisterous inauguration in January 1829. At this point, the Democracy (or worse) of the Frontier displaced the older, settled world of the Virginia gentleman. Perry Miller has argued that the turning-point came in 1815. After the textile mills opened in New England, America was set to become a business civilization; capitalism and selfishness, rather than Indians and crude manners, were to be the new enemies. In 1898, when America went to war with Spain, it became, like the nations from which it revolted, an imperial power. By this time too, America could claim to be like any other industrial civilization – only more so. The absence of a feudal past meant there was no aristocratic class to challenge the claims of Mammon. Jefferson's dream was gone.

The past is gone in a double sense. With greater awareness of American history, we can see that the America of Heine, like the America of Mrs Trollope, is a land that never was. The reality of the past is far more complex than any dream or nightmare could encapsulate. If the South had its intellectual aristocrats, it also had its Simon Legrees. If the North had grasping merchants, the same Yankee civilization also produced men who grasped and groped to find what transcended commerce, in a search for the soul of man. The frontiersmen were both incredibly brave and adventurous, and incredibly crude and violent.

A second reason for the disappearance of the dream is that at some point in the nineteenth century the line of continuity between past and present wore thin, then snapped. The pressures were multiple: expansion across a vast continent, the growth of industrialism and, not least, the gathering-in of tens of millions of new immigrants from unfamiliar parts of the Old World. Previous chapters in this volume have emphasized how incomparable the American past is with the European past. My point is different, and perhaps more disturbing: the American past has now become largely irrelevant for an understanding of contemporary America too.

II. THE PRESENT WAKEFULNESS

The wakefulness that is about in America today reflects worries often grounded in myth. The present seems worse than the past, because both friends and critics have forgotten what the American past was really like. Americans have been repeatedly reassured by historians of the righteousness of the nation's foundations, because it is one of the functions of historians to act as nationalist pietists. This role is specially important in America because Americans cannot take their history for granted. Unlike European inheritors of a feudal past, Americans inherited a world which they could make their own. The boast was that it would be bigger and better than anything that had gone before. Whatever Americans make of their society today, they have only themselves to praise or blame. The children of Genesis, once expelled from the Garden, lament and repent of their past with a vehemence and hyperbole characteristic of America at all ages.

Europeans eavesdropping on this *Schadenfreude* can become confused about the future of Europe, as well as about the present condition of the United States. If the problems of America today are unique to that society, then they are not infectious. But if the problems of America stand out because the United States has been the first to reach the end of the line of Western industrial society, then European nations can expect to arrive at the same destination in a few more decades. There is another possibility, namely that the things about which Americans protest today are not new at all. Instead of representing the zenith or nadir of the nation's progress, they are nothing more than familiar stops in a circular course of American history. If this is the case, then European societies are much less threatened by the course of American history. If Europeans could survive American slavery, America's Civil War, the burgeoning of industrialism and foreign trade, and a world depression led by Wall Street in 1929, then Europeans may reckon that they can also survive the present 'downs' in the roller-coaster course of American history.

Europeans as well as Americans should find reassurance in the fact that many of the problems that trouble American society today are not unique in time and place, but have their counterparts in earlier eras of the American story. If the 1960s found Vietnam, racial violence, the hippy culture and draft-dodging terrible problems, the 1950s found the beat generation, and the witch-hunting of Joe McCarthy, equally distasteful and inexplicable. In the 1930s the Depression drove many jobless emigrants to America back to their European origins. In the 1920s some American intellectuals left the United States in their own protest against its Babbitry, against the Ku Klux Klan and the judicial murder of Sacco and Vanzetti, making Paris for a while the intellectual capital of the United States. The 1890s might in retrospect seem to be the years of the full dinner-pail, but they were also the years of the Pinkertons and strong-arm methods in strike-breaking, of Big Bill Haywood and the Wobblies, who did not stop short of dynamiting. The 1830s and 1840s found it hard to tolerate causes as diverse as the Mormons, the immigrant Irish, the Utopian New Harmony community and Elijah Lovejoy, the white abolitionist preacher. The outlaw, the eccentric and the Utopian, the extremists of Right and Left, have a long history and a proud pedigree in America, north and south of the Mason–Dixon line. In American history the gun, rather than the Bill of Rights, is 'the great equalizer'. Violence is a recurrent theme in the American story; it is, as Rap Brown said in 1967, 'as American as cherry pie'.

Another persistent theme of American history is revivalism and high emotion. The America of the Enlightenment was never far from the America of the Great Awakening – as the writings and sermons of Jonathan Edwards testify. The tradition of Whitfield and Edwards, of Moody and Sankey, and of Billy Graham also has a long pedigree. 'The language of excitement', to use Reinhold Niebuhr's phrase, 'is as important as the appeal to reason.' If institutions are to be reformed, men also must be called to an individual salvation. Tocqueville noticed in America 'a sort of fanatical spiritualism':

In all states of the Union, but especially in the half-peopled country of the Far West, itinerant preachers may be met with who hawk about the Word of God from place to place. Whole families, old men, women and children, cross rough passes and untrodden wilds, coming from a great distance, to join a camp-meeting, where, in listening to these discourses, they totally forget for several days and nights the cares and business and even the most urgent wants of the body.

Moralism, revivalism and populist politics are another legacy of the Great Experiment. Men such as William Jennings Bryan and Tom Watson of Georgia, Gene Talmadge and Theodore Bilbo, Joe McCarthy and George Wallace are in each generation as much in the American grain as the Unitarians (or the latter-day non-Unitarian intellectuals) of Harvard. Any explanation of American politics has to pay as much attention to the evangelism of the Burned-Over District and the Bible Belt as to the cool and faded elegance of Beacon Hill. Populist politics is quicker to recognise enemies than allies; it is especially prompt to recognize or invent conspiracies. Yet the demand to know the truth because it is believed to be liberating, the demand for total freedom of speech, the idealism of Fighting Bob La Follette and the Wisconsin Idea of the early 1900s, this moralist politics is far more typical of the American grass roots and more truly democratic than anything taught in Ivy League colleges or New York City law firms. When President Kennedy consciously sought to surround himself by an elite, a praetorian guard of intellectuals, he was defying the American tradition. One of their legacies, the Vietnam war, is a monument to the fact that the people whom David Halberstam has termed *The Best and the Brightest* are not always the wisest when profound issues are at stake.

The presence of the black man in America has always cast a dark shadow across American professions of equality. No modern European societies had to live half slave and half free. Indeed, Russia freed the serfs – and faced an infinitely more complex economic problem in doing so — before the United States freed the slaves. Lincoln carried through Emancipation in 1863 only in those states at war with the North and as a military tactic, not from an absolute set of ethical convictions. The strange career of Jim Crow is a reminder that there has been nothing hypocritical in the eyes of many Americans about the status of America's blacks. For generations, many states maintained laws that defined their status as separate *because* unequal. It was a narrow band of intellectuals, living several removes from the largest concentrations of blacks and whites, who believed that Americans faced a dilemma in their race relations. In almost every generation, both whites and blacks have differed among themselves about the best form of race relations. Nor are the black separatists of today unique in American history. Mormons, Fourierists, Mennonites and settlers of foreign-language communities everywhere on the Prairies have also fought, usually unsuccessfully, to build a fence around their own plot of Eden.

But in an age of national dissatisfaction, there is danger that Americans as well as foreign observers will overlook the achievements of contemporary American society. Concurrent with the rise of anxieties about national policies many things were done and done well, whether judged by American or European standards.

The affluence of America is taken for granted by Americans today, in a way that would not have occurred to a generation raised in the Depression, whose first experience of economic laws taught them about scarcity rather than abundance. Europeans raised on the shortages of war and the austerity of reconstruction, as well as upon depression, still cannot take their eyes off the evidence of well-being in American society today. For example, Americans cannot be said to have a housing problem, when American housing (old or new) is judged against European counterparts. The only problem that Americans can claim is a problem of the people who live in houses in such a way that buildings with a solid fabric become slums long before their useful life need be ended. The basic problems of America today are those of a 'post-affluent' society.

The decade of discontent has also seen great advances in civil rights. The civil rights legislation passed by Congress with strong executive leadership has gone far beyond anything previously enacted in American history, and far beyond what a British government has yet seen fit to provide for British blacks. Notwithstanding the rhetoric of black militants, the majority of blacks are proud, and have increasing incentive to be proud, of their American citizenship. Millions have entered the solid, staid ranks of middle American society, for they too are 'unpoor, unyoung and non-violent'. The civil rights movement stimulated great welfare and education programmes in the administration of Lyndon Johnson.

The United States Supreme Court, a uniquely powerful institution asserting the subordination of the executive arm of government to some form of higher law, has continued to assert itself. In 1971 the court upheld the right of the *New York Times* and other newspapers to print the Pentagon papers, despite the wish of the Nixon administration that they remain confidential. In 1973 the combined probings of judges, prosecutors and newspaper reporters broke the Watergate scandal. If some revelations of this scandal have been disturbing evidence of how politicians may attempt to mislead the American people, the disclosures are a sharp reminder of the independence of the press. Reason of state has never been accepted as a basis for censorship in America, unlike Britain, France and other European societies. Yet Americans can use their freedoms in ways that might strike foreign observers as odd. They have also been used by opponents of the Vietnam war to rewrite contemporary history, to ignore the many achievements of the Democratic White House of the 1960s and, specifically, to deny credit to Lyndon Johnson for his great domestic achievements.

The American achievements that have most significance for Europeans are in diplomacy and defence. Here the record is mixed. Until well *after* the outbreak of the Second World War, the American attitude towards foreign policy was ambivalent. Some politicians were for an interventionist policy, but others were against having *any* foreign policy. Senator William Borah, a prominent Republican isolationist, boasted that he avoided foreign travel in order to keep his mind free from any prejudices that might result from contact with foreigners. Americans who recalled what happened after Woodrow Wilson had entered a European war to make the world safe for democracy were anxious not to be tricked again. America entered the war in Europe by courtesy of Adolf Hitler. The Japanese attack on Pearl Harbor not only thrust America into action in the Pacific; it also constituted an argument against diversionary efforts across the Atlantic. Notwithstanding Japan's failure to support Hitler by delivering a potentially fatal stab in the back to the Soviet Union earlier in 1941, Hitler declared war upon America. In the belligerent climate of December 1941, the American Congress reciprocated by accepting a war on two fronts.

After the Second World War there were again uncertainties about America's role in world affairs. The Labour government of Britain took the lead in drawing America back into Europe. In 1946 it passed its commitments in Greece and Turkey to the United States. The following year the Marshall Plan, originally open to Eastern as well as Western Europe, commenced. As the Cold War grew more intense, the military alliance of NATO followed. By June 1950 American troops were in action in Korea, and European nations were beginning to rearm as part of a global alliance against Communism. Harry Truman, a populist rather than a professor's idea of a diplomat, had in his own term of office made the American system into a world system, at least as far as diplomacy and defence were concerned. The Eisenhower Presidency consolidated what its predecessor had started.

Nothing recedes like the recent past. The brief and tragically ended Presidency of John F. Kennedy quickly became a subject of myth. The reality, especially in foreign affairs, is far different. The Kennedy administration opened inauspiciously with the abortive invasion of Cuba at the Bay of Pigs. The message of the first inaugural was not a call to peace abroad and justice at home, but for patriotism and sacrifice. There was martial talk of 'friend and foe', and of America standing as the watchman on the walls of freedom. 'Let every nation know, whether it wishes us well or ill, that we shall pay any price, bear any burden, meet any hardship, support any friend, oppose any foe to assure the survival and the success of liberty.' The assumptions were outgoing and belligerent, the parallel was with Theodore Roosevelt rather than Franklin D. Roosevelt.

It was John F. Kennedy who began the escalation of the war in Vietnam. In 1960 the United States had 685 advisers there; by 1963 it had 16,500. The Pentagon papers show clearly that Kennedy and his advisers first conspired with South Vietnamese military plotters against President Diem, then backed away from an active role and, in the end, stood by and allowed the coup against him to take place. Over this story of the real Kennedy – power-conscious, ruthless and opportunistic – the assassination has cast the glamour of a King Arthur, the glow that never was on sea or land.

America's involvement in the Vietnam war put great strain upon its relationship with Europe. The strain did not arise from the stones thrown by demonstrating students, but from the doubts cast by their elders upon the wisdom of American involvement in a land war in South-east Asia. They doubted this for reasons of self-interest as well as larger considerations. Inevitably, an Asian war, especially one fought at such a massive cost, would turn America's attention away from Europe. Few anticipated but few were surprised to see the domestic politics of the war turn Americans towards isolationism once again.

In the establishment of great empires, European countries led America. The founding of America was a by-product of imperial expansion. Its successful fight for independence and continental expansion was aided by diplomatic events in Europe, as well as by forces within America. Can Americans find lessons from Europe in how to build or lose an empire? Neither France nor Germany can offer anything but lessons about what to avoid. Britain is perhaps different.

In the achievement of world-power status, Britain led America by more than a century. Napoleon's Waterloo was the beginning of Britain's triumphant century. In exercising world influence, Britain relied on the advantages of geography and a strong navy to protect its homeland from invasion, just as America has done. Its basic method of influence differed greatly from that of America. Britain avoided direct engagement in many international conflicts. It did not wish to fight wars itself, but to hold the balance of power, ensuring that no other country won 'too many' wars. The role of umpire or ultimate court of appeal required less force than the American strategy of containing Soviet Communism. It was morally neutral as between other nations. First France, then Germany, was perceived as the nation threatening to 'overbalance' the international system. By comparison, American readiness to define a single enemy creates rigid commitments to weak or dubious allies. Harassed American diplomats might point out that it was easier for the British to play a balance of power role than for the United States to do this. After all, the British could count on European nations to check each other in a way that has not been possible since 1945. Moreover, the British have also counted on the United States entering to redress the balance with a force that the British cannot provide today.

The sun set on the British Empire decades ago. Some observers now think that it is late afternoon on the Potomac. Can Britain's disengagement from empire offer any lessons for Americans to follow? In so far as history offers any lessons, its message is stoic: the less attempted, the less lost. The British managed gracefully their retreat from imperial eminence, because the government did not seek to hold sovereign authority, once native groups showed – peacefully or otherwise – that they would no longer accept alien rule.

Perhaps American Presidents might try to avoid comparisons with a Churchill, whose record on the invasion of Gallipoli in 1915 and opposition to Indian independence in the 1930s was as bad as his later hours were splendid. Instead they might emulate the architect of Britain's withdrawal from empire, Clement Attlee, the Labour Prime Minister from 1945 to 1951. If Americans reject this model, then they might ponder the record of an American President who really knew what Winston Churchill was like: Dwight D. Eisenhower, after all, had been Commander of Allied Forces in Europe. In the White House he was a man of peace, initiating a period of benign neglect and détente, with a rhetoric that was as distasteful to intellectuals as the substance of his policy is, in retrospect, appealing.

III. YOU CAN'T GO HOME AGAIN

When writing an essay, a historian can pick and choose among his materials. Desirable features of the past and present can be brought together in one paragraph, and the sins and shortcomings can be segregated in another, or left out altogether. Neither Americans nor Europeans can enjoy such a luxury of selection among the facts of life today. We must accept the inheritance of our past, good and bad. The passage of time not only bears away many errors, but it also means that much good is irretrievably lost. This message is specially true for a nation of immigrants. The trials of the crossing and settlement behind them, the third and successive generations seek to retrieve the positive elements of their European origins. Notwithstanding the conscious efforts to promote ethnic identity in a society that is avowedly pluralist, these offsprings of immigrants cannot find their way home again. Their Old World was buried in two massive land wars. In the polyglot New World the Jew is less Jewish, the Irish less Irish and the German less German than their hyphenated grandparents.

Whatever Americans use to face the future, they must, for the most part, fashion themselves. In so far as America is unique, it cannot learn from the experience of others, except by considerable feats of reasoning. In so far as American experience is comparable with other societies, then often it pays the price of leadership: it has no country to follow. It is precisely in the vision of its leadership that American society appears most in need today. There are, as at every point in the past, thousands of men of intelligence and goodwill, anxious to serve their country. But the question is: in what way? The desire to lead is inhibited by the awareness that the old remedies are not good enough.

At one point in the recent past there was little need for doubt. The philosophy of leadership was often that of the labour leader Samuel Gompers. He summed it up in one word: more. More of what, one might ask? Why, more of everything. This was the way in which a continent was settled. In the 1930s it was the way in which the New Deal led the country away from depression, and a decade later led its allies to military victory. It was also the philosophy of John F. Kennedy who, with an assumption of limitless national resources, asserted a readiness to 'pay any price' to achieve national aims ten years before the dollar was devalued in consequence of over-extended military adventures.

Today it is clear that more is not enough. Americans face

the future wondering, like their ancestors before the primeval forest or the Great Plains, whether the way ahead gives comfort to friend or foe. The mood is that of Melville or Poe or Faulkner, rather than Walt Whitman, Norman Rockwell or some other celebrator of America's greatness. The dream is not over, but a period of wakefulness has clearly begun. Even if Europeans cannot understand the moods that now possess this troubled giant, they cannot remain indifferent to what he does or what he is. In a world that is increasingly interdependent as well as uncertain, there are many on both sides of the Atlantic who continue to endorse Emerson's claim that America, in all its energy, violence and anguish, indeed because of its capacity for self-questioning questing and sudden change, is still the last best hope of suffering mankind.

The Contributors

REYNER BANHAM, b. 1922, England. B.A., Ph.D. (Courtauld Institute of Art, University of London). Engineer, Bristol Aeroplane Co., 1939–45, and avid reader from childhood of *Scientific American* and *Mechanix Illustrated*. Formerly on editorial staff, *Architectural Review*. First went to America in 1961 to see things for himself. Fellow, Graham Foundation, Chicago, 1964–6. Visiting lecturer at University of California at Los Angeles and University of Southern California. Board member, International Design Conference, Aspen, Colorado, since 1963. Author of *Theory and Design in the First Machine Age, The New Brutalism* and *Los Angeles*. Professor of the History of Architecture, University College, London, since 1969.

MARCUS CUNLIFFE, b. 1922. England. M.A. (Oxford). First went to America as Commonwealth Fund Fellow, Yale University, 1947–9. Visiting Professor, Harvard, Michigan, City University of New York. Author and editor of many books on America, including *George Washington: Man and Monument, The Nation Takes Shape, 1789–1837, Soldiers and Civilians: The Martial Spirit in America* and *The Literature of the United States*. Professor of American Studies, University of Sussex, since 1965.

NICHOLAS DEAKIN, b. 1936, England. M.A. (Oxford), D.Phil. (Sussex). First went to America on a student exchange with Milton Academy, Massachusetts. After reading History at Oxford, entered Home Civil Service and then went to Institute of Race Relations. Returned to America to study Poverty Program in 1969, and subsequently as Visiting Fellow, Adlai Stevenson Institute, University of Chicago. Head of Social Studies, Department of Planning and Transportation, Greater London Council, since 1972.

HUGH HECLO, b. 1943, Marion, Ohio. B.A. (George Washington), M.A. (Manchester), Ph.D. (Yale). First came to Britain in 1965 to study at the University of Manchester on a Rotary International Fellowship. Returned to study comparatively the evolution of welfare policies in Britain and Sweden. A former assistant on domestic affairs to the Vice-President of the United States. Author of *Modern Social Politics in Britain and Sweden: From Relief to Income Maintenance*, and co-author of *The Private Government of Public Money*. Since 1973 Research Associate at the Brookings Institution, Washington DC.

TOM HOOSON, b. 1933, Wales. M.A. (Oxford). First went to America in 1961 to work with Benton & Bowles Advertising, after a career in London advertising and publishing. Former chairman of the Bow Group of British Conservatives. Moved from New York to Paris in 1971 to become director of European operations for Benton & Bowles International.

ALAN N. LITTLE, b. 1934, England. B.Sc., Ph.D. (London School of Economics). First went to America in 1956 as a graduate student in sociology at the University of Wisconsin. He has returned since on a Ford Foundation grant to examine educational problems. Consultant to Organization for Economic Co-operation and Development, Paris, on educational problems. Formerly Lecturer in Sociology, London School of Economics, and director of research, Inner London Education Authority. Author of *Secondary Education: Trends and Development*, and co-author of *Strategies of Compensation*. Since 1972 Head of the Reference Division of the Community Relations Commission.

H. G. NICHOLAS, b. 1911, England. M.A. (Oxford). First went to America in the New Deal years as a Commonwealth Fund Fellow at Yale University. Returned to work in the Ministry of Information, London, and British Embassy, Washington, during the Second World War. Visiting Professor, Brookings Institution, Johns Hopkins University; Institute of Advanced Studies, Princeton; Institute of Politics, Harvard. Author of *The American Union, Britain and the United States* and

The American Past and the American Present; edited Tocqueville's *De la Démocratie en Amérique.* Rhodes Professor of American History and Institutions, Oxford University, since 1969.

JIM POTTER, b. 1922, England. B.A., M.A. (Manchester). First went to Sweden to do comparative study in economic history. Since 1952 a visiting faculty member at Yale, North Carolina, Indiana and Kansas universities. Author of a variety of articles on the economic and population history of America. Reader in Economic History with special reference to the United States at the London School of Economics since 1964.

RICHARD ROSE, b. 1933, St Louis, Missouri. B.A. (Johns Hopkins), D.Phil. (Oxford). First came to England in 1953 to attend the London School of Economics during the day, and London's theatres during the evening. Reporter, *St Louis Post-Dispatch*, 1955–7. Acquired a speaking and written knowledge of English at Oxford, 1957–60. Visiting appointments at University of Illinois and Stanford University; Fellow, Woodrow Wilson International Center, Washington DC. Author of many books about the politics of the English-speaking peoples, including *Politics in England Today, People in Politics: Observations across the Atlantic* and *Governing without Consensus: An Irish Perspective.* Since 1966 Professor of Politics at the University of Strathclyde, Glasgow, the basis of his Scotch–Irish perspective on Anglo-American relations.

JOHN WHALE, b. 1931, England. M.A. (Oxford). First went to America to teach English at the University of Minnesota, 1957. Washington correspondent, Independent Television News, London, 1967–9, and correspondent in residence, University of Missouri, 1973. Author of *The Half-Shut Eye: Television and Politics in Britain and America* and *Journalism and Government.* Since 1969 with the *Sunday Times,* London.

ESMOND WRIGHT, b. 1915, England. M.A. (Durham). First went to America as a Commonwealth Fund Fellow at the

University of Virginia, 1938. Founder-member and past chairman of the British Association for American Studies. Conservative Member of Parliament, 1967–70. Author of many books, including *George Washington and the American Revolution, Benjamin Franklin and American Independence* and *Causes and Consequences of the American Revolution*. Director, Institute of United States Studies, and Professor of American History in the University of London since 1971.

Index